Dangerous Dreamers

THE FINANCIAL INNOVATORS FROM
CHARLES MERRILL TO MICHAEL MILKEN

ROBERT SOBEL

BeardBooks
Washington, D.C.

Library of Congress Cataloging-in-Publication Data

Sobel, Robert, 1931 Feb. 19-
    Dangerous dreamers : the financial innovators from Charles Merrill to Michael Milken /
by Robert Sobel.
        p. cm.
    Originally published: New York: Wiley, c1993.
    Includes bibliographical references and index.
    ISBN 1-58798-029-0 (pbk.)
    1. Milken, Michael. 2. Stockbrokers--United States. 3. Securities industry--Corrupt
practices--United States. I. Title

HG4621 .S65 2000
332.6'2'0973--dc21

                                                                    00-057977

For
Vincent and Miranda Sabia

PREFACE

In the late summer of 1987, I received a telephone call from Les Levi, at the time a public relations officer at Drexel Burnham Lambert. Levi was familiar with my work, and wanted to talk with me about a project. Out of this came a series of articles regarding the evolution of high-yield securities and a historical section for one of Drexel's annual reports.

The following spring, at Levi's invitation, I attended the Drexel Institutional Research Conference. There I appeared on a panel dealing with the future of high-yield securities, which was chaired by Michael Milken. Afterward, Milken and I spoke about the substance of my paper, especially about my thought that junk bonds were close to the end of their cycle, to be succeeded by different kinds of paper.

Although I did not know it at the time, this was the message Milken already had been suggesting to his clients and customers. He wanted to know whether I could prepare a presentation on the subject for the next conference. I could and did, and "The Use of High-Yield Securities in Corporate Creation" was delivered in April 1989, by which time Milken had been dismissed and Drexel was under siege.

I met with Milken several times during the next year, once for a two-day session to assist in a book he was preparing. I last saw him a week or so prior to his going to prison, when in the midst of all his troubles, he was concerned with yet another project.

In this period of less than three years, I attended several Drexel functions and conferences, and came to know some of the major players in this book. I was on a panel with T. Boone Pickens, for example, dealing with methods of financing takeovers.

I do not claim the kind of intimacy with Drexel I enjoyed with the subjects of some of my earlier works, such as those on the stock exchanges, Salomon, and ITT, among others. But these experiences as a bystander served me well when I commenced work on *Dangerous Dreamers*.

In the process of my research, I have scoured court records, magazines, newspapers, and journals. I also have interviewed other observers, most of them academics, along with some journalists who covered the story from the start.

I have tried to document all of my sources. All information given to me on a "not-to-be attributed basis" was weighed carefully, and if unverified, excluded. There are no reconstructed conversations in the book. Anything quoted was reported in the press, books, or other printed material, or said directly to me.

ROBERT SOBEL

Long Beach, New York
January 1993

CONTENTS

III.　DEBACLE

INTRODUCTION

Live the normal span of three score and ten, and you likely will experience two or three periods during which activity on the financial scene accelerates and Wall Street lures some of the smartest, slickest, and most entertaining characters imaginable. The honeypot of quick and easy wealth attracts both flies and grizzly bears. Whenever large amounts of money are to be made, both clever scoundrels and brilliant innovators are drawn to finance, and during hard times they seem to vanish.

After the Civil War, during what Mark Twain called the Gilded Age, Jim Fisk, Daniel Drew, and Jay Gould made fortunes with wile and cunning. Meanwhile, banker Jay Cooke and businessmen James Hill and Cornelius Vanderbilt, among others, were building the world's finest railroad system. At the turn of the century, a clutch of rogues, including Thomas Lawson and Charles W. Morse, wheeled and dealed on Wall Street. At the same time, J. P. Morgan, Jacob Schiff, and their kind shaped the outlines of modern industrial America. In the 1920s, Joe Kennedy and Jesse Livermore organized pools and manipulated stocks, while Henry Ford and David Sarnoff pioneered the modern automobile and radio industries. During the 1950s and 1960s, while Bernie Cornfeld bilked tens of thousands of investors and professional dancer Nicholas Darvas became a much-followed and widely admired market tout, Thomas Watson, Jr., created the computer age, Edwin Land realized his ambition of recreating the photography industry, Charles Merrill concocted "People's Capitalism," and James Ling dazzled Wall Street with his financial pyrotechnics.

Most recently, in the Junk Decade of the 1980s, we had inside trader Ivan Boesky and scores of arrogant young Wall Streeters, whose ethics were, to put it charitably, dubious. But firms like Forstmann Little and Kohlberg Kravis Roberts played major positive roles in the largest restructuring of American industry since the turn of the century.

Money manias, then, are hardly new. The so-called conglomerate commotion of the 1950s and 1960s had the flavor, if not the substance, of the Junk Decade. There were similar developments in the 1920s and at the turn of the century. Doubtless, we have not seen the last of them.

And there is Michael Milken. Should he be ranked with the Morgans and Merrills, or with the Cornfelds and Boeskys? Judge Kimba Wood, who sentenced Milken to ten years in prison, was ambivalent. "There may some day be enough information for another entity, be it a court, or, as Mr. [Arthur] Liman [Milken's attorney] suggested, a historian, to judge whether most of your business was conducted lawfully, but I cannot make that judgment today either way."

Whether Milken should be considered a positive or negative force—or both—is one of the central questions addressed in this book. I hope to demonstrate that Milken, T. Boone Pickens, and others of the era were merely the vehicles through which the phenomena of junk finance and leveraged buyouts played themselves out.

In 1989, the *Wall Street Journal* listed those businessmen the editors considered the nation's most important. On the list were Lee Iacocca, Steve Jobs, Henry Kravis, Peter Lynch, William McGowan, Fred Smith, Ted Turner, P. Roy Vagelos, Sam Walton, and Mike Milken. In describing Milken, the *Journal*'s reporter wrote:

> Not since J. P. Morgan has any financier influenced Wall Street and the nation the way Michael Milken has . . . . Not surprisingly, Mr. Milken, 42, aroused the fear and loathing of industrialists whose companies fell to his onslaughts or seemed likely candidates for his attentions.

Another reporter asserted that Milken was "arguably the most important financier of the century." Yet, for all his creativity and power, Milken was never as influential as Morgan—given the complexity and scope of modern banking, no one could have approached that banker's power; although what Milken might have accomplished had the Justice Department not gone after him will always be debated. At Milken's age, Morgan's greatest accomplishments were yet to come; he then was a promising but not commanding banker.

On the other hand, attorney and business writer Benjamin Stein called Milken "probably the most successful master criminal of the last century," and a chorus of critics echoed the charge. But both admirers and critics agreed that he was consequential. Turner and McGowan were on the *Wall Street Journal* list by virtue of having created Turner Broadcasting and MCI. Both were financed by Milken. Some of Henry Kravis' biggest deals at KKR were made possible by Milken's fund-raising abilities.

Milken was a meteor who flashed across the investment skies, only to burn out—or, perhaps more properly, he was brought down by forces he didn't fully comprehend. He was scarcely known outside of financial circles as late as 1983, when he came to prominence by assisting Pickens in his attempted takeover of Gulf Oil. There was some stir in 1978 when Milken moved his operation to Beverly Hills; note was taken in the press because, at the time, the move appeared so odd. Otherwise, the media ignored him; *Wall Street Journal* articles dealing with his firm, Drexel Burnham Lambert, rarely mentioned Milken. Relative anonymity suited him. Milken granted few interviews, and those to which he submitted dealt strictly with his position on junk bonds as a proper investment medium.

This was not surprising, for two reasons. When people ask, "How did the market do today?" they mean stocks, not bonds. Milken was a bond man. Bonds were and are a more substantial investment arena than stocks. The government bond market alone is several times larger than the stock market. But it is largely a professional market, in which small investors tend to operate through mutual funds. Milken only became famous when he assisted in hostile takeovers, which affected the stock market.

The other reason is Milken's personality, which is totally unlike that of any other major figure of the 1980s. He disliked publicity, and seemed to enjoy only three things: his work, his family, and meditating. Milken's mind was always working, leaving him oblivious to much around him. He truly was fascinated with problem solving. While awaiting incarceration, he developed a scheme whereby Japan would assume the Mexican debt in return for a free trade zone in Mexico. He was able to interest the Mexican and Japanese governments in this idea, but it fizzled when Washington rejected it.

While Milken was riding high, Drexel resembled a graduate school because he invited so many academics to write papers, chair seminars, and lecture to clients, customers, and professionals. This was genuine research: There were questions Milken wanted answered, information he wanted to integrate into one of his plans. So the academic would go off for several months, sort out concepts, gather material, and then present the results. It was as if Milken were saying, "Look, I'm awfully busy. I only have one brain, and it can't work on all I want to know. Could I rent your brain for a while?" And so he did.

This obsessive curiosity comes out in conversations with Milken. Most of Wall Street's great figures are interested in themselves and their work, not in the person with whom they are talking. Milken will ask questions, listen, ask more questions, and then come back with additional ideas. Even people much older than he say that a conversation with him reminded them of the talks they had when they were students. Milken is at the same time exuberant, enthusiastic, and, what is unusual for one in his position, modest. On one occasion, said a Drexel banker, Milken was at a dinner meeting when the cleanup squad came into the room and started work. "Mike, take care of that mess," said one of the supervisors to a young employee, who was also present. Milken immediately turned around and started bussing a table. This sounds far-fetched, but to those who know

Milken, it is at least plausible. He is a person to whom the words "please" and "thank you" are not alien.

None of the above could be written about his contemporaries Felix Rohaytn, John Gutfreund, Nick Brady, and other important Wall Street figures. They possessed *gravitas*. But Milken reminds one of the child who asked, "Why is the sky blue?" and still wonders about it.

This is not to suggest that Milken is a candidate for canonization. He is as complicated a figure as any in our time, and, as will be seen, he has his dark side. Milken is highly competitive and intelligent. The desire to win often has proved more powerful a force in him than a willingness to play by the rules.

Milken and Pickens were opportunists in a neutral sense. Transported to another era, say the 1960s, they might have become involved with the conglomerate movement, which not only resembled the leveraged-buyout craze of the late 1980s, but helped cause it. Both came after periods during which financial values were out of line, encouraging outsiders to make plays for all sorts of undervalued assets.

Both the conglomerateurs of the 1960s and the raiders of the 1980s recognized an imperfection in American capitalism. The separation of management and ownership resulted in a loss of responsibility by the corporate CEO, who would not be punished for a mediocre record. Accordingly, those firms whose net worths exceeded their equity prices were ripe for takeover. The conglomerateurs and raiders learned to profit from this situation—in the process, distressing managements. In the 1980s, CEOs fought back through the forum of public relations, establishing the impression that the raiders and their bankers created nothing useful. The latter were depicted as crooks, scavenging sound businesses, earning enormous fortunes and ruining the economy, starting with the S&L crisis and culminating in the recession of the early 1990s. In my view, these conclusions are unwarranted distortions.

In the late 1960s, threatened CEOs had demanded an end to the conglomerate movement, and legislation was developed. But the movement ended before it was passed. The massive LBOs of the mid-1980s resulted in similar demands for legal reform. Congress considered ways to force Milken, Pickens, Icahn, and the rest out of the arena. Then, unexpectedly, the Securities and Exchange Commission uncovered a ring of inside traders, with connections leading to Milken. This opened a second front against the raiders, one far more effective than the first. In the end, the raiders were brought down, while government acted to make takeovers more difficult in the future.

Battles like these occur during most money manias. In 1912–1913, the Pujo Commission vilified the bankers and industrialists who oversaw the major overhaul of the banking industry and the railroads in the 1890s and the early years of the twentieth century. The Pecora Investigation of the early

New Deal tried to make criminals of the tycoons and bankers of the 1920s. During the 1950s and 1960s, two innovative businessmen, Louis Wolfson and James Ling, who threatened the status quo and angered establishment bankers and their allies in government, were driven from business for minor, technical transgressions. Today, both are largely forgotten; rare is the person under 50 who has heard of them. I believe that by the second decade of the twenty-first century, Pickens and Milken will be mere footnotes in the business history of our times, mentioned, if at all, to illustrate the use of junk bonds during the 1980s.

If the United States faces difficult economic times throughout the 1990s, the blame will be placed on the big players of the 1980s, including Milken. Yet, Milken was not wrong in his assumptions, inexpert in his operations, or foolhardy in his financial management. Rather, he was toppled from power by forces he probably didn't fully comprehend, for reasons secondary to his real importance as a financier. History is written by the winners. The winners in this struggle already have incarcerated and demonized Milken.

As Judge Wood acknowledged, it is the task of the historian to analyze just why Milken was brought low. Part of that task is to find out who had a stake in seeing him fall. It may be too early still for the kind of analysis that requires historical perspective. When one deals with a contemporary human legend, composed of unequal parts of talent, truth, and myth, objective analysis becomes particularly difficult. This book, then, is a first draft of the definitive history of the Junk Decade, for a later generation of historians to complete.

I

PRECURSORS

1

LOUIS WOLFSON— THE JUNKMAN

The middle-aged man stood before the judge in a courtroom on Foley Square in New York City. He had been convicted of securities crimes. Now he was to be sentenced, and those who had followed this curious case watched, enthralled by what seemed the final chapter in the career of the most colorful businessman of his time. No one was more closely identified with raids on corporations than the person known on Wall Street as "the junkman."

His attorney had argued that the defendant had been victimized by a vendetta on the part of those who felt threatened by his activities. In his heyday, he had challenged the leadership of several large corporations, making powerful enemies. For years, federal officials had attempted to indict him on one charge or another; some said the Justice Department had been influenced by his opponents. He was an outsider, and he was being penalized not so much for violating laws as for attempting to crack the complacent facade of entrenched business. "When you soar like an eagle," his attorney expounded, "you attract the hunters," adding that government officials were using "bureaucratic muscle to destroy people they don't like."[1] Moreover, the charges against the defendant normally would result in civil, not criminal, indictments. This man was being victimized because of his celebrity and to set an example.

The lawyer was not describing Michael Milken, once "junk bond king" at Drexel Burnham Lambert, and the date was not 1990. It was 1967, and the man on trial was Louis Elwood Wolfson, a now-forgotten businessman, who briefly blazed his way across the corporate firmament of post-World-War-II America.

He had been indicted for several minor, technical offenses. Wolfson and his close associate, Buddy Gerbert, had been found guilty of 19 counts of conspiracy and sales of unregistered securities, for which each might have been sentenced to a maximum of 95 years in jail and fines of $95,000.[2]

What crimes would have justified such a sentence? Look at just what Wolfson was supposed to have done.

One of Wolfson's many business interests was Continental Enterprises, which owned movie theaters and real estate, and an assortment of other holdings. Continental posted revenues of around $1 million a year at the time the crimes (sales of unregistered securities) occurred. Wolfson's attorney, Milton Gould, called it "a little-nothing company," adding that this marked the first time since passage of the federal securities law that anyone had been prosecuted on criminal charges for selling unregistered stock; all earlier and later indictments for this offense were on civil charges.[3] Indeed, William Casey had been found guilty of the same crime, and had paid a fine. Later, Casey headed the Securities and Exchange Commission (SEC).

U.S. Attorney Robert M. Morgenthau asserted that Wolfson had capitalized on his control of Continental to license to the company an aerosol packaging patent he also controlled. Publicity regarding the device ran the stock up from $2.75 to $8.50 a share, and Wolfson and Gerbert sold into the market.[4] Between 1960 and 1962, they sold 690,000 shares of unregistered stock on the open market, for a profit of more than $1.6 million.

Wolfson conceded that he did make the sales, but claimed he didn't know he was doing anything illegal. Indeed, he had reported the transactions on his income tax forms for the years involved. "Anyone who violates a rule or regulation has to be insane," he said. "Especially a man in my position. Why would I want to violate any rule or regulation when I could register stock and sell the stock?"[5]

During the trial, U.S. Attorney Michael F. Armstrong had called to the stand former Assistant Regional Administrator for the SEC James Duncan, who testified that in 1950 he had had a two-hour conference with Wolfson concerning registration provisions of the securities law. Wolfson said he could not recall what happened at a meeting 17 years earlier. More damaging, however, was testimony from 15-year Wolfson confidant Alexander Rittmaster, who turned states' evidence to prevent being named a coconspirator. Rittmaster testified that he had placed several sales orders for the stock, as a favor to Gerbert. But nothing he said indicated that Wolfson had committed criminal acts.[6, 7]

Wolfson maintained his innocence, suggesting that others in his organization had committed wrongful acts without his knowledge. It was true that he was known for a lack of interest in details. Rittmaster, his financial consultant and investment counselor, generally handled such matters on his own. Before the sentencing, Gould told the court his client had been "a leading citizen in the community" and "a benefactor to the needy and oppressed not only in his own community but in other parts of the United States." Prosecutor Armstrong's comeback was that the crimes demanded a stiff sentence for its deterrent effect. In so doing, he revealed the government's true motives in bringing the criminal indictment: "There are people down in the street right now on Wall Street, awaiting the outcome of this case to govern their actions."

The judge sentenced Wolfson to a year in jail. Wolfson ultimately served nine months and a day at the prison at Eglin Air Force Base.

The Wolfson sentence was to serve as a warning to others. "The case also has put Wall Street on notice that the Government is taking a firmer stand on law enforcement involving the registration requirement of the Securities Act," wrote Terry Robards of the *New York Times*. "New surveillance procedures by brokerage houses may result."[8]

There were surface resemblances between Wolfson and Milken. Both were alternately shy and assertive, curious about all sorts of subjects but able to focus on business with intensity. They were loyal and patriotic, and were contributors to a wide variety of medical and charitable programs—Wolfson through the Wolfson Family Foundation, and Milken through the Milken Family Foundation. Wolfson was involved with civil rights before it was a popular cause. In 1946, he endowed a children's clinic at a Baptist hospital in Jacksonville, Florida, open to all regardless of race. Milken has attracted criticism for his support of programs involving Jesse Jackson, and he was the first recipient of the Marcus Garvey Award for Economic Freedom, bestowed by 100 Black Men of America. Both Wolfson and Milken were staunch benefactors of Jewish causes and of the state of Israel.

Both were also family-centered men. In 1961, Louis Wolfson told a reporter his father "knew right from wrong, and he didn't spare the rod to teach it to his sons." All who know Milken testify to his sturdy familial ties. "My father had a very strong sense of what was right," he said in 1987. "I grew up in a family that asked why you got Bs."

"What's wealth?" Wolfson asked, and provided his answer: "My wealth is my health, my family, and my friends." In discussing his friend and fellow billionaire, Carl Lindner, Milken stated that the most impressive thing about him was not the companies he owned, but that "his children are outstanding human beings."[9]

Both men had their defenders. In the late 1960s, a group called "Friends of Lou Wolfson" contributed toward the publication of a full-page advertisement supporting the indicted man. In 1989, "Friends of Michael Milken" did the same.

Even the rhetoric used to describe them was strikingly similar. In 1955, *Forbes* referred to Wolfson as a 43-year-old tycoon with "a host of spectacular followers, a reputation for skillful opportunism, unproved charges of sharp dealing, and a widespread distrust among many U.S. corporation executives." According to the magazine, "The legend Wolfson himself has built up assiduously and flawlessly.[10] So flawlessly, indeed, that although countless attempts have been made to produce the 'real' Wolfson, none has succeeded in producing the slightest tear in the legend itself. The enigma—what makes Wolfson run and what is he after—is also intact and unresolved."[11]

Such was Wolfson in his prime. Substitute the name Milken for Wolfson, and the article could have run in 1986, when Milken was 43 years old and at the pinnacle of his success.

The two men operated in substantially different business environments; also, Wolfson was a businessman, and Milken was a banker. Takeovers and their management were central to Wolfson. Corporate takeovers were one of Milken's occupations, and, to his mind, the least important. Milken would serve the likes of Carl Icahn and T. Boone Pickens in the 1980s; without an individual who could raise enormous amounts of money on short notice, their activities would not have been possible.

That Wolfson never achieved the power of the latter two was due to the fact that there was no one like Milken on the scene in the 1950s. Had Milken arrived in the financial district, like Wolfson, in the aftermath of World War II, he would have been frustrated, for the time wasn't right for many of his ideas; had Wolfson been born a quarter of a century later, he might have come to epitomize rampant capitalism run amok in the 1980s.

Milken did not know—or know of—Wolfson. But he sensed that the time hadn't been right for takeovers before the 1980s. In 1986, he told a group of students of the wonders that awaited them. "There are phenomenal opportunities for everyone no matter what you're doing. If we had lived 20 or 30 years ago, those opportunities wouldn't have been open to us." Wolfson's tragedy was having been born too soon.

From the vantage point of a quarter of a century later, it seems clear that Wolfson had no criminal intent, that the government had come after him with guns blazing, determined to rid the business scene of a dangerous raider. There are no subtle shadings here; Wolfson was the victim of a zealous prosecutor. Toward the very end, he was being assured by his attorneys that he had nothing to fear, certainly not a prison sentence.

It would be different with Milken. Wolfson pleaded not guilty; Milken agreed to a plea bargain on six felonies. No matter that all six were minor, or that he was the only person ever tried on criminal charges for such minor transgressions as parking securities. Milken was an admitted felon, while Wolfson was convicted despite maintaining his innocence. Such was the distinction between the more sedate and secure business atmosphere of the 1950s and 1960s and those of the 1980s.

The government could pursue Wolfson without fear of any economic consequences, since he was not connected with other businessmen. It was different with Milken, who helped finance a clutch of takeover artists. The government *wanted* to remove Wolfson from the scene. In the late 1980s, prosecutors felt they *had to* eject Milken in order to preserve the positions of many leaders of major American corporations. Wolfson was a victim of circumstances; Milken was a casualty of history.

Grasp how his era produced Louis Wolfson and you will better appreciate why the opportunities of the late 1970s conspired to create Milken.

THE POWER OF "CREATIVE DESTRUCTION"

The arrival on the scene of the likes of Lou Wolfson often is a sign that a new period of creativity is about to begin. The Wolfsons of the world recognize when values are out of line. Considerable profits are possible for those who understand this and are prepared to take relatively minor risks for large rewards. They and others, who follow their leads, are often brought low by excesses. Yet without them, business creativity would not be rewarded, incompetent managers would sleep soundly, and the economy would stagnate. There would be little of what economist Joseph Schumpeter called the "creative destruction" so necessary to capitalist development.

To understand Wolfson, one must first appreciate the kind of business atmosphere he faced. The United States had emerged from World War II as the world's preeminent economic power. One might assume the business scene would have been bubbling with optimism and innovation, but it was not. It was the time of novelist Sloan Wilson's "man in the gray flannel suit" and social critic William Whyte, Jr.'s, "organization man." Each was a man who worked for a large corporation, rose to middle management in his 30s, lived with his wife and children in suburbia, and went to work on the 8:10 and came home on the 6:07. He was steady and unimaginative, viewed creativity with suspicion, and was more comfortable executing orders than giving them. Whyte argued that this new businessman had largely abandoned the old "Protestant ethic," based on a strong belief in work, frugality, and absolute values, to embrace what Whyte called a "social ethic," in which he took on the standards of his peers and avoided confrontations. He got ahead by going along.

In this atmosphere, Louis Wolfson was a peacock at a convention of sparrows. For one year, 1955, he provided the kind of business excitement encountered regularly at the turn of the century and in the 1920s, and later in the 1960s and 1980s. His admirers thought him a wonder worker. Everything he touched seemed to provide rich rewards for himself and his followers. But his enemies, including leaders of the nation's major corporations and their political allies, considered Wolfson a menace. He was dangerous and exciting.

Like many business mavericks, Wolfson was the quintessential outsider, a first-generation Floridian whose parents were poor Russian Jewish immigrants. Shortly after he was born in 1912, the family moved from St. Louis to Jacksonville, where the elder Wolfson established himself as a dealer in junk and scrap metal. Louis entered the University of Georgia on a football scholarship, dropped out due to an injury, and entered the family business. Hence Wolfson's nickname—"the junkman." Together with his father and older brother, Sam, he organized the small construction firm of Florida Pipe & Supply Co., which scraped along during the Depression, but did better after the United States entered World War II.

In this period, Wolfson learned to appraise the value of assets, purchasing those he considered underpriced and then selling them, often for substantial profits. Once he bought what seemed a heterogenous collection of fencing, barbed wire, and plumbing parts, for $275, which he sold over the next few months for a profit of over $100,000. During the war, Wolfson occasionally bought supplies from one company and sold them to another for a large profit. By 1945, Florida Pipe was doing business at a $4.5 million-a-year clip.

Wolfson had become a local celebrity. Tall, strikingly handsome, with piercing eyes and a slow drawl, he was aggressive, hard-working, and determined to succeed. He would do so by applying the simple lessons he learned in scrap metal and building supplies.

Wolfson taught himself to scan balance sheets and recognize businesses worth far more dead than alive. As a butcher might purchase a side of beef and carve it up into parts to be sold for a profit, he found properties that could be purchased at low prices, and then, disassembled, resold for a profit, or managed into prosperity.

Though Wolfson might have thought he had a totally novel approach, he, too, had predecessors. Benjamin Graham and David L. Dodd, in their classic work, *Security Analysis* (1934), wrote of the desirability of locating stocks whose share prices did not reflect their true value. Wolfson became famous for ferreting out stocks selling substantially below the worth of their net assets. In the 1980s, T. Boone Pickens, Carl Icahn, and others would think the same way.

THE FIRST CONGLOMERATEUR

In 1946, Wolfson purchased two surplus shipyards, Tampa Shipbuilding and St. Johns River Shipbuilding, which he eventually liquidated at large profits. He also purchased an interest in Monogram Pictures for $400,000 and a few years later sold it for $1.2 million.[12, 13] Three years later, Wolfson eyed Merritt Chapman & Scott (MC&S).

MC&S was in the business of marine salvage and a wide variety of construction. The market value of the common stock came to under $6 million, while the firm's net worth was at least $8 million, and it held $3.4 million in cash alone. Management was old, weak, and unable to adjust to the postwar environment. Like many other men of their generation, they were unassertive, psychologically scarred by the Great Depression.

Wolfson quietly purchased 20,500 shares for something under half a million dollars, which made him MC&S's largest shareholder. A proxy fight ensued, which he and his associates won for three reasons: (1) they had so large a stake to begin with, (2) there were relatively few other stockholders, and (3) management had no idea of how to conduct a defense. From this experience, Wolfson learned the rudiments of raiding.

Some time later, a commentator described the technique:

Repeatedly he [Wolfson] has demonstrated an uncanny ability to sniff out old, conservative corporations with over-all hardening of the assets and which have been all but overlooked by the investing public. Wolfson's strategy: to buy into the old firm (secretly registering stock in the names of brokers and trusted friends in order to allay suspicions), wrest control from stodgy management, then boom the stock's price by skyrocketing dividends or waging proxy warfare.[14]

Even though MC&S was quite small, the proxy battle captured the attention of the business community. Such contests were rare in the 1950s. Unless they were singularly incompetent, corporate managers were virtually assured of continuity in office. Boards of directors were rubber stamps. In theory, shareholders owned the corporation, and managements were their employees. In fact, however, ownership of shares gave the holder only the right to dividends (if management decided to pay them) and capital gains if realized. Should shareholders be disappointed with performance, they could sell their holdings.

Nor surprisingly, Wolfson felt the system was unfair, since, until this time, he had functioned either as sole or majority owner, had no experience with publicly owned companies, and had never worked for anyone but himself. In late 1955, he offered his ideas on proxy fights to an academic researcher:

Proxy contests are wholesome because similar to public elections they serve to focus attention on the stewardship of those holding and aspiring to office. They are a form of surgery sometimes necessary to effect [sic] the cure of corporate ills. Just as the cure for any physical condition must start with the patient himself, the cure for corporate ills must start with management.[15]

A few months after winning control of MC&S, Wolfson went after Capital Transit Co., the firm that operated the Washington, D.C., streetcars and buses. Capital was a dependable money-earner that paid small dividends. Management wanted it this way, piling up surpluses for the rainy days so many expected after the war. In 1949, Capital had $6.7 million in cash and securities and another $22.5 million in its depreciation, injury, and damages accounts, while the market value of the total shares outstanding came to only $4.8 million.

With permission of the Interstate Commerce Commission, Wolfson bought 46 percent of Capital's shares for $20 a share, which came to under $2.2 million. He then ousted most of the old management, had himself named chairman, and placed his nominees on the board. Wolfson paid out the company's surplus cash, along with most of the new earnings that came in. He split the stock four for one in 1952 and paid a special dividend of $15.60 a share. During his five years in control, Wolfson had Capital pay a total of $44.95 a share in dividends, which averaged 150 percent of earnings. The shares soared, rising as high as 70. And, in 1954, Wolfson spun off Continental Enterprises, which became a holding corporation for a grab bag of his companies.

Wolfson had no desire to run a company as small as Capital; rather, he expected to grow MC&S quickly. He went back on the acquisition trail, sometimes using MC&S stock as currency for purchases, other times borrowing or selling bonds to raise cash.[16]

In 1953, MC&S purchased Milton Electric Steel and Fitz Simons & Connell Dredge & Dock. The following year, it acquired Newport Steel and C.A. Pitts General Contractor, Shoup Voting Machine, Marion Power Shovel, and Osgood. In 1955, MC&S took over three sizable companies: New York Shipbuilding, paint maker Devoe & Raynolds, and Tennessee Products & Chemical. Then Wolfson purchased Savin Construction. Additional holdings included Highway Trailer and Nesco (the latter made pans for roasting and frying). MC&S now had revenues of $375 million and earnings of $25 million, and was paying a dividend of $2.00 plus stock per share. Wolfson's once-small company was a member of the Fortune 500.

Wolfson had, in effect, put together the first modern conglomerate, namely a corporation with diverse, unrelated interests. He was not credited with this innovation, however, due to the randomness of his acquisitions. In this period, he was on the prowl for unrealized values; he was not trying to build an industrial empire with a coherent agenda. Even so, he already had built MC&S rapidly when Royal Little was still attempting to make Textron, which many deem the first true conglomerate, a dominant factor in the textile industry. Little would provide conglomeration with a rationale, as would others who followed, but Wolfson got there first.

THE GREAT MONTGOMERY WARD RAID

In August 1954, Wolfson started accumulating shares in the Chicago-based department store chain and mail order operation, Montgomery Ward, an undervalued, cash-rich concern. It was headed by the cantankerous, 80-year-old Sewell Avery, one of the nation's most conservative businessmen, who, early in his career, had nursed U.S. Gypsum through the Great Depression. Like the old Capital management Wolfson had ousted, Avery believed the nation was due for a repeat of that disaster. He intended to accumulate cash, which would be utilized to expand once land and construction prices fell. Avery was not alone in his philosophy during the immediate postwar period, but when a minor recession in 1945–1946 was followed by a recovery, others changed their minds. Not Avery, who added to his pile, even as he saw profits slide. In 1954, the company had $50 a share in cash and securities alone, at a time when the stock was selling in the high 40s. Its price/earnings ratio was under 10, indicating just how out of favor the shares had become. The wonder of it all to today's bankers would be that no one went after Montgomery Ward before Wolfson. But a takeover contest was difficult in the timid business atmosphere of the 1950s.

At an August 1954 press conference, Wolfson went public with his intention to make a play for Montgomery Ward and revealed that he had already accumulated a sizable stake in the company. There was no way Wolfson could have raised the funds necessary to make a serious bid on his own without divesting himself of some of his properties, and he didn't do this in 1955. So when Wolfson sketched his plan, it was obvious there was only one way such an assault could be mounted: There would have to be a proxy battle.[17]

Undoubtedly, Wolfson would have done it differently 30 years later. After taking slightly less than a 5 percent position in the stock (just below the limit requiring formal notification), and lining up financial support from banks and institutions, he would have made a tender offer at a premium price—say, 60 for the 6.5 million shares, coming to $390 million or so. Or he might have confronted management and offered to sell his shares to them for a profit, this being the "greenmail" approach that became so notorious in the 1980s.

Such procedures were unthinkable in 1955. None of the unassertive bankers of the period would have extended short-term financing for the undertaking. Try to imagine how a conventional banker at Chemical or Irving Trust would have reacted to a person who sketched the true value of Montgomery Ward and suggested there would be a successful tender. Wolfson then might have observed that the tender offer really wasn't so high considering the $320 million in cash and equivalents owned by Montgomery Ward. Once in control, he could sell $500 million or so in bonds and use part of the proceeds to repay the loan. The average yield on Baa rated bonds in 1955 was 3.5 percent. Those new Montgomery Ward bonds would be offered to yield 4 percent, making the total interest payment $20 million. Montgomery Ward had earned $34 million the previous year, so there would have been ample assets to cover the interest payments.

But even if the loan were granted, who would have bought such bonds? Certainly not the institutions, or the conservative mutual funds, or individuals with deep pockets.

If the Montgomery Ward situation had arisen in 1986, the company would have lasted as long as a wounded goldfish in a tank of piranhas. The risk arbitragers, or "arbs," and the institutions would have provided Wolfson with the needed proxies. The banks would have had no trouble coming up with the money (even if adjusted for inflation, which would have meant $1.6 billion or so). A Michael Milken could have raised that amount in a day from customers wanting to purchase Montgomery Ward bonds, and a latter-day Wolfson could have used the proceeds to pay off the bank loans. It was done that way repeatedly and with amazing ease in the 1980s.

In 1986, First Boston and Citicorp each advanced $900 million to Robert Campeau to finance his acquisition of another retail giant, Allied Stores. Before it was over, Campeau would expend $4.1 billion for the company, including fees and expenses of $612 million. Less than two years later, he purchased Federated Department Stores for $6.8 billion. All of this was made possible through junk bond financing. Campeau, who was barely known outside of Toronto earlier in the decade, became the world's largest department store tycoon.[18] But none of this was possible in the 1950s, which was why Wolfson had no choice but to engage in a proxy contest.

Proxy contests in Wolfson's time were dangerous and difficult. Small shareholders then retained their holdings for long periods and identified strongly with the company. Stories of middle-class Americans buying and squirreling away shares of AT&T, General Motors, and the local utility company for their dividends, and then passing them down to their children, were common. They would purchase products turned out by *their* firm, believing that by so doing they were adding to their own profits.

Montgomery Ward had approximately 68,000 shareholders in 1955, 55,000 of whom owned fewer than 100 shares.[19] Most lived in and around Chicago. Montgomery Ward shareholders shopped in *their* stores. They looked upon Wolfson as an interloper. A deeply tanned Jewish southerner, he looked more like a movie star than a businessman. He had an accent that sounded foreign to Chicagoans. Wolfson surrounded himself with friends and relatives with backgrounds like his own. This didn't help. The stockholders weren't going to permit the likes of Lou Wolfson to become master of Montgomery Ward.

The price of Montgomery Ward stock rose immediately after Wolfson's announcement, and, by December, the common stock price was close to 80. The reason was evident. People bought shares in the expectation of a rise during the struggle, after which they would sell. This often happened in such circumstances, and didn't necessarily assist one side or the other.

Wolfson spent some time courting the institutional shareholders, but not as much as raiders would have in the 1980s. In this period, pension funds had just started dabbling in stocks. Insurance companies had a bit more exposure, but stocks were still a small fraction of their portfolios. Mutual funds were yet to become popular; the general rule among the institutions was to vote for managements.

Since Montgomery Ward's fate would rest with the independent owners of some 3.5 million uncommitted shares, Wolfson would have to woo them assiduously. So he did. He met with shareholder groups in Florida, Los Angeles, San Francisco, Chicago, Detroit, and New York. The campaign resembled presidential politics more than a fight for corporate control.

It was the business story of the year. Newspaper readers who earlier had no interest in such matters wondered just what it was Wolfson was attempting, why he was going about it in that way, and what it had to do with them. People who previously demonstrated little or no interest in the subject started reading the financial pages, and some were tempted to jump aboard the Wolfson bandwagon to profits.

Wolfson presented a carefully constructed business program for Montgomery Ward, to be implemented by experienced managers. Most of the agenda involved the deployment of the cash reserve. As had been the case at Capital Transit, part of the cash would go to the shareholders, who would have the right to tender 2 million shares at book value, some $93 a share (this being 12 points higher than in late February, when Wolfson mailed his proxy material). This maneuver, he said, would have the effect of increasing earnings per share.

Wolfson also wanted to restructure Montgomery Ward in a novel fashion, which demonstrated the kind of imagination one associates with some of the leveraged-buyout people of the 1980s. He would organize a separate company, initially capitalized at $50 million, to which would be transferred Montgomery Ward's fixed assets plus $18 million in cash. Shares of this new company would be distributed on a pro rata basis to the company's shareholders, who now would own two pieces of paper, one for the operating company, the other for the real estate firm. The latter, which had the hard assets, would be permitted to borrow up to $200 million to help finance Wolfson's program of construction and renovation.[20]

SEWELL AVERY FIGHTS BACK

Montgomery Ward offered no alternative plan. Instead, management responded with a personal attack on Wolfson, repeating themes heard in the business community since his purchase of the two Florida shipyards and Capital Transit. Wolfson's intent, Avery claimed, was to strip Montgomery Ward of its assets. The board was attempting to protect "honest and capable managements" from "financial pirates," whose sole aim was to "loot" successful companies and leave small stockholders "only the skin and bones." Avery indicated this was not merely a fight for Montgomery Ward. If successful there, Wolfson would turn to new targets, and other raiders would be encouraged to enter the field. The Montgomery Ward contest had wide implications for the future of American capitalism. Therefore, Avery would fight long and hard.

Montgomery Ward President Edmund A. Krider reiterated the theme. "Montgomery Ward may be the battleground for the war on all legitimate industries," he said. On several occasions, he called Wolfson an "irresponsible raider," who would loot the Montgomery Ward treasury. Company spokesmen made ominous references to the "eastern interests" behind Wolfson, suggesting he was backed by Jewish bankers out for no good.

Wolfson shot back that "vilification is a poor substitute for legal argument," and that the owners—the shareholders—should be protected against "people who perpetuate themselves in office by taking a stranglehold on a corporation."[21]

Wolfson would later claim that Montgomery Ward had hired private detectives to dig up dirt on his personal and business operations. Ward executives denied this, but information released and leaked to the press would indicate there was some substance to these rumors. Wolfson was subjected to anonymous telephone calls threatening kidnapping, which were reported to federal authorities. For a while, FBI agents traveled with the Wolfson party.

In reality, Avery had little to fear from Wolfson. The numbers and the nature of the shareholder population indicated that the odds were decidedly in the company's favor. Wolfson was deeply in debt as a result of his stock purchases and the campaign, and he still directly and indirectly controlled less than 3 percent of the votes. The outcome depended on success with small shareholders, and indications were that they remained loyal to management.[22]

The showdown took place on April 22 at the Medinah Temple, a Shrine auditorium on Chicago's North Side. The meeting was well attended and covered in detail by the press. The board tried to restrain the elderly Avery, but he would have none of it, insisting on personally answering questions. He appeared weary and confused, rambling at times, rarely responding directly. Wolfson was courteous, content to permit Avery to damage his credibility with this kind of performance. No one there could have failed to conclude that the chairman was ill-equipped to continue in office.

Nevertheless, when the votes were counted, it was obvious management had won by a landslide. The Wolfson slate received 31 percent of the ballots, which, under the Montgomery Ward bylaws, entitled it to three board seats. Wolfson and two lieutenants joined the board.

The contest had attracted so much attention that two private concerns analyzed the ballots. They concluded that the institutions had voted overwhelmingly for management; 92 percent of the shares owned by banks had been voted for the present board. The Wolfson group received 74 percent of the votes of shares in brokerage accounts. Most shareholders in 1955, aware of the brokerage firm failures of the early 1930s, took physical possession of their securities, so these brokerage shares represented the individuals who had bought in hope of a Wolfson victory, as indicated by the fact that the number of broker-held shares increased from 500,000 to 1 million between March 1954 and March 1955. Only 27 percent of the individual shareholders who held their shares came down for Wolfson. This may seem small today, but it was a large percentage in that period of shareholder loyalty.[23]

After it was over, Wolfson told reporters he intended to be an active board member. The fight for control would continue, he said.[24] But, in reality, he had lost interest in the battle. Wolfson started selling his shares, and in less than a year he left the board.

WOLFSON'S FALL

Meanwhile, matters were unraveling at Capital Transit, where Wolfson had delegated too much authority to subordinates. Although he had moved to Washington, he had never devoted much attention to Capital Transit. Problems mounted. Wolfson continually clashed with members of the Committee on the District of Columbia and the Public Utilities Commission of Washington, who oversaw activities at the firm. Capital Transit long had been a source of secure jobs for relatives of well-connected individuals. Wolfson ended this, antagonizing some of the powerful. His high dividends were accompanied by requests for fare increases, which usually were rejected. The *Washington Post,* the city's dominant newspaper, regularly criticized him, and Wolfson snapped back with lawsuits. A 1951 strike led to demands the company be taken over by the government.

During the Montgomery Ward contest, Capital Transit entered into contract negotiations with the District of Columbia Transit Workers. With Wolfson away, management gave the union an ultimatum, which was rejected, and another strike began on July 1, 1954. There was a storm of criticism in the press and in Congress. Senator Wayne Morse (R. Oregon), once a Wolfson booster, was irate, suggesting that the government seize the company. Wolfson got into a shouting match with several legislators. On August 4, President Eisenhower signed a hurriedly drafted measure to make Capital Transit a public utility. A year later, the battered Wolfson sold Capital Transit to a syndicate headed by O. Roy Chalk. Wolfson left Washington wealthier than when he arrived, but also embittered by the experience and having made many enemies there.

The Montgomery Ward and Capital Transit experiences soured Wolfson on business. He spent much of the 1960s winding down matters at MC&S, dabbling in other ventures, and, toward the end of the decade, defending himself in the Continental case. There also were charges of felonies involving MC&S, with Wolfson losing the first trial. There were inconclusive retrials, and he finally agreed to a plea bargain to one charge of filing false statements in an MC&S annual report. All other charges were dropped. On November 30, 1972, Wolfson received a suspended 18-month sentence and a $10,000 fine.

Wolfson returned to Florida after serving his time at Eglin, and, except for the MC&S retrials, dropped from public sight. Today, at age 81, he remains bitter for what he regards as an outrageous miscarriage of justice.

Always interested in racing, Wolfson raised horses on his farm near Ocala. Because of his criminal record, he was initially unable to obtain licenses to race, but these finally were granted in 1971. Eight years later, one of his horses, Affirmed, won the Triple Crown.

On June 10, 1978, after Affirmed won the Belmont Stakes, the last of the Triple Crown events, the dapper, still ruggedly handsome, 66-year-old Wolfson strolled to the winner's circle with his wife to accept the victor's cup. F. Scott Fitzgerald was wrong. Some American lives have second acts. Perhaps it will be so with Mike Milken as well.

2

CHARLES MERRILL
AND THE REBIRTH
OF WALL STREET

Like corporate America, the American financial community was a conservative, risk-averse group in the period immediately following World War II. Bankers close to their primes had hunkered down, hoping merely to survive; after a decade and a half during which venturesome activities were not encouraged, they had emerged orthodox and unimaginative. "When the crash came in the thirties, no banker would admit where he worked," recalled Citibank's Walter Wriston. "Nobody wanted to work for a bank from 1933 to 1939. Then the war started. So there was nobody coming into the business from 1933 to 1946."[1]

Wall Street was in disfavor. Soon after World War II, Elmo Roper conducted a poll for the New York Stock Exchange to learn what people thought about that institution. He discovered that most believed Wall Street was home to some of the nation's slickest and most accomplished crooks. And a substantial segment thought the stock market was a place where cattle were sold.[2]

Bright, ambitious college graduates of the late 1940s and early 1950s considered careers in law and medicine. If they went into business, they sought trainee posts at some large corporation. Few without relatives in the field considered banking. This wasn't because bankers were poorly remunerated, but rather because there were yet higher returns to be had from corporate America. And more prestige as well.

The NYSE and the brokerage firms were dull places. Personnel stationed on the Exchange floor sometimes played baseball with rolled up newspapers and crumpled quotation sheets. Vacancies caused by retirement went unfilled. During the dismal year of 1940, average daily volume on the NYSE was 751,000 shares, and 5,855 people worked in New York's financial district. Volume doubled by 1946, but the labor force declined to 4,343.[3] In those days, the New York Curb Exchange, later to be renamed the American Stock Exchange, had average daily volume of only 550,000 shares.

The NYSE was open for business five full days with half-day trading on Saturday. From early June to late September, the exchange closed on Saturdays to give the community the long weekend, at a time when office air conditioning was still in its infancy.

Million-share days were not unusual, but at a majority of sessions fewer were traded. There were 26 trading days in March 1947. Four of them saw more than 1 million shares traded. On Saturday, March 15, 368,000 shares changed hands—typical volume for a winter day. Activity slowed considerably during the summer. There were no million-share days that August. Occasionally, the ticker tape would remain silent for minutes at a time, indicating that no trades at all had taken place. For the year as a whole, 254 million shares were traded, which is what volume can be on a single active session nowadays.

Investment bankers at the more distinguished houses were Ivy Leaguers whose fathers and uncles had worked there before them. At Morgan Stanley, partners tended to be Princeton men; as late as 1965, almost half were in the Social Register. First Boston had a Yale image, and Dillon Read bankers came from Harvard and Princeton. These scions of wealth conducted a leisurely business with contemporaries who had attended the same schools and belonged to the same fraternities. There was a name for what they were engaged in: "relationship banking."[4]

For the most part, these bankers were not the sharpest minds in their college classes. They didn't have specialized training; few majored in business or economics. This was no drawback, since the work was fairly simple. Ordinarily, the newcomer would start in "the cage," where back-office work was done. There they would function as glorified clerks, perhaps for several months, occasionally longer. Then, when an opening appeared, they might assist in a deal, or move on to trading or sales. The pay started around $50 a week, but after a while there would be year-end bonuses, and shares of profits when a partnership was achieved.

Trainees expected to remain at the same bank throughout their careers. There was a strong sense of loyalty and professional ethics at this level, one of the legacies bestowed by the elder J. P. Morgan and the other bankers of his generation. The gold watch awarded on retirement after several decades of service was not uncommon.

Clients, too, were steadfast, their fees negotiated in a gentlemanly fashion. Bankers led leisurely lives, marked by long summer weekends in the Hamptons or Newport and pleasant lunches with clients in private clubs. Things hadn't changed much since Otto Kahn told a congressional committee in 1933, "It has long been our policy and our effort to get our clients, not by chasing after them, not by praising our own wares, but by an attempt to establish a reputation which would make clients feel that if they have a problem of a financial nature, Dr. Kuhn, Loeb & Co. is a pretty good doctor to go to."[5]

What of bankers at the second- and third-tier houses? Here, one might have found graduates of the City College of New York, St. John's, and Long Island University, or, more likely, individuals who had never seen the inside of a college. Richard Schmeelk, one of the up-and-coming young men at Salomon Brothers & Hutzler, was a high school graduate. Billy Salomon, who had taken the firm into its position of prominence, had not attended college, and confessed to rarely reading anything other than a newspaper, magazine articles, and reports. "We weren't high school dropouts," said one old-timer there. "We were elementary school dropouts."

To be sure, Salomon was a minor force then, concentrating on selling bonds to institutions. But First Boston, one of the oldest, largest, and most distinguished investment banks, was headed by George Woods, who had taken a job as office boy at Harris, Forbes after graduating from Brooklyn Commercial High School.[6] This was not considered unusual.

Sidney Weinberg left school in the eighth grade with little more than a letter from his teacher at P.S. 13:

> It gives me great pleasure to testify to the business ability of the bearer, Sidney Weinberg.
> He is happy when he is busy, and always ready and willing to oblige. We believe he will give great satisfaction to anyone who may need his services.[7]

Weinberg got a job as assistant to the janitor at Goldman Sachs, where he caught the eye of Paul Sachs, who sent him through business college at night. Weinberg eventually headed that bank, became known as "Mr. Wall Street" in the 1930s, and engineered the initial public offering of Ford Motors in 1956—the underwriting of the decade.

THE ERA OF SAFETY FIRST

Financing in the 1950s meant stocks or bonds—that was all there was. Which it would be was determined by tax considerations, the company's debt structure, and the climate of the marketplace. To the bankers of that period, convertible debentures, warrants, and preferred stock were exotica. The idea of creating a new type of security for a client, or even playing a variation upon one of the main themes, would have been considered daring.

Foreign currency translations were not a factor; America was on the gold bullion standard, and all other western currencies were pegged to the dollar. As for interest rates, these barely moved. A bond salesman who set out on the road to meet with potential clients would carry lists of his firm's holdings and their quotes in his breast pocket notebook. He would make sales from it for weeks without consulting the home office, so stable was that market.

These bankers wanted little to do with initial public offerings of stocks, since such issues would be difficult to sell to prudent customers. "Common stock in small, young corporations can't as an ordinary matter be sold at all," wrote journalist Martin Mayer in 1955. Mayer, who would become one of the premier analysts of American finance in the decades that followed, was then feeling his way around Wall Street. He thought such companies might sell preferred stock, especially if it were convertible into common and paid a large dividend:

> It may be possible to sell a little common stock by giving the underwriter a quarter or a third of the proceeds, and of course, some corporations, even small ones, can sell additional stock to those personal friends who got them started in the first place. Without such friends a corporation will find that the price for "venture capital" is high as a gallows.[8]

The message was that small businesses seeking capital would have a tough time of it. Bold leaders of young companies could not hope to obtain much help from bankers like these. Even if the bankers had the will to underwrite their paper, who would buy the stocks and bonds? Not individual investors, who had deserted the Street in the 1930s and still hadn't returned.

Institutional investors were not interested in pioneering. They wanted high-rated bonds that would cause them no trouble. Like the bankers, the money managers were cautious, prudent, and risk-averse. Little wonder that activities like mergers, acquisitions, and proxy fights were rare. This was why Wolfson had paid little attention to bankers when going after Montgomery Ward.

Those firms too small to sell new issues and without financial resources had only one source of financing: venture capitalists. A handful of firms, the best known being the Rockefeller brothers' operation, specialized in securing funds for such companies and were on the prowl for promising situations. One venture capital concern, American Research & Development (AR&D), made the most spectacular investment of the time, in 1960 giving MIT researchers Kenneth Olsen and Harlan Anderson $70,000 in exchange for a 60 percent share of their embryonic company, Digital Equipment. Olsen and Anderson had no choice but to accept AR&D's proposition. Without that $70,000, there would have been no Digital Equipment. When AR&D later spun off its DEC shares two decades later to stockholders, this stake was worth more than $350 million.

Investors immediately after World War II were as timid as the businessmen and bankers. Those who purchased and held securities wanted the safety of high-rated corporate and government bonds. For the more daring, there were the bluest of blue chips, like American Telephone & Telegraph, Pennsylvania Railroad, or General Motors. Most Americans who had some extra cash put it into time deposits at savings banks, pleased to get an insured 3 percent return. Or they bought government savings bonds, the smallest of which cost $18.75 and in ten years returned $25. (Those were zero coupon bonds, although the term didn't exist at that time.)

Common stocks other than those of the major industrials, stable utilities, and railroads, were thought to be speculative. In the 1953 edition of one of the most popular finance textbooks of the period, Professor Julius Grodinsky of the Wharton School (where Milken would study two decades later) warned students of the dangers inherent in common stocks:

> The investors in common stocks . . . are the genuine risk bearers in the system of capitalism and free enterprise. Profits, like the ripples in a brook, are forever changing. Common stockbuyers are entitled to no contractual return. They receive only a participation in profits, and even then, only if such profits are declared in dividends. Nobody knows what future profits will be. Though everyone guesses, neither the management nor the shareholders, nor the public and private forecasters, soothsayers, or astrologers know the answer. There is a never-ending difference of opinion about future profits.[9]

In 1934, Benjamin Graham and David Dodd had set down the accepted dictum regarding dividends, which they called the "overshadowing factor" in common stock investment:

> The prime purpose of a business corporation is to pay dividends to its owners. A successful company is one that can pay dividends regularly and presumably increase the rate of return as time goes on. Since the idea of investment is closely bound up with that of dependable income, it follows that investment in common stocks would ordinarily be confined to those with a well established dividend. It would follow also that the price paid for an investment in common stock would be determined chiefly by the amount of the dividend.[10]

The greater the risk, the greater the reward. Stocks were riskier than bonds, and so investors expected a higher yield on stocks than that available from bonds. They got it. In 1949, U.S. government bonds yielded an average 2.3 percent, high-grade corporate bonds 2.7 percent, preferred stocks 4 percent, while the Moody's composite index of common stocks returned 6.6 percent.[11] One bought stocks when the economy seemed to be improving, and one bought bonds during declines. It was that simple.

The average price/earnings (P/E) ratio for the Dow-Jones Industrials that year (1949) was 7.6, and blue-chip stocks were selling around that level, offering unusually high yields. U.S. Steel, one of the top ten high-volume

stocks, earned $5.40 a share, paid a $2.25 dividend, and closed the year at
26$^1/_8$. General Motors earned $14.65 a share, paid an $8 dividend, and ended
at 71$^5/_8$. Other well-regarded stocks were selling for similar P/E ratios and
offering equally high yields. American Tobacco and CBS sported P/Es of 9,
and Sears Roebuck's was 8. Both had yields of around 6 percent.[12]

The most active stocks on the NYSE were not blue chips, but high-risk,
low-priced issues. This was because people interested in the quality stocks
would buy and hold. Outside of that handful of investment-grade issues,
common stocks were considered almost as speculative as lottery tickets. They
appealed to the kind of person who was not a long-term investor, but was
more akin to a contemporary habitué of off-track-betting parlors. Among
the ten most active stocks (and their closing prices) of 1949, for example,
were Benguet Consolidated (1$^5/_8$), United Corporation (5), Commonwealth
& Southern (5$^1/_2$), and Pepsi Cola (8$^1/_2$).

The media of the time reflected the general lack of interest in securities
and, for that matter, almost anything regarding business and economics.
The *Wall Street Journal* was a minor newspaper with a limited circulation
outside of the East and California. Its legendary editor, Barney Kilgore, was
striving to turn a narrow, parochial publication into a national one with a
broad circulation. In the late 1940s, it certainly was not in the same league
as the *Herald Tribune,* the *Journal American,* the *World Telegram,* or close
to a dozen other New York newspapers that now are only memories. Dow
Jones monitored the markets, but updated its famous averages only once an
hour. Radio news programs did not carry market quotes. Market research
was close to nonexistent, and what did exist was fundamental in nature.
Technical analysis existed, of course, but the number of indicators was quite
small—the information simply wasn't being generated—and so it was not in
vogue. The larger newspapers had business pages, and some even had sec-
tions. The reporting was inadequate, the analysis flimsy, and the quality of
the writing poorer than was to be found in other parts of the newspapers.
The reason was not difficult to find. Business was one of the least desirable
assignments on most newspapers: the doghouse at some, the bullpen at others, but for all, clearly, not the place to seek a splendid career.[13]

All this was about to change.

Money was tight during the summer of 1949, though the discount rate
was 1$^1/_2$ percent, where it had been since the previous August. But the talk
on Wall Street was that the economy was recovering from a mild slump. The
Treasury had a hard time selling long-term bonds, because if the recovery
occurred, money would move from bonds to stocks.

On June 13, the Dow Industrials posted an intraday low of 160.95 on
volume of 1,345,000 shares, and the average fell by three points. There
was nothing in the news to account for this sell-off. The Berlin Blockade
remained a dangerous situation, and a trial of American Communist Party

leaders continued. The Council of Foreign Ministers meeting in Paris ended without agreement on the unification of Germany. Baseball scores were more interesting to the vast majority of Americans than anything happening at the New York Stock Exchange.

The Dow never again would close so low. Stocks opened down on June 14, with the Dow at 160.60 by 11:00. Then a small rally developed, bringing the average to 162.51 shortly before the close. Volume that day was 1,123,000 shares.

Prices moved higher thereafter, ending the year at 200.52 on volume of 2,086,000 shares. Most people on Wall Street understood that a bull move had begun. Even so, no one quoted in the major publications predicted a cracking of the 381.17 record posted some 20 years earlier on September 3, 1929.

By then, there were faint stirrings among the vast majority of Americans who had not shown much interest in securities since the 1920s, and still feared the return of hard times. As more people came to believe that the long-anticipated postwar depression would not take place, this indifferent attitude was beginning to change.

THE COMING OF PEOPLE'S CAPITALISM

The public's reintroduction to the securities markets came slowly. The initial impetus was the promotion of "people's capitalism" by Charles E. Merrill, CEO of the banking firm of Merrill Lynch, Pierce, Fenner & Beane.

Merrill saw his major task as convincing the public that investment in stocks was not only sensible, but prudent. He was concerned with attracting the "33-year-old veteran with a wife and children, a small home and mortgage, and a $5,000-a-year job."[14]

One of the major problems was getting that person into a brokerage office. At the time, brokers came in two varieties. In the first group were those akin to the amiable investment bankers, although usually not as intelligent, sophisticated, educated, or well-connected. In his 1954 novel, *A World of Profit,* Louis Auchincloss has an unimaginative character say the following: "When it's profit you're after, why go about it the hard way? I intend to be a stockbroker. It is a profession that is devoid of hypocrisy. One attempts to make the most money with the least work. It is clean. It is pure. It is without cant."

Such brokers made sales to college chums, members of clubs they frequented, relatives, and others in that milieu. Their idea of a large deal might be the sale of 300 shares of General Motors to a client who took the purchase as seriously as he might that of a new Pontiac. Some brokers did a substantial amount of trust or money management business, investing funds by rote in governments, railroad bonds, and the like. They were janissaries for old money, handling mechanical details, like making certain bond coupons were clipped and dividends and interest were either remitted or reinvested.[15]

In the second group were out-and-out hustlers, who switched clients in and out of stocks and bonds frequently in order to earn commissions. The sleazier ones worked out of marginal houses, making calls on the telephone, hoping to snare the unsuspecting. The respected institutions deemed such brokers mendacious and shifty, having more in common with racetrack touts than bankers. Their customers didn't mind, however, since they were gamblers, hoping one or another of the low-priced stocks they favored would be a fast double. But there weren't many of them.

In Merrill's view, the most important task facing Wall Street was rebuilding the public confidence that had been shattered by the Great Crash and Depression. If anything positive was to be accomplished, the public would have to be convinced that brokers, the key figures in the investment process, were scrupulously honest.[16] Merrill believed that if potential small investors could be persuaded that the broker was a professional in every sense of the term, they might be induced to use his services. Brokers had traditionally ignored this market; they had discouraged individuals with only a few hundred dollars, who were hardly worth the trouble of consultation, planning, and management, from investing.

Merrill argued that while novice investors usually started small, in time, if the experience proved salutary, they might become more substantial investors. In effect, he hoped to do for the brokerage business what chain stores had done for retailing: Make smaller profits per client, but lure many more of them to the operation. "Our business is people and their money," Merrill said in 1946. "We must draw the new capital required for industrial might and growth *not* from among a few large investors but from the savings of thousands of people of moderate incomes. We must bring Wall Street to Main Street—and we must use the efficient, mass-merchandising methods of the chain store to do it."[17]

Merrill instituted a rigorous training program, at a time when most new brokers were given little more than a day of orientation and the examination to become a broker was a joke. In an era when few could hope for much success except those who came with family and other accounts, Merrill began to hire bright young men who showed promise, and he provided them with leads garnered from responses to his extensive advertising campaigns—another first.

The NYSE mandated minimum commissions, but there was no maximum, and most brokerage firms extracted what the traffic would bear. Not Merrill Lynch, which not only charged the minimum but campaigned for yet lower rates. Research operations were beefed up, and, at a time when other brokerage firms charged for such material, reports were offered free to interested individuals. Other brokerage firms had fee schedules for monthly statements, for holding securities and for clipping coupons on bonds, and for practically any other service rendered. Merrill Lynch waived such charges.

In this period, Merrill Lynch brokers were paid salaries, not commissions, and Merrill made certain the public knew this. Brokers at other firms might use the hard sell to increase their income, but not at his firm. Merrill even changed the employee designation from "broker" to "account executive." The company's offices were bright, cheerful, and comfortable, unlike some of the older places that were somber, dark, and forbidding.

This approach worked. Merrill Lynch became a powerhouse of finance. By 1955, when Louis Wolfson made his play for Montgomery Ward, the firm handled 10 percent of the transactions at the NYSE and 18 percent of the odd-lot business. Its gross income came to $45.6 million in 1950; four years later, the figure was $73.3 million.

Merrill Lynch had an elan rare on the Street, and it engendered customer and employee loyalty. Charles Merrill did for brokerage what Tom Watson had done for IBM and Ray Kroc would later do for fast food; he made it efficient, trouble-free, and trustworthy. "If you took a group of IBM salesmen and Merrill Lynch brokers and mixed them up, you couldn't tell one from the other," remarked William Schreyer, a future Merrill Lynch CEO, who arrived in this period. "Their principles were so similar. When people came to Merrill Lynch in those days, they never thought about going anywhere else."[18]

Merrill Lynch's success led other wire houses to imitate its methods and, in this way, set the tone for the industry. They would pattern themselves after Merrill Lynch in all matters except broker commissions. As volume increased and commissions rose, Merrill Lynch, too, abandoned fixed salaries and paid commissions—the one area in which the firm bowed to tradition.

The alteration of public attitudes toward stock investing that Merrill sought took time. As late as 1952, according to a NYSE census, there were only 6.5 million shareholders, which came to one of every 24 Americans.[19] By 1970, there were 30.9 million shareholders, or one out of every six Americans.[20]

More than anyone until then, Charles Merrill remade the face of the American securities business. No longer was the broker a second-class business citizen. In that age of fixed commissions, when the purchase or sale of 1,000 shares of stock generated ten times the income of a 100-share trade in the same stock, brokers made a great deal of money. By the 1960s, it was not at all unusual for brokers to draw larger paychecks than investment bankers. The best became superstars with large followings that could be transferred should the broker decide to move to another company. Brokers at major houses no longer had to be hucksters. Backed by a large staff of researchers, the broker of the 1960s was deemed a professional in every sense of the word.[21] Now bright young college graduates flocked to Wall Street, where they hoped to become brokers.

CHARLES WILSON AND
PENSION PLAN SOCIALISM

Around 1950, Walter Reuther, head of the United Automobile Workers, and General Motors CEO Charles Wilson set into motion forces in institutional stock sales similar to those Charles Merrill generated for small investors. During the 1951 contract negotiations, Wilson suggested a pension program, which was approved. Moreover, under terms of the agreement, the GM plan would be permitted to invest in common shares.

Management-provided pension plans were themselves not a new idea; a Bureau of Labor Statistics study indicated that there were several hundred of them in place in 1919, and there were about 2,000 in 1950. Almost all plans invested their funds in corporate and government bonds, a policy considered prudent by a generation wary of anything that smacked of speculation, especially when it came to a pension plan. Moreover, the "prudent-man rule" in many states mandated the purchase of high-quality bonds and, in some cases, preferred stock. This was easing, however, as the older trustees retired. By the late 1940s, some pension funds were buying common shares. In 1949, they owned a grand total of $500 million of common stock; in 1971, this figure was over $900 billion, while the total for all institutions rose from $11 billion to $219 billion in the same period.[22] It was the beginning of what business analyst Peter F. Drucker would call "pension plan socialism."[23]

In the same year as the General Motors pact, some New York life insurance companies petitioned state regulators for the right to invest up to 2 percent of their assets in common shares. The state agreed. Other states followed. By 1955, life insurance companies owned more than $3.6 billion in common stock, while the property and casualty companies, which always had the right to own common shares, held another $5.4 billion.

In its 1952 census, the NYSE found that only 11 percent of all common shares were owned by institutions and nominees.[24] This was a time when critics of capitalism frequently complained that a small group of powerful individuals—the DuPonts, the Mellons, and others—controlled American business through nominees on the boards of many companies. As late as 1962, one of the nation's leading radical scholars, Gabriel Kolko, could write, "The concentration of economic power in a very small elite is an indisputable fact."[25]

Yet, even then the situation was changing. The old money retrenched, and a new group of billionaires was coming to the fore. Within two generations the wealthiest Americans would be Bill Gates (Microsoft), Sam

Walton (Wal-Mart), Warren Buffett (Berkshire Hathaway), and John Kluge (Metromedia), all of whom had come from humble origins. Yet none was considered a dominant force outside of his own industry. True power was passing to a new force.

By 1976, pension plans owned more than a third of the nation's equity; by the early 1990s, they had investments of $2.5 trillion and owned more than half of the nation's equity. Were they of a mind to become active owners, faceless pension plan managers could decide the fates of the managements of most medium-sized and large corporations.[26]

What was not realized in the 1950s, but became obvious later, were the differences between the Merrill version and that of Wilson and Reuther. The former spoke of shareholder democracy. Wilson used similar language, but felt the process would be accomplished collectively rather than individually.

The Merrill version prevailed in the 1950s and 1960s. The 1970s were a period of transition. In the 1980s, it became clear that the Wilson variant had triumphed—that individual investors, frightened by the uncertain markets of the 1970s and bewildered by the multiform methods of investment that followed, were seeking safety in mutual funds and other large aggregations of capital. This meant that account executives would have fewer clients, while anonymous institutional managers would become prime stock purchasers. Big money, not small, would come to dominate markets, even though it was often made up of the accumulated resources of many small investors. The big money wouldn't be the wealth of men like Bill Gates or Warren Buffett, but of those janissaries of the small investors, who managed the huge pension funds, mutual funds, and insurance funds. This had not been the case in Lou Wolfson's time, but it would be bedrock reality for Mike Milken.

None of this was clearly perceived in the 1950s and 1960s. It simply appeared that Merrill, Wilson, and Reuther, among them, had created a new demand for common shares, which had the effect of boosting stock prices. The demand for equity encouraged companies to provide it. Investment bankers now stepped forward to take young companies public with the lure of attractive stock prices, as well as to sell new issues of established concerns. The statistics told the story. During no year of the Great Depression and World War II did the value of newly issued common stock come to as much as $400 million; it would rise above $1 billion in 1952, $2 billion in 1955, and $3 billion in 1961.[27]

THE GREAT BULL MARKET

The increased demand transformed common stocks as an investment vehicle. At the beginning of the decade, those venturesome individuals who purchased shares did so for the dividends. If the stock rose, the yield declined. Thus, they might buy shares at $10 with a $1 dividend for a yield of 10 percent. If the stock went to $20, the yield would have declined to 5 percent, and at that point the investors might sell and look for another high-yielding stock.

In the process, they would learn the delights of capital gains, and they might be converted from Graham and Dodd value investing to the search for more rapid rewards from growth stocks, whose P/Es were higher and yields were lower. As the 1950s wore on, such investors were prepared to pay a higher price for earnings and forego dividends entirely in the hope of capital gains. Indeed, some argued that the payment of dividends, once considered a sign of business strength, was really a weakness, since the payouts meant the company no longer needed funds for growth, the new leading investment objective. Such growth stocks as Texas Instruments, Litton Industries, and Varian Associates sported P/E ratios of over 50 and paid no dividends. IBM had a P/E of better than 50, and offered a yield of just one half of one percent. Interest in mutual funds had shifted from portfolios balanced between bonds and stocks to those emphasizing growth. Never before or since have common shares been as popular as they were in the 1960s.

As the mania gathered steam, and demand for stocks expanded, Wall Street produced what should be called "junk stocks." Of course, they were not known by that name; more often than not, they were referred to as "emerging growth stocks." Just as the pension funds, mutual funds, and insurance companies of the 1980s would line up to purchase junk bonds with enormous amounts of money coming in regularly, so the mutual and pension funds of the 1960s, along with those new individual investors wanting to participate in America's industrial boom, sought stocks in young companies with "a story." By the early 1960s, a period of high optimism for America, the junk stock market had become the focus of speculative attention for individual investors. It was there that one found the highest level of risk and possible rewards.

Fortunate indeed were young firms in need of funds during this period, or even "concept companies"—those with nothing more than ideas and a small circle of personnel. "Going public" was simple when the appetite for stocks was so great. In January 1961, initial public offerings were coming to market at the rate of two per day. Such now-forgotten companies as Chemtronic, Madigan Electronics, Pneumodynamics, Vacuum Electronics, and Varitab were the early-1960s analogue to the failed junk issues of the late 1980s. They were promoted by Michael Lomasney, Charles Plohn, Donald Marron, and Stephen Fuller, "hot" underwriters of the period, who evoked the same kind of admiration bestowed on some of the (much larger) junk underwriters two decades later.

THE GROWTH MANIA

Seeking assistance in locating the next story stock, investors increasingly turned to "performance," or "go-go" mutual funds managed by hot analysts adept at ferreting out emerging growth stocks. There were more than a score of these individuals, including Gerald Tsai, who managed Fidelity Capital Fund; Fred Mates, who immodestly called his vehicle Mates Fund; Fred Alger, whose company selected stocks for Security Equity Fund; and Fred Carr of Enterprise Fund, which was managed by Shareholders Capital. These were new men, the kind Wall Street usually saw during manias. They were definitely not establishment types—they had no use for existing selection criteria and were certain of their own abilities.

Carr was probably the best known of the lot and the longest-lived professionally. His career ran from the era of go-go stocks to that of junk bonds, from Lou Wolfson to Mike Milken. An Angeleno who disliked New York but had to go there since it was the nation's financial hub, Carr was born Seymour Cohen in 1931. He grew up in the Depression as the son of parents who ran a neighborhood fruit stand. He entered college but soon dropped out and held a variety of jobs, from pumping gasoline to selling insurance.

In 1957, Carr got his first financial job as a trainee at Bache & Co. The other brokers there were right out of the Merrill tradition—clean-cut, obliging, and dependent upon the firm's vast research facility, which in this period concentrated on the big, proven companies. These held little allure for Carr, who liked to do his own research, usually consisting of observing what was going on around him; this implied investing in companies with new products and services.

The market was moving, and so were the young people who arrived at the right time. Soon Carr was director of research for Ira Haupt & Co., and when that firm collapsed a few years later, he took a similar job at Kleiner, Bell & Co., one of the hottest of the new-issue houses. Now he was making $100,000 a year, considered very good money in this period. Still, Carr wanted to be his own boss, so he left Kleiner, Bell to take over management of the $21 million California Fund. While continuing there, he organized Shareholders Management Co., whose only asset was the talent of Carr and several other hot shots, who would later be known as "the dirty dozen" and "the twelve angry men." One of the several mutual funds they organized was Enterprise, which, toward the end of the 1960s, became one of the best performing funds in the nation.

Carr specialized in uncovering special situations, or stocks with an unusual story. In the late 1950s and early 1960s, this included, among other businesses, fast-food companies. His first big coups came in this area, with such stocks as Winchell's Donuts, Kentucky Fried Chicken, and McDonald's. He then went on to Tonka Toys, Jostens, and Kelly Services.

The appetite for shares of small- to medium-sized enterprising growth companies was demonstrated by shareholders in Enterprise and other mutual funds. By then, some American businessmen, especially in smaller companies, and mavericks uncomfortable with established firms, had become more confident, not only of the future, but of their own abilities. Business new-comers who chafed at operating within old constraints and who sought chal-lenges were concluding that skills acquired in one industry might easily be transferred to another, and there was no reason one company couldn't be in several simultaneously. They also prized growth, and the fastest way to achieve it was through company acquisitions. There was nothing new about this, but wedded to the new philosophy of transferable management skills, the concept of acquisition came to suggest that a firm could profitably take on and absorb just about any company within its sights. Out of this vision came the conglomerate movement, led by several remarkable businessmen, none of whom was more imaginative and daring than James Ling.

3

JAMES LING AND THE CONGLOMERATE ERA

The conglomerate movement had several origins. First, there was a renewal of the antibusiness atmosphere of the late 1930s, which had been suspended during the war. Federal legislation aimed at halting horizontal and vertical mergers was sponsored by Congressman Emanuel Celler (D. New York), an octogenarian who had represented the same district since 1923, and was chairman of the House Antitrust Committee of the Committee on the Judiciary. His cosponsor was Estes Kefauver (D. Tennessee), a politically ambitious senator who was fashioning a reputation as a southern liberal. The Celler-Kefauver Act of 1950, intended to supplement existing antitrust legislation, made it difficult for companies to expand through acquisitions of companies in related areas. Intent was discounted. If a firm had a large share of the market as a result of mergers, the courts could dissolve it even if no restraints of trade were involved. Size alone mattered. But conglomerates did not dominate single industries, and so did not fall under the perview of the law.

Then, too, fears of a new depression led some businessmen to seek diversification in order to hedge economic bets. By the 1950s, when it became increasingly apparent that there would be no depression and the stock market started to rise, newly optimistic businessmen came to believe they might manage just about any type of company. The high price of their stocks provided them with a means to acquire other companies. So they did. By the mid-1960s, several old-line firms had abandoned or added to their traditional businesses. (See Table 3–1.)

Studebaker left the automobile industry to manufacture industrial machinery; Philadelphia & Reading moved from coal to clothing; W.R. Grace, a steamship line, became a force in chemicals and fast foods. Beatrice diversified from its dairy base to purchase firms manufacturing luggage, lamps, and even Avis, the car rental company. All the tobacco companies, fearful of governmental bans on cigarettes, diversified into such areas as food, liquor, office equipment, petroleum, and transportation.

Table 3–1

DISTRIBUTION OF MERGERS BY TYPE
AND PERIOD, 1940–1968
(figures in percent)

	1940–47	1951–55	1956–60	1961–65	1966–68
Type of Merger					
Horizontal	62.0	39.2	30.1	22.5	8.6
Vertical	17.0	12.2	14.9	17.5	9.8
Conglomerate	21.0	48.6	55.0	60.0	81.6

Source: Staff Report of the Federal Trade Commission, *Economic Report on Corporate Mergers,* Hearings on Economic Concentration, Subcommittee on Antitrust and Monopoly, U.S. Senate, 91st Congress, 1st Session (Washington, 1969), p. 63.

The same happened at some of the newer companies. Gulf + Western began in auto parts, and wound up with a cigar company, a sugar plantation, and a motion picture studio. Litton started with electronics and took over companies in publishing, shipbuilding, and industrial machinery. Teledyne was an electronics operation that purchased insurance companies and the firm that manufactured Water Pic. International Telephone & Telegraph was, literally and figuratively, all over the map.

THE BIRTH OF LTV

Harold Geneen, the CEO of ITT from 1959 to 1976, who came to symbolize the conglomerate phenomenon in the popular imagination, was renowned for the number and scope of his takeovers and purported managerial skills— not for his originality. From the vantage point of another generation, one may wonder at the celebrity afforded Geneen in the 1960s. The same could not be said for James Ling, whose boldness continues to impress those who have studied his accomplishments.

Ling was another of the brash, self-assured young men from the provinces who arrive during periods of financial opportunity. He was even more of an outsider than Wolfson. Ling was born in 1922 in Hugo, Oklahoma, a town not found on many maps. His father, Henry, was a Bavarian immigrant, a railroader who, after killing a man and being acquitted on grounds of self-defense, converted to Catholicism and entered a monastery, abandoning his wife, Mary, and his six children.

Like many others during the Great Depression, young James drifted from place to place, and, somehow or other, was able to obtain an electrician's license. After service in the Navy during World War II, this self-described "bum" found himself in Dallas with few prospects. So, with initial capital of

$3,000, he founded Ling Electric and cast about for small contracts wiring homes.

Dallas was in the midst of a major expansion in both residential and commercial construction, and business was there for the taking. Through aggressive salesmanship, Ling won a few assignments and then some more. Ling Electric grossed $70,000 in 1947. The following year, revenues rose to $200,000, and the year after that, to $400,000. By the early 1950s, Ling Electric was bidding for contracts throughout the region and had construction units in New Orleans and San Diego. In 1955, the firm grossed $1.5 million.[1]

Ling knew next to nothing about finance when he started out; he picked up what knowledge he required when the need arose—when he required capital for expansion. Like Wolfson, Ling came to realize that a company can grow faster through acquisitions than by expanding upon an existing base. And he learned there was more to business than wiring houses and office buildings. Indeed, why concentrate on a single industry? After all, the rationale for business was to make money, not specific products, and Ling meant to make a lot of money.

Ling decided to sell some shares to raise capital for his schemes. He took his company to Wall Street and tried to talk some small underwriters into making an offering of common stock. They shrugged him off, and so he went about it his own way. Taking a booth at the Texas State Fair, he was able to peddle 450,000 shares at $2.25. This taught him that people were demanding stock, and he intended to provide them with plenty of it.

Ling started out by purchasing L.M. Electronics, a manufacturer of testing equipment, an area he suspected held great promise. He changed his firm's name to Ling Electronics and celebrated by purchasing United Electronics and Calidyne. Other acquisitions followed, among them Altec Electronics, University Loudspeakers, and Temco (formerly Texas Engineering and Manufacturing Company).

Ling soon cast his eye on Chance Vought (CV), the largest defense company in the Dallas region, which itself had diversified into other areas. In this, his first attempt at a major acquisition, Ling showed that, like Wolfson, he sought assets undervalued in the marketplace. CV had both strong earnings and a low stock price—in the 1950s, its earnings averaged close to $6.00 a share, while in 1960, the stock had a book value of more than $36 a share and was selling in the low 20s.

CV was Ling's first hostile takeover. He started by borrowing short-term from several insurance companies to finance a tender offer, which he initiated in the spring of 1961. CEO Frederick Detweiler replied by initiating a civil antitrust suit, arguing that the merger would lessen competition in the aircraft industry. Using his considerable clout in Washington, Detweiler urged the Justice Department to institute a suit of its own, which was done.

In the end Ling acquired CV—and changed the name of his company to Ling-Temco-Vought (LTV). But Ling would claim that from that point on, the government was out to destroy him, because he threatened the established forces in American industry.

Ling had gone deeply in debt with these acquisitions. Now he set about to clean up his balance sheet in preparation for additional forays. He sold several CV subsidiaries, using the proceeds to pay off part of the debt, and transformed short-term debt into longer-term obligations.

Ling did this because he had discovered a truth that later would be rediscovered by the junk bond practitioners of the 1970s and 1980s, and that earlier had made Wolfson's career. The price of a firm's stock need not be a valid measure of its worth. Carve up the company, sell off the parts, or invade the treasury, Ling realized, and the parts might prove to be worth more than the whole. So it had been with Montgomery Ward and Capital Transit in the 1950s, and so it was with LTV's targets in the mid-1960s. It would be the same with Beatrice and RJR Nabisco in the 1980s. Ling performed precisely the kind of leveraged buyout that would become familiar in the 1980s. The difference between the CV takeover and that of RJR Nabisco by Kohlberg, Kravis, Roberts & Co. (KKR) was a matter of scope, not form.

Proxy solicitor Arthur Long, who worked with some of the major players in the 1980s LBO contests, got his start with Ling and reminisced about this in 1984. "The first thing Jimmy looked for was value," recalled Long. "But in a different way. He'd say, 'Here's an undervalued company. I could leverage the whole thing, and the company could buy itself.' James Ling did the first leveraged buyout 25 years ago."[2]

In the 1980s investors would want high-yield junk bonds, and bankers issued them. And just as the highly leveraged companies of the 1980s had to monitor their credit ratings to be able to issue bonds with lower coupons, so Ling's first task in the 1960s was to strengthen his common stock, since, along with convertible debentures based on common, this was to be his prime means of acquiring companies.

To enhance the price of LTV common, Ling would have to increase earnings per share. There were two methods to accomplish this: LTV could either generate higher earnings with the same amount of shares outstanding, or maintain earnings while shrinking the number of shares. The former method would be accomplished through operations and the acquisition of companies with good earnings. The latter might be achieved by breaking down existing holdings into independent companies and exchanging part of their capitalizations for LTV common, in this way winding up with lower capitalization and partial ownership of subsidiaries. By so doing Ling could combine diversification with a radical restructuring such as the nation had never seen. His ultimate goal was enlargement of per share profits, which would boost the price of the common stock.

Ling started in a fairly conventional fashion. In 1964, he offered to exchange one share of convertible preferred stock that paid $3 in dividends plus $15 in cash for three shares of LTV common. It was an attractive offer, since the common stock was paying 50 cents in dividends and the preferred could be converted into 1.25 shares of common at the option of the owner. Those who accepted would have the cash, and twice the dividend income, and they still would have a stake in LTV common through the conversion process. In this way, Ling would slash the equity base, and so boost earnings per share. It worked. He would repeat the process four more times.

On this occasion, LTV decreased its capitalization from 2.8 million shares to 1.9 million. The effect was dramatic. LTV's 1963 net income had been $6.2 million, which worked out to $2.12 per share. Income for 1964 actually declined to $4.9 million, but since the capitalization was so much lower, per share earnings came in at $2.32 per share. As Ling anticipated, LTV stock responded by staging a respectable advance. Everyone seemed to have won in this, the first of Ling's machinations.

PROJECT REDEPLOYMENT

Later that year, Ling announced what he called Project Redeployment, a highly original plan to transform LTV into a pure holding company. The purpose was not production efficiencies or return on investment, but once again to enhance the stock price.

The first step was to establish three wholly owned subsidiaries—LTV Aerospace, LTV Ling Altec, and LTV Electrosystems, whose only assets were their common stock. Next, Ling divided LTV into three unequal portions, and exchanged the appropriate ones for the common shares of the three new entities. Aerospace received most of CV and a substantial portion of Temco, Ling Altec obtained Altec and some miscellaneous properties, and Electrosystems got the leftovers.

In April 1965, LTV offered one-half share of each of these three companies, plus $9, for every share of LTV common tendered to the parent. He hoped that 800,000 shares would be tendered. Some stockholders, however, held back, since they had difficulty figuring out whether or not it was a good deal, a not uncommon situation with Ling's offers. In the end, LTV received only 245,000 shares from the exchange offer.

The three new entities now had public shareholders, greater visibility, and, eventually, listings on the American Stock Exchange. As it turned out, those who accepted Ling's offer did quite well for themselves. The book value of the three companies at the time of Project Redeployment was $7.9 million. The market values of the shares a year later came to $35 million.

In this way, Ling performed for his company in 1964 a version of what the LBO practitioners would do a quarter of a century later. After their leveraged buyouts, they would sell assets and realize immense profits. The difference between them and Ling was that in Project Redeployment he sold partial ownerships, not entire businesses.

Ling plunged ahead. In October 1965, he acquired Okonite, a major manufacturer of copper wire and cable, for $31.7 million in cash. He financed this deal by having LTV raise $20 million from a consortium of banks, putting up as collateral $73 million worth of its own securities. Then, as share prices advanced, Ling sold additional stock in all its subsidiaries, with LTV borrowing the money to pay off some of the loans needed for the Okonite purchase. Finally, he sold 17 percent of Okonite and used the money to pay off the rest of the loans. Okonite common responded by advancing.

In this way Ling provided LTV with a fourth subsidiary, gave Okonite a market valuation, and secured funds to pay for the purchase. In effect, LTV had 83 percent of Okonite for virtually no cost save that of time and effort, and approximately $3 million in market value of subsidiary stock. Okonite was able to contribute immediately to LTV's earnings, which made its common stock seem more appealing than ever.

In 1965, LTV reported a modest net sales increase to $336.2 million from the prior year's $332.9 million. Earnings were up sharply, however, to $6 million vs. $4.9 million the year before, while per share earnings rose from $2.32 to $2.82. Without the Okonite deal, LTV's figures would have declined across the board. As it was, investors responded by pushing the price of LTV common from 17 to 58, with the P/R ratio rising to 20.

GOLFBALL, GOOFBALL, AND MEATBALL

The next step was even more audacious. In 1966, Ling fixed his gaze on Wilson & Co., the nation's third-largest meat packer, with sales of more than $1 billion, more than twice the income of LTV. Wilson was also a major manufacturer of sports equipment; from hides and skins came coverings for footballs. There was, additionally, a pet foods business, which obtained its raw materials from meat unfit for human consumption. From the fats came soap. Finally, Wilson had developed a small but rapidly growing unit in pharmaceuticals derived from animal organs. By extrapolating its core business rather than by acquiring other businesses, Wilson had become a conglomerate. Moreover, the parts seemed to be worth more than the whole. Sporting goods and pharmaceuticals were glamor businesses. Meat packing was not. Freed from the meat operation, the other units might fetch large sums. From this staid company might be sliced three, four, or even five units. Since the stock was selling for around 50 and there were 2.4 million shares outstanding, Wilson was valued by the marked at $120 million.

Ling struck in December 1966, offering $62.50 in cash for each of the 750,000 shares of Wilson common. Wilson's CEO Roscoe Haynie objected strenuously and vowed there would be a battle. Management's campaign contained an echo of the Montgomery Ward broadsides against Wolfson. There were advertisements imploring shareholders to demonstrate loyalty and attacking Ling as being unfamiliar with the industry. But something had changed in the 11 years since Wolfson's attempt on Montgomery Ward. Those loyal shareholders had been replaced by owners to whom a stock was a piece of paper to be bought and sold; it was not a marriage contract.

The Ling offer was oversubscribed. He purchased more shares on the open market and within days had half of Wilson's stock at a cost of slightly less than $82 million. Then he exchanged $115 million worth of LTV $5 preferred stock for the remainder of the Wilson shares. (This procedure would come to be known as a two-tier takeover, in which those who came in on the first offer would do better than those who followed.)

The Wilson acquisition transformed LTV into a $1.8 billion corporation, but the balance sheet looked shaky. There were 4.7 million shares outstanding, while the long-term debt came to $363 million. Ling's next step would be to rectify this situation.

First, LTV stripped Wilson of its cash and set aside four packing plants to be leased to a newly created Wilson & Co. for high fees. Ling also transferred $50 million in debt from LTV to Wilson.

He then implemented a strategy that might have been (but wasn't) inspired by Wolfson's scheme to restructure Montgomery Ward. Ling organized three new shell companies: Wilson Sporting Goods, Wilson Pharmaceutical & Chemical, and the new Wilson & Co. In exchange for their shares, LTV provided each with the relevant portions of the old Wilson & Co. Wall Street wags soon dubbed these new firms "Golfball," "Goofball," and "Meatball."

Ling sold 18 percent of Wilson & Co. to the public, realizing $21.8 million. A quarter of the shares of Sporting Goods added another $17 million, while 23 percent of Pharmaceutical & Chemical fetched almost $6 million. In all, LTV gained more than $44 million from these sales.

With these funds, Ling paid off a portion of the debt incurred in the Wilson purchase. Within months, the shares of the three companies had risen substantially. Sporting Goods and Pharmaceutical & Chemical became semiglamour stocks in the great bull market of the period. By autumn, LTV's equity in these three companies had a market value of approximately $250 million. The cost, as Ling calculated it, came to around $6 million in short-term debt and the $5.7 million required annually to service the $5 preferred issue. This was the miracle of junk stock in a market that had an appetite for such paper.

No 1980s practitioner of leveraged buyouts had anything on Ling, whose record is all the more impressive since he thought up most of his maneuvers on his own, and was not helped (or, some might say, encumbered) by an MBA or reliance on Wall Street brains. The fundamental explanation for all of this strategy was that Ling realized that the followers of people like Merrill and Charles Wilson—the small investors and the institutions—were hungry for common stock. All he did was give them what they wanted. A similar mania would exist in the 1980s, when Mike Milken dumped bundles of junk bonds on eager purchasers at high-yield mutual funds and insurance companies.

So it went. Ling structured, restructured, and re-restructured LTV, acquiring firms, spinning them off into new entities, and coming up with new approaches every season or so. All of this had the expected impact on the price of the shares. In early 1964, LTV common sold for under 10; in 1967, it peaked at 169½ before declining, and then rallied once more. The stock's 1963 P/E was as low as 5; in 1967, it reached 24.

In 1968, Ling set about acquiring Greatamerica Corp., which was controlled by a friend, Troy Post. Greatamerica was an umbrella for a wide variety of companies, most of them financially oriented. These included Franklin Life, American Amicable Life, Gulf Life, Stonewall Life, and First Western Bank & Trust. Greatamerica also had a bundle of smaller companies, including a controlling interest in Braniff Airlines, and was preparing to buy National Car Rental.

With Post's encouragement, Ling made a tender offer for Greatamerica common, then selling in the low 20s. This was too large a firm to be acquired for cash, and a tender based on common stock would cause major dilution in per share earnings, so Ling had to take another route. For every 100 shares of Greatamerica he would exchange $3,000 in LTV 5 percent debentures maturing in 1988, plus a warrant to buy ten shares of LTV common at 115. It was an appealing submission that, with Post's blessings, was readily accepted.

The takeover was soon completed, whereupon Ling arranged for the familiar deployment. Stonewall Life was sold for $15 million, First Western for $62.5 million, and American Amicable for $18 million. Ling received funds equal to 20 percent of the debentures, and still had most of Braniff, all of National Car Rental, and a grab-bag of insurance companies.

As a result of these activities, LTV's total long-term debt had risen to $1.2 billion. Troubled by large interest payments, Ling decided to cut back on this front. This worried many investors, and their doubts bothered Ling. On learning that a top analyst had questioned his balance sheet, Ling asked him to come for a talk. On seeing that the man had a touch of gray in his temples, Ling snorted, "What could I expect from someone over 40?"

Anyone who doubted Ling's wizardry would have come around after learning of his next moves, which required greater input from Wall Street than he had been accustomed to. In October 1968, with his bankers, Goldman Sachs and Lehman Brothers, Ling put together a "unit" composed of the following:

1 share of Braniff Class A stock

0.6 shares of National Car Rental common

1 share of National Car Rental Class A

1.1 LTV warrants exercisable at 103.35 expiring in 1978

0.3 share of Computer Technology.

The last firm named was a small entity Ling had recently put together, which now would become a public company.

The following is what Ling offered under his plan:

1.1 units for 1 share of LTV common

9.75 units for $1,000 of LTV 6.5 percent notes

10 units for $1,000 of LTV 6.75 percent debentures

6.7 units for $1,000 of LTV's 5 percent debentures

9.5 units for $1,000 of LTV's 5.57 percent debentures

In essence, Ling proposed to exchange shares in subsidiary companies with warrants for LTV common and debt. He was trying to lower both the debt and the equity base, which would relieve him of interest payments while increasing per share earnings. This would make the common more attractive, enabling him to use equity-based securities in his next foray.

The impact of the offer was electric. Owners of LTV paper called their brokers to have the deal explained and ask for advice, and the brokers simply didn't know how to answer. Was it or was it not a good deal? No one quite knew, but all agreed that if the plan was successful, LTV would have a much lower debt and perhaps significantly less equity, while retaining important blocks of Braniff, National Car Rental, and the new Computer Technology.

As this was going on, Ling set about targeting another large company. There was talk it would be Westinghouse, Bendix, North American Aviation, one of several petroleum and natural gas companies, or Youngstown Sheet & Tube. The last was closer than the others. His target turned out to be Jones & Laughlin Steel.

Few could understand why Ling wanted the company, which wouldn't lend itself easily to divestitures and partial sales as had Wilson and Greatamerica. But Jones & Laughlin common was selling for around 50, while the shares had a book value of $85, which appeared understated. The company had just completed a $400 million capital improvement program, which worked out to another $50 a share. From the first, Wall Street doubted the wisdom of the purchase. Yet, so elevated was Ling's reputation by then that few challenged him.

Ling met with J&L CEO Charles Beeghly to discuss a deal. To Ling's surprise, Beeghly agreed to support the sale if the price was right, which to him meant a cash offer, not an exchange for LTV paper. After some discussion,

Table 3–2

LING TEMCO VOUGHT, 1957–1969

(revenues, net income, and shares in millions)

Year	Revenues	Net Income	Senior Capital	Shares Outstanding	Earnings per Share	Price Range
1957	$ 130	—	—	—	$ 1.59	7–3
1958	133	—	—	—	1.30	19–5
1959	148	—	6.5	2.4	1.16	44–16
1960	148	3	5.7	2.6	1.25	42–20
1961	193	(13)	70.2	2.8	(4.82)	42–23
1962	325	9	68.7	2.8	3.03	25–15
1963	329	7	39.1	2.8	2.44	19–13
1964	323	5	41.8	1.8	2.32	20–14
1965	336	6	42.9	1.8	2.82	58–17
1966	1459	20	147.6	2.1	6.47	80–38
1967	1833	34	511.9	4.7	7.11	169–109*
1968	2769	36	748.5	2.1	6.39	135–80
1969	3750	(38)	752.6	2.4	(10.15)	97–24
1970	3709	(70)	616.9	2.8	(17.09)	29–7
1971	3359	(57)	602.9	7.1	(9.28)	27–7

Source: Moody's Industrials, 1967; Moody's Industrial Manual, 1968–1971.
*After 3–2 split.

they agreed on $85 a share in cash. Ling said he wanted 63 percent of the stock, which would require a tender offer of $425 million.

Ling had already raised part of the money from the sale of Greatamerica assets. He then sold 600,000 shares of LTV common, bringing in $60 million. The placement of short-term notes supplied another $200 million. And, the unit exchange was geared to sop up part of the debt in preparation for the final absorption of J&L. (See Table 3–2.)

The first sign of weakness came when J&L shareholders tendered 6.8 million shares of the 7.9 million outstanding, and Ling accepted only 5 million. Then, due to industry pressures and weak markets, the price of hot-rolled steel, one of J&L's major products, was slashed by 22 percent, and other company products also fell under price pressures. It became clear why Beeghly had been willing to sell. Ling had gotten in at the top of the cycle.

THE UNRAVELING

All of this bad news came together at the end of 1968, when the bull market of the 1960s was running out of steam. The topping out coincided with

Ling's complex exchange offer, and made it less attractive. An insufficient number of bondholders tendered their debt for what was coming to be considered chancy equity, so that failed. Ling found himself strapped for cash to pay interest on the debt. He was obliged to liquidate holdings to raise money.

The clearance sale began in February 1969 with the sale of 2 million shares of Braniff and continued throughout the year. Computer Technology went in April, followed by National Car Rental. By December, the three Wilson companies were selling assets and remitting funds to the parent. Wilson & Co. conducted its own version of Project Redeployment by organizing four subsidiaries: Wilson Beef & Lamb, Wilson Certified Foods, Wilson Laurel Farms, and Wilson-Sinclair, to be followed by Wilson Agri-Business Enterprises. Portions of all were sold, but the offerings failed in a developing bear market. Nor could Ling sell additional shares in order to raise funds, since LTV itself was declining.

The J&L situation went from promising in 1968 to disastrous two years later. There were problems at Braniff due to declining ridership, and other units were also in trouble as the nation entered a recession.

Ling's problems—and those of other conglomerateurs—were compounded by political difficulties. Just as government would decide something was wrong with LBOs and junk bonds in the late 1980s, so in the late 1960s, Washington suspected chicanery on the part of those who were fashioning conglomerates with junk stock. On what hook might the new Nixon administration hang its opposition? The antitrust laws? Conglomerates like LTV did not dominate any single industry and so appeared immune from antitrust prosecution. Donald Turner, who had been head of the Antitrust Division of the Justice Department during the Johnson years, was convinced that there was nothing in the existing laws to prevent conglomerate takeovers. "I do not believe Congress has given the courts and the FTC a mandate to campaign against 'superconcentration' in the absence of any evidence of harm to competition," he wrote, rebuking those who wanted him to act without such legislation.[3]

But if the government could not halt conglomeration through the antitrust laws, it could make unwelcomed acquisitions more difficult. In the vanguard of the attack were some legislators whose antibusiness approaches dated back to the New Deal, and who made no distinction between the old and new breeds of business. Emanuel Celler, for example, had been vocal in denouncing the accumulators of great wealth in the 1930s; now the coauthor of the Celler-Kefauver Act was almost as impassioned regarding "corporate raiders."

In February 1969, Celler scheduled hearings on conglomerate takeovers, which would investigate five conglomerates, including LTV. The objective was to determine the following: "If a multi-industry company merger does not substantially lessen competition or tend to create a monopoly, and thus does not violate the antitrust laws, is there any effect that nonetheless needs to be corrected by legislation?"[4]

Still more significant than the upcoming Celler Committee investigation were actions against conglomerates instituted by conservatives in the Nixon government. After Nixon's inauguration, Richard McLaren, a close aide to Senator Barry Goldwater (R. Arizona), took over as head of the Antitrust Division. A senior partner at a large Chicago law firm, McLaren had devoted the past 20 years to defending corporate clients against Justice Department criticisms, and recently had served as chairman of the Antitrust Section of the American Bar Association. He was close to Attorney General John Mitchell, who was formerly a senior partner at Nixon, Mudge, Rose, Guthrie, and Alexander, famed for its roster of blue-chip corporate clients; and, of course, Mitchell was one of Nixon's closest confidants.

McLaren energized the department and embarked on one of the most vigorous antitrust crusades the nation had ever seen. Reformers were puzzled; they asked, Didn't Nixon represent "the entrenched interests"? And the answer was, Certainly. That was one of the reasons for accelerating antitrust activities and putting McLaren in charge. McLaren was going after companies that threatened corporate America, which were led by businessmen prominent in the Nixon campaign.

From the first, McLaren indicated his disagreement with Turner regarding the need for new legislation before acting against the conglomerates. "We would follow my beliefs with regard to what the Supreme Court cases said on conglomerates, and the restructuring of the industry that I thought was coming about in an idiotic way." McLaren targeted those who, like Wolfson earlier and Milken later, were threatening the power of conventional businessmen, not only by taking over their companies, but, in some cases, by doing so through unfriendly bids.[5] Mitchell, who once said, "This country is going so far right you won't recognize it," echoed McLaren, decrying "super-concentration" in American business; to put a fine point on it, Mitchell added that conglomeration "discourages competition among large firms and establishes a tone in the marketplace for more and more mergers." No one at the time seemed to notice that high on the list of potential takeover candidates were many on the roster of clients at the law firm of Nixon, Mudge.[6]

Thus, conservative businessmen who were fighting the conglomerate movement for their own reasons welcomed a new ally. The struggle now would be conducted on what amounted to a second front. McLaren was the 1960s counterpart of Rudolph Giuliani in the late 1980s. Each man used government weapons at his disposal to rid American business of what he deemed to be contaminating elements. In Giuliani's case, there were actual crimes to prosecute; in McLaren's situation, the aim was to ban specific business practices. Yet, they were alike in targeting disturbers of the business peace. Note, too, the curious alliance of the political Old Left and the

New Right, which brought together liberals like Celler and conservatives like Mitchell, and would reappear in the assault on the LBO practitioners in the late 1980s.

Not waiting for Celler Committee action, on March 22, 1969, McLaren telephoned a member of the law firm representing LTV to inform him of an intention to file an antitrust brief to prevent the J&L takeover. Ling reacted with what he later described as "absolute, utter disbelief," not unlike what Wolfson said he felt upon learning it was illegal to sell unregistered shares of unlisted common stock. Ling said, "You consult your attorneys before you make any move that might involve those laws, and unless they think you are in the clear, you don't make the move."[7] This he had done, and Turner hadn't said anything regarding the purchase. Ling discovered what Wolfson had learned to his dismay, and what Milken would learn later: When the government comes after you, whatever rules exist will be twisted as necessary so that a zealous attorney can achieve his ends.

McLaren really had to stretch on this one. The April 14 filing charged that the J&L takeover would lessen competition in the steel industry and increase aggregate concentration. But how could this be, when LTV had no steel operations? The question was asked, but McLaren never responded. In addition, he charged that the merger would involve reciprocity violations—claiming this *prior* to the consummation of the deal.[8]

Now everything went on hold. But not for long; in May, the Justice Department's request for a preliminary injunction against LTV was denied. Still, Ling's major concern in this period was not the government but servicing the large debt LTV had accumulated in search of companies. He had been prepared to pay the interest, always thinking that when the dust settled he would sell off assets and use the proceeds to call in the bonds, or make the kind of convoluted exchange offers for which he had become famous. As recently as 1965, LTV had only $40 million in long-term debt, actually down from the $64 million of 1962. In 1969, as Ling struggled to stay afloat, LTV's long-term debt came to $1.5 billion. In addition, the various LTV subsidiaries had another $767 million in long-term debt. All of this was on an equity base of 3.8 million common shares.[9]

ENDGAME

The antitrust case prevented Ling from making longer-term plans, and even warped his judgment. Ling conceded as much. "I think I can beat McLaren if I stick with it," he said in June, adding, "but that would be just to satisfy my ego." Ling asked, "Is it—trying to look at it from a historic point of view like in Vietnam—a matter of getting so engaged in it to win my point that I might hurt other people, when there is really no other point in staying in the fight?"[10]

Ling twisted and turned, devising new exchange programs and spinoffs. When all these ideas failed, Ling assented to a settlement with the Justice Department. In March 1970, LTV agreed either to divest itself of both Braniff and Okonite or to dispose of its shares of J&L. In addition, LTV pledged itself not to acquire a company with assets of more than $100 million during the next ten years.

The terms dictated by the government were almost laughable. LTV didn't have to be prevented from acquiring companies. Rather, it was itself a takeover candidate, with Chapter 11 bankruptcy a definite possibility. In fact, J&L proved to be Ling's downfall. He had expected the steel company to earn $38 million for 1969. The figure came to only $22 million. There were further complications at Braniff. Expected to earn $25 million, its earnings came in at $6.2 million. LTV revenues for 1969 came to $3.8 billion, up by $1 billion as a result of the J&L acquisition, but LTV posted a loss of $38.3 million as against 1968's profits of $29.4 million. At the time of the announcement, LTV common was selling for 12. The company had an empty treasury. Its 5 percent bonds were going for 25, to yield 20 percent. By May 1970, LTV common was under 10 and those 5 percent bonds were being offered at 15.

The end of the greatest and longest bull market in Wall Street history came gently, not with the crash that had been expected by those who looked for parallels to the 1920s. It started to wind down shortly after the tumultuous 1968 election. On Monday, December 2, 1968, Chase Manhattan Bank raised its prime rate to 6½ percent, causing a sell-off at the NYSE. The next day, the Dow rose to 985, but then declined. On December 18, the Fed raised the discount rate to 5½ percent, and the banks immediately followed with a prime boost to 6¾ percent; the Dow declined to 954 before recovering to 975. At year end, 1968, the average was at 944. There was a steady but orderly retreat into spring of 1970; on May 26, the Dow finally found support at 631, after some $300 billion in market value had evaporated.

By then, the prices of most conglomerate stocks had declined by one-third to one-half. Their managers could no longer offer inflated paper for real assets, and this resulted in a leveling off of earnings, which no longer were boosted by assistance from that source. The leveling off prompted additional sell-offs.

The conglomerate age ended on a sour note. More than $40 billion in deals had been done in 1968; in 1975, the figure came to just $12 billion.[11] The period when initial public offerings were all the rage died simultaneously.

On May 17, 1970, LTV's outside directors asked Ling to step down as chairman, which he did, although he continued on as president for a while. Ling was finished as a force in American business. The company made additional divestitures, and later merged J&L with Republic Steel. It limped along through the 1970s and the early 1980s, still a conglomerate as far as

Wall Street was concerned, but better known as the nation's second-largest steel company. Plagued by several inefficient plants and a generally uncompetitive position, LTV filed for Chapter 11 bankruptcy protection on July 17, 1986, the largest industrial bankruptcy in American history to that time. By then the LBO movement was in full swing. To some, in retrospect, the LTV failure was the cap to the conglomerate movement. To others, it was a portent of what was to come for the LBOs.

As for Ling, he attempted several comebacks. In 1980, he organized Matrix Energy, which explored for oil and natural gas in Oklahoma and Texas without much success. In 1981, Ling was stricken by Guillain-Barré syndrome, a little-known, debilitating illness. While still recovering, he became involved with L.G. Williams, another exploration company and, for a while, seemed on the way back. But this amounted to little.[12]

The other conglomerateurs have faded as well. Royal Little, Tex Thornton of Litton Industries, and Charles Bluhdorn are dead. Harold Geneen is still in business but not at ITT; instead, he is on his own with a variety of enterprises. Once considered the premier businessman of his time, Geneen's reputation today is much lower. He is a relic.

Geneen was a guest at the 1989 Drexel Burnham Lambert Institutional Research Conference. He strolled through a hall full of mostly young, aggressive bankers, traders, salesmen, and clients, talking deals. None except a few friends his own age recognized him. None sought his advice or wanted to hear the ruminations of a man who once was considered one of the most powerful forces on the business scene. There was a new game in town, played by new rules—or so it appeared to the new players.

Actually, many of those people were reinventing ploys developed earlier by Wolfson, Ling, and a few others. But toward different ends. Some of the companies the conglomerateurs put together were being surgically disassembled. The conglomerates had come into being because stock prices were so high. They were sliced apart in the 1980s because prices were so low. And the scalpel was junk bonds. Warren Buffett, arguably the shrewdest investor of our times, put it this way:

> Wall Street never voluntarily abandons a highly profitable field. Years ago, there was a story about the fellow down on Wall Street who was standing on a soapbox at noon, and giving lectures like they do. He was talking about the evils of drugs. And he ranted on for 15 or 20 minutes to a small crowd, and then finally he finished, and he said, "Do you have any questions?" And one very bright investment banking type said to him, "Yeah, who makes the needles?" Well, the needles of the acquisitions game are now junk bonds, just as they were phony equity securities in the late sixties, and Wall Street makes the needles.[13]

II

MICHAEL MILKEN AND THE JUNK DECADE

4

MICHAEL MILKEN—
THE OUTSIDER

The longest-lived bull market in American history ended gently. While trading volume remained high, other business declined. There were still good earnings to be made in brokerage, but profits at the investment banks eroded. Many of these banks had expanded rapidly during the boom years, and now they either merged or closed.

The consolidation began when Hayden Stone merged with Cogan, Berlind, Weill & Levitt. The new CBWL-Hayden Stone didn't last long. After picking up H. Hentz & Co. and Saul Lerner, it joined with Shearson Hammill to produce Shearson Hayden Stone. Then came the acquisitions of Lamson Brothers; Faulkner, Dawkins & Sullivan; Reinhardt & Gardner; and Western Financial. In 1977, the enlarged Shearson Hayden Stone merged with Loeb, Rhoades, Hornblower, and then with Lehman Brothers. Eventually it would be taken over by American Express.

Jackson & Curtis, which traced its origin to 1889, and Paine Webber, whose founding was the following year, combined to form Paine Webber, Jackson & Curtis. Merrill Lynch acquired Goodbody. Blyth joined Eastman Dillon Union to form Blyth Eastman Dillon. Later, Lehman Brothers would merge with Kuhn Loeb. Sears Roebuck bought Dean Witter Reynolds.

Hundreds of professionals lost their jobs. It had happened in the 1930s, and it would happen again in the late 1980s. As recently as 1972, there had been some 600 NYSE member firms; over the following six years, almost 250 of them vanished. In the process, the kind of investment atmosphere fashioned by Charles Merrill and those who emulated him deteriorated and, ultimately, all but disappeared.

THE GREAT INFLATION

Since Merrill's heyday, clever young men and, occasionally, women had been drawn to Wall Street careers. Now the flood of talent slowed to a trickle. Bright MBAs sought the safety of employment at Fortune 500 companies. Those who remained in the industry had to suffer through a bizarre period.

Just as the United States had endured the Great Depression in the 1930s, so it experienced what should be called the Great Inflation in the 1970s. The inflationary virus had been introduced into the economy by the Johnson administration's decision in the second half of the 1960s to finance the Viet Nam War through borrowing rather than taxation. The inevitable result was the debasement of the dollar, and the necessary abandonment of the gold bullion standard and fixed-currency parities in 1971, which set the stage for the gyrating interest rate market of the 1970s.

The problems were compounded by two severe oil shocks. In the early summer of 1973, a barrel of Arabian light crude cost $3.00. During the Arab-Israeli War, OPEC embargoed oil deliveries to the United States and raised its price; in January 1974, a barrel of crude sold for $11.65, and the United States was tumbling into recession. By the decade's end, oil was selling in the mid-$30 range, and this price event, along with economic lags, resulted in high inflation. Soon, the public was introduced to a new term: *stagflation.* Economists once thought such a phenomenon to be impossible over more than a short interval. It wasn't. There was a moderate recovery, followed by more hard times.

In this period, the stock market traced a winding path. The Dow went from 627 in the summer of 1970 to 1067 in early 1973, then collapsed to 570 in late 1974. The index rose to 1026 in the autumn of 1976, and fell to 736 in early 1978, only to advance to 917 by late summer of the year. After bouncing around for a while, it stood at 759 in April 1980.

The Dow was below where it had been in late 1963. Moreover, the Consumer Price Index (CPI) had more than doubled in this period, so the dollar had lost approximately half its purchasing power. The stock decline, in real terms, from 1969 to 1980 was almost as severe as that of the 1929 to 1932 period, although, of course, it was played out over a longer interval and was masked by inflation.

As had happened during the Great Depression, common stocks lost their allure. In 1963, the Dow's P/E ratio had been more than 17; in 1980, it was slightly higher than 7, about where it had been in 1950. If stocks were a bad investment, bonds were even worse. In 1969, when the CPI rose 5.6 percent, AAA corporates yielded an average of 7 percent. In 1974, AAA bonds returned 8.6 percent, but the CPI rise was on the order of 14.6 percent, so the return on the AAAs was actually a negative 6 percent. Moreover, bondholders were double losers, since the high interest rates caused those old bonds to lose half their value.

This decline affected the entire bond market. Investors who had been delighted to purchase 5 percent 20-year government bonds in the early 1960s found themselves with huge losses from their supposedly safe investments. As defenders of junk bonds would argue in 1990, when the government pressed the thrift institutions to mark their bonds to market, had they done so ten or eleven years earlier, these institutions might have been forced into illiquidity due to the reduced value of U.S. government paper.

Yet, all was not bleak on the bond front. The wide swings in rates provided opportunities for traders to profit from their timely purchases and sales. Therefore, for the first time since the early 1930s, the bond market became the arena for "action" for out-and-out speculators.[1]

Faced with negative returns from high-rated bonds, investors switched to the higher-yielding, low-rated issues, which had captured the attention of financial journalists. On April 1, 1974, in one of the first articles on the junk bond phenomenon in a national magazine, a *Forbes* writer observed that the Recrion 10s of 1984 was one of the most actively traded bonds in the first quarter of the year, advancing from 68 on its first trade on January 23 to more than 80, in a period when the Dow bond index actually declined.

These were not the same junk bonds that were to become an important source of financing for medium-sized companies and used as the vehicles for takeovers in the 1980s. Rather, they were of two varieties. The larger group were known as "fallen angels," bonds originally issued with investment grade ratings that had been downgraded due to business setbacks. In 1970, there were only $7 billion worth of high-yield bonds outstanding, virtually all of them fallen angels. The other type was bonds issued by smaller or less substantial companies, which either were unrated or had been given a low credit rating by the agencies. Many of these bonds were sold for conglomerates, either to raise money for a cash offer or, more often, in an exchange for the acquired firm's equity. Some fast movers included those LTV 5s of 1988 issued in the Greatamerica takeover, McCrory 7⅝ of 1997, and Western Union 10¾ of 1997. "Big money is being made in junk bonds," one trader told the *Forbes* writer. "If you're a businessman and you want to play the bond market," said another, "this is one way you can do it." The original-issue junk segment was also expanding: "There are now new junk bonds coming out every few weeks—APL, M-G-M, Reliance Group and Gulf & Western."[2]

As we have seen, conglomerateurs attempted to utilize stock when their P/E multiples were high; they resorted to borrowing when the P/Es were low. Thus, in the late 1960s, AVCO acquired Seaboard Finance with 7½ percent bonds, and Loew's took Lorillard with 6⅞ percent bonds, which, in that period, were high-yield, low-rated instruments. Today, these would be called junk.

Some well-regarded bonds tanked during the 1974–1975 economic collapse. Then, New York City failed to pay interest on a series of notes, prompting a general rout in the bond market, with issues of lower-rated or unrated companies performing very poorly. Grolier 9½, for example, above par at the beginning of the year, fell to under 20 in early 1975. The malaise spread to the real estate market. A decline there prompted a sell-off of securities of real estate investment trusts (REITs), which, in turn, affected securities of banks that made loans to the REITs. Several REITs went bankrupt in early 1975, and as the year wore on, more than a third of REIT loans stopped making interest payments.

Bonds improved after the recession, with no major bankruptcies, and some of the REITs performed quite well. Low-rated bonds came through the bear market in particularly good shape. Yet, the residue of fear remained, and interest rates remained high, making it difficult for midsized, low-credit-rated or unrated companies to raise money. Such firms rarely engaged in public borrowing but, rather, would seek funds at banks where they had lines of credit. Since banks were loath to lend money in an uncertain interest rate environment, new business creation declined sharply.

CREATIVITY ON DEMAND

Unwilling to purchase either stocks or bonds, investors turned to short-term government paper and other safe holdings. Probing for ways to attract investor attention, Wall Street invented and promoted money market funds. These were mutual funds that invested in short-term financial instruments offering attractive returns that fluctuated with the general level of short-term rates. There was just one money market fund in 1971, Reserve Fund, with assets of under $100 million. As interest rates rose (and stocks and bonds fell), more such funds came to market. By 1981, when yields averaged around 16 percent and went as high as 20 percent, these funds had assets of $170 billion. Four years later, there were more than 300, with assets topping $215 billion, and they accounted for close to half the total assets of all mutual funds.

It made abundant sense to leave stocks and bonds for the money market funds. Why purchase a stock at 100 with a 6 percent yield, when it would have to rise 10 points a year to equal the return on a money market fund? Why even buy a 20-year bond at par with a 10 percent coupon, when a far better return was available from the funds?

Add one more ingredient to the mix that was transforming the investment arena: deregulation. This did not come all at once, and it wasn't devised by Reaganites in the 1980s. Rather, deregulation evolved from several forces during the 1970s.

The first was the search for a means of ending stagflation. Conventional macroeconomics wasn't the answer, so, in the second half of the 1970s, government turned to the micro approach. Under the intellectual leadership of Cornell economist Alfred Kahn, the Carter administration advocated sweeping deregulation, with the idea that market forces would bring an end both to inflation and unemployment.

There was another compelling rationale for deregulation: the growing awareness that some of the concepts put into place during the New Deal had become outdated. Practices that made sense during the famous Hundred Days of the Roosevelt administration, a year when GNP was $56 billion, appeared outdated during the 1970s, when nominal GNP rose from $1 trillion to $2.5 trillion. Legislation enacted by one of the most liberal administrations and Congresses in American history was reexamined by far more conservative government leaders and legislators in the late 1970s and 1980s, who demanded less governmental intervention in the economy. These factors would conspire to alter profoundly the operations of the securities and banking industries.

The initial challenge to regulation came through a change in the structure of investment banking; it was little noted outside the financial district, but it would bring an end to several key elements of the old order. From the 1930s through the early 1960s, Wall Street had been a clubby place. Commissions were fixed, and bankers maintained close relationships with clients. It was generally assumed that when an over-the-counter stock met requirements, it would apply for listing on the American Stock Exchange. When an Amex stock passed muster, it would be admitted to the NYSE. Market makers and brokers at the OTC, Amex, and NYSE did not trade in stocks listed at the other markets.

For some years, a few brokerage firms that the establishment called "renegades" had been trading NYSE stocks over the counter at lower charges, doing an institutional business in blocks of 10,000 or more shares, on what was known as the "third market." Try as it might, the NYSE could not halt this practice, and its member firms could not compete with the renegades, since, under the terms of the long-standing Rule 394, they could not engage in off-the-floor trading. The renegade trading eroded profits at the large wire houses, but it had little impact at those investment banks that concentrated on providing counsel and related services. In 1962, a case seeking to prevent harassment by the NYSE against the third market came before the Supreme Court. In *Silver v. New York Stock Exchange,* the Court decided that the NYSE did not enjoy the status of a protected monopoly.

As the decade wore on, institutional participation increased, and the third market expanded. This posed a threat to the NYSE's commission structure. Around the same time, the SEC began to discuss whether fixed rates should be eliminated.

Yet another threat appeared from within the establishment itself. In May 1969, the NYSE member firm of Donaldson, Lufkin & Jenrette announced its intention to become a publicly owned company by selling stock; it would raise $24 million for the 10 percent of shares it sold, the money to be retained in the company. The plan made good sense, since the partners would have a public market for their shares, while multiplying their own net worth many times. The trouble was that this procedure was against NYSE rules. The partners, upstarts all, said that, if necessary, they would sell their NYSE seat, intimating that DLJ would become a third-market concern.

The NYSE did not rise to the bait. DLJ remained a member. In 1971, Merrill Lynch followed suit. Soon after, other firms went public, with Bache and Reynolds leading the way. Morgan Stanley, White Weld, and Lehman became incorporated. Later, Salomon would turn the trick by merging with Phibro, which already was a publicly owned concern. In the process, the banks became cash-rich, and the bankers themselves became multimillionaires.

Bankers and clients noted a different tone at those newly public investment banks. While the firms had been private, their leaders had nurtured them, avoiding undue risks. After all, they were playing with their own money, and a false step could lead to personal disaster. Things were different now that they had cashed out. Not only were the firms wealthy, but with their full coffers, the banks also could take larger risks, and failure would mean only lower bonuses.

In January 1971, the Dreyfus Corporation, a mutual fund organization, applied to become a member of the NYSE. A week later, Jefferies & Co., the brokerage affiliate of another mutual fund operation, Investors Diversified Services, submitted its application. Others followed, and rumor had it that insurance companies and pension plans would do the same. The reason was obvious: These institutions would trade for their own accounts, eliminating the need to pay fixed commissions. If this happened, the NYSE could be doomed as a haven for the conventional brokerage firms. The choice was simple: Find some way to adapt or die.

The double challenge from fixed-commission structure and public ownership of investment banks prompted the SEC into action. The agency took the matter of commissions out of the stock exchange's hands, and so the NYSE was able to avoid a painful choice. The SEC decided that, as of April 1, 1971, commissions could be negotiated on trades of more than $500,000; the figure would be lowered in stages, culminating in fully negotiated commissions on May 1, 1975, which came to be known as "May Day" on the Street.

This action jarred the comfortable brokerage firms that had thrived in the hothouse atmosphere of the 1950s and 1960s, but it opened paths for more aggressive ones. The institutional investors withdrew their applications, but now the industry was flooded with scores of discount brokerage firms, who were prepared to transact business on a "no-frills" basis for a fraction of the old fixed rates. Brokers at full-service houses retaliated by cutting their fees, but they couldn't go as low as the discounters. In the process, the full-service houses created a variant of what Charles Merrill had attempted to accomplish in the 1950s—low-cost, full-service brokerage.

The results were striking. In 1966, brokerage commissions accounted for almost 62 percent of securities firms' revenues; by the end of 1977, despite an increase of total commission revenues by 59 percent, these earnings accounted for only 41 percent of revenues. Moreover, an increasing amount of commissions came from commodity and options contracts, instruments used by more sophisticated investors (the kind of people likely to be lured to discounters). The brokerage firms tried to respond by offering additional research, to little avail. In the three years after May Day, an estimated $600 million in commissions were lost because of negotiated commissions.[3]

Until May Day, the large salaries on Wall Street had been made in the brokerage of equities. This now ended. Brokers who had made huge salaries and bonuses saw in negotiated commissions the end of the world as they had known it. The future would belong to traders and investment bankers.

The markets chugged along during the 1970s, but those brokers with better opportunities went elsewhere. The disgusted, confused, and disillusioned small investors also were leaving. If they remained in the market at all, it was through mutual funds, on the principle that when hunting in the jungle, it pays to have an expert guide. The growth of computerization, the proliferation of instruments, and the altered international environment all would accelerate this movement.

If not quite dead, by the end of the 1970s, people's capitalism had evolved from direct to indirect investment in what seemed to be the beginnings of pension plan socialism. In the 1970s and 1980s, institutional power multiplied. From 1983 to 1989, individual investors reduced their stock holdings by $550 billion, which was 40 percent of their 1983 portfolios. That portion went to the institutions, which, by 1989, owned more than half the stock in American corporations.[4]

Faced with the loss or deterioration of a major source of revenue, investment banks opted for several solutions. Some attempted to win a larger share of a dwindling market by taking business from other bankers. Some downsized and sought new products to peddle to old and new customers. Some tried all three approaches. To do nothing was to invite disaster, so they acted—and, in the process, they changed the face of the industry.

The new business the investment banks so desperately needed came in two forms: the revival of interest in the debt market, and mergers and acquisitions. The later notoriety of junk bonds made it appear that they were the most innovative new financial instrument of the period. Lost in this interpretation is the fact that junk was a response to the altered financial and business environment. This new playing field encouraged others to innovate in different ways. Charles Schwab did it with discount brokerage firms; Fidelity did it with mutual fund families. At Salomon, Bob Dall and Lew Ranieri made Ginnie Maes the most important new security of the decade, the first of many types of asset-backed debts. Commodity traders in Chicago organized the Chicago Board Options Exchange. It was a time when the financial community reinvented itself in a dozen different directions.

ENTER MILKEN

Michael Milken appeared on Wall Street a full decade before the advent of the "yuppie bankers" of the 1980s. Like Wolfson, Ling, Carr, and others who arrived during that earlier sea change in financial markets, Milken was an outsider. His father, born Bernhard Milkevitz in Kenosha, Wisconsin, had a difficult life.[5] His mother had died in childbirth, and he lost his father to a car crash seven years later. Milkevitz spent his early years with relatives, contracted polio, and later was sent to an orphanage. Somehow, he persevered. He attended the University of Wisconsin during the Great Depression, studying for a degree in accountancy and working his way through by selling peanuts and waiting on tables at a sorority house. There he met his future wife, Ferne Zax.

Milken doesn't like to talk about his parents, not because of shame but out of a dislike for the past. He told one writer his father had not really been in an orphanage: "It was a sort of home. I prefer to think of it as a boarding school."

After graduation, Bernhard and Ferne married and moved to Encino, California, to start fresh. To symbolize this beginning, they changed their name to Milken. It was there that Ferne gave birth first to Michael, then to Lowell and Joni.

All three children attended the local Birmingham High School in Van Nuys, performing well academically. Through effective campaigning, Mike was elected head cheerleader. He and Lowell went to college at Berkeley, where they were superior students. Mike now demonstrated the qualities that would make him a star banker. He was elected head of his pledge group and president of his fraternity, using the same approach as in high school. "I don't think you would say he was popular in the fraternity," recalled Jeffrey Unickel, another member. "It wasn't charisma. He campaigned very hard and won people's respect. It was like running for public office—kind of Machiavellian. He was as driven to succeed as anybody."

According to those who knew him then, Milken was brilliant, erratic, single-minded, and intensely ambitious. One of his few pastimes was marathon card games. Another fraternity brother spoke of an all-night gambling session in which Milken participated. "I remember he was down one time by maybe a thousand dollars—that was an astounding amount in those days. But he didn't care. He was the house—the one taking all the bets. He knew the odds were in his favor and that he'd get his money back." Even then, Milken showed signs of avarice. The brother continued, "He was monomaniacal about money. To be a millionaire by age thirty was his goal. I thought I shared the same goal, but Mike was different. He wanted to be *rich*."[6]

Later, Milken would say the happiest period of his life was the time at Berkeley. The school was a yeasty place. In 1964, while he was a freshman, the university experienced the first of its many rallies and riots. Sproul Plaza, the gathering place for those wanting to argue for or against a cause, was filled daily with a milling mob. The Free Speech Movement was born there and later was transformed into the Filthy Speech Movement. Sproul was a supermarket of opinions, most of which were superficial and trendy, but this suited Milken, who had the same qualities. It was a jittery time, when attention spans were short and moods were mercurial. And these, too, were qualities one could ascribe to Milken, both then and later.

Politically, however, Milken had little in common with the agitators of Berkeley in the 1960s. In his last year at Berkeley, he didn't attend rallies but, rather, took a job at the Touche Ross accounting firm. Later, Milken would find the means of combining his own reforming streak with business, and demonstrate that the two went well together.[7] For the time being, however, there were more important things, like work, grades, activity in his fraternity, the management of a few portfolios, and his relationship with his childhood sweetheart, Lori Anne Hackel, whom he married upon graduation.

The dedication to career continued at the University of Pennsylvania's Wharton School, which Milken later said he selected in 1968 for graduate work because he was able to receive credit for some courses merely by passing exams. Yet, he couldn't have found a business school more suited to his talents. While Harvard was famous for turning out general managers; Northwestern was the place for marketing people; and the University of Michigan was a breeding ground for future leaders in the automobile industry; Wharton was one of the nation's best places for those concerned with finance and accounting. Said alumnus Donald Trump in 1987, "I took a lot of finance courses at Wharton, and they first taught you all the rules and regulations. They then taught you that those rules and regulations are really meant to be broken; it's the person who can create new ideas who is really going to be the success." To this, Gilbert Harrison, future managing director at Shearson Lehman added, "When we got out of Wharton, we felt like we could conquer the world. And, in fact, we did."[8] Among other Wharton graduates in Milken's generation were Saul Steinberg, Ron Perelman, and Martin Lipton, all of whom would figure in his business life. Jon Burnham, the son of I. W. (Tubby) Burnham, founder of Burnham & Co., also received his MBA from Wharton.

Throughout his years at Berkeley and Wharton, Milken had many acquaintances but few friends. Perhaps this was because he lacked the talent for small talk and became animated only when speaking of business-related activities. Later, he interacted with colleagues, clients, and customers in the same fashion. When he became the most celebrated figure in the financial industry, Milken was surrounded by acolytes, and scores of hungry young people were eager to work with him—after all, that was the route to financial success. But his only true friends were members of his family and a handful of others from his youth. He didn't regret this. The work was what mattered.

Milken never had a wide-ranging intellect. Instead, he concentrated on a subset of a single market and its implications. His desire was to encompass all knowledge and all business experience relating to his kind of financing. He was the consummate workaholic—intense, humorless, even grim, when on the job. Milken promised his wife he would not work past noon while on their one-week annual vacation to Hawaii. Keeping his word, Milken would take two suites, one for business, the other for the family, and he would put in close to a full day's work—New York time—before noon. His only affectation, if one could call it that, was wearing a toupee, which was strangely ill-fitting.

Those who know Milken best speak of his many interests, his intellectual curiosity, and his tendency to jump abruptly from one topic to another, unrelated one. Conversations with him can be exciting but also exhausting and frustrating. To a stranger, he seems interested in virtually everything. In time, however, one comes to realize that while his curiosity is huge, his information is shallow, derived from conversations and magazine and newspaper articles—material he can digest quickly. On most matters, he is superficial, resorting to analogy, anecdote, and carefully selected statistics, rather than relying on a subtle and complex knowledge of the subject. This style may have developed because of his intensely focused days in the office.

In his book *The Hedgehog and the Fox*, Sir Isaiah Berlin quotes the Greek poet Archilochus as writing, "The fox knows many things, but the hedgehog knows one big thing." Berlin would have classified Milken as a hedgehog—one "who relates everything to a single central vision."[9] Milken took ideas adumbrated by others, added his own native abilities and a capacity for work that astonished all who knew him, played variations on that one big theme, and, from such a mix, fashioned his reputation.

THE ACADEMIC FOUNDATIONS OF MILKENISM

While in his spare time, Milken had helped his father with an accounting client who, as it happened, was particularly interested in low-rated convertible bonds. Fascinated with their high yields and relative unpopularity, and hoping to learn more about them, Milken walked library corridors in search of more information. In 1967, Milken discovered the works of an obscure professor by the name of W. Braddock Hickman—in particular, his *Corporate Bond Quality and Investor Experience,* an abstruse tome that sold a grand total of 934 copies, most of them to college and university libraries, when released by Princeton University Press in 1958. Hickman was one of a handful of academics who provided the intellectual underpinnings for much of what Milken did.

Though barely known outside of academia, Hickman was one of the pioneers of modern bond analysis. Writing in a dry, scholarly fashion, laboriously putting together tables in the precomputer era of the 1950s, Hickman had reached several conclusions that intrigued Milken.

Analyzing the gap between bond ratings and performance, Hickman had determined that at certain times in the economic cycle, lower-rated bonds performed significantly better than the higher-rated ones. He concluded that "issues in the high-quality classes (including large issues of large obligators) had the lowest default rates, promised yields, and loss rates; but the returns obtained by those who held them over long periods were generally below those on low-grade issues."[10] In other words, purchasers of high-quality bonds usually were safer from defaults than purchasers of low-rated bonds, but, over the entire market cycle, low-rated bonds, even taking defaults into consideration, did better, due to their more generous coupons.

This basic insight later would be vulgarized by proponents of junk bonds as meaning that low-rated issues outperformed higher-rated bonds. Junk bond proponents explained the phenomenon by saying that the rating agencies had only an imperfect concept of the worth of bonds they investigated. Hickman seemed to be saying as much: "The errors in rating corporate bonds [are due] . . . principally to the business cycle and to the difficulty of forecasting industry trends."[11]

In their reasoning, the defenders of junk failed to take into account another of Hickman's findings. Addressing the question of when low-rated bonds should be purchased, he wrote, "One of the most persistent and most pronounced phenomena observed in the data is the propensity of the market to undervalue corporate bonds at or near the date of default."[12] This meant that while low-rated bonds did well over the entire cycle, the best results came when the market was overly gloomy regarding their prospects. The corollary had to be that the *worst* time to buy was when investors became overconfident and issuers had no trouble selling their paper. That's when bad deals came to market. Those who entered the market on the buy side late in the cycle would lose.

In 1967, Thomas R. Atkinson of the National Bureau of Economic Research updated and amplified Hickman's efforts. In general, Atkinson's studies confirmed the earlier conclusions and stated explicitly what Hickman only suggested: "The greatest number and volume of defaults occurred in bonds offered one year prior to peaks, presumably a time of greatest optimism."[13] Atkinson went on to demonstrate that such bonds performed poorly in 1912–1913 and 1928–1931, suggesting that the same thing would happen the next time the public became optimistic regarding high-yield bonds.

This caveat would be crucial in the late 1980s and early 1990s. Milken understood this. What Hickman and Atkinson were saying was familiar to students of market history. Bull markets begin with pessimism and end with wild, unrealistic optimism. The time to get in is at the beginning, and the time to leave is before the end. It is that simple.

Even earlier than Hickman's writings, and even more obscure, were the studies of University of Oregon Professor O. K. Burrell. In a 1947 paper, Burrell tracked bond performance in the period from 1927 to 1939. He demonstrated that the average AAA-rated industrial bond declined from $1,000 in June 1927 to $886 in June 1932, while BAAs fell from $977 to $355. Yet, those who purchased the lower-rated bonds at their bottoms did better than they would have with the high-rated issues, as the BAAs rose to $625 by December 1934, while the AAA issues appreciated to $1,063. From June 1932 to December 1934, the AAAs appreciated 19.9 percent; the BAAs, 75.8 percent.[14]

Burrell also noted that during the market's decline from March 1937 to March 1939, the AAAs fell by only 0.7 percent, the BAAs by 5.6 percent, while Bs declined a sickening 23.1 percent.[15] From this fact, he deduced the following:

> It is sometimes urged that the additional income available on lower-grade securities will average out, over a reasonably long period, to be sufficient compensation for actual losses incurred by reason of the greater risks. Thus the difference between the riskless rate of interest, say 2½ percent, and the return available on, say, BA grade bonds of perhaps 5½ percent would, over a decade or so, compensate for losses sustained in instances where default in interest or principal occurred. . . . .

> From the very nature of things proof of such a theory is difficult or impossible. In any event it is a matter of no particular consequence to the individual investor. The individual investor who suffers a loss of income or principal through default may not have received a compensatory risk premium, even though a generalized group of investors may have received an adequate premium to compensate for the loss.[16]

Burrell, therefore, concluded that because losses cannot be accurately predicted, the idea of yield differentials being an insurance fund against losses is useless for individuals.[17]

There, Burrell understandably missed the mark. How could he have predicted the swinging markets of the 1970s and 1980s? Nevertheless, there was a precedent established. As it turned out, the bond market of the 1970s was a new version of the market for depressed bonds in the early 1930s.

This market was analyzed by Barrie Wigmore in 1985, in his monumental *The Crash and Its Aftermath*. An investment banker, Wigmore was drawn to the subject through his interest not in the current market, but rather in the period of the 1929 crash. At a time when junk bonds were the talk of Wall Street, Wigmore was examining the markets of more than half a century earlier, and he came to conclusions regarding bond performance that echoed those of Hickman, Atkinson, and Burrell.

Wigmore noted that the yield spread between AAA and BAA rails in 1929 had been between 90 and 142 basis points; by 1934, the spread had risen to 433–497 points. In the same period, AAA and BAA industrials went from a spread of 38 to 111 basis points to 225–599. Yet, the default rate even for those issues whose ratings declined sharply was quite low. According to Wigmore, not a single railroad issue of more than $40 million went into default, and the same was true for industrial issues of over $20 million.[18]

Most of the damage to the market had been done in the early 1930s, when the effects of the Great Depression were broad and deep. Subsequent recovery was sharply hindered by the unwillingness of businessmen to assume added risks in an uncertain environment. There were fallen angels galore, due largely to the decline in price of paper that once had been highly regarded. In 1932, one might have obtained a yield of more than 10 percent on what had been an A-rated railroad bond but had fallen to Ba. For example, Shell Union, still a strong company, had its rating lowered from A to Ba; its 5 percent bond, maturing in 1947, fell to 47, for a better than 10 percent yield at a time when Treasury bills were yielding 2.25 percent. Investors were uncertain, dumping whatever they could in the quest for quality. By 1934, the Shell Union bonds were back over par. Those bonds downgraded to low ratings that offered high yields performed well in the 1930s, in the second and third legs of what Sidney Homer, the leading student of interest rates, has called "our greatest bull bond market."[19] Thus, confidence in bonds increased, and their popularity continued.

Even so, low-rated issues still sold at depressed prices, and companies unable to obtain credit ratings of at least A had trouble finding investment bankers willing to underwrite their paper. Doubtless, this difficulty contributed to the continuation of the Depression, but it certainly was understandable given the traumas that generation experienced between 1929 and 1933.

Milken relied heavily upon Hickman's and Atkinson's works; whether he also knew about Burrell's efforts is not known. He recognized that the spreads between lower-rated or unrated bonds and investment grade bonds had widened since the mid-1950s, and he considered the resulting risk/reward ratios very attractive.

Milken's fellow students at Wharton cared little about the low-rated bonds that so intrigued him. Only a few firms on Wall Street considered them worth more than a passing glance. One of these, BEA Associates, a New York-based advisory firm, showed that during periods of tight money and financial stringency, low-rated bonds offered returns of over 30 percent, and that investments in them paid off better than those in other instruments. Salim "Cy" Lewis of Bear Stearns had prowled the fallen-angel market since the 1940s and had done very well purchasing bonds of distressed railroads.[20] Lewis's reasoning was simple enough: All the bad news about those railroads was public and was fully reflected in the prices of their securities. Few people had any faith in their recoveries; yet, some were bound to come back. Even if they didn't, the companies would be restructured, not put out of business. The common stockholders probably would lose all, and the same might be true for the owners of preferred stocks. But bondholders could come out of the restructuring with new equity, which, given the prices of the bonds, often would be worth substantially more than the investment. Indeed, Lewis and others hoped for restructurings rather than prolonged delays during which the bonds would hardly move.

During the 1970s, it was difficult to sell new stock issues to disillusioned individual and institutional investors. To convince companies to sell bonds, however, further evidence was needed of their value. The theoretical foundation was provided by other academics, most notably Franco Modigliani and Merton Miller, in a series of scholarly papers starting with "The Cost of Capital, Corporate Finance and the Theory of Investment" in 1958.[21]

One of the many facets of "Modigliani-Miller" concerned the attractiveness of debt over equity for raising funds. The government treated dividends on stocks and interest from bonds differently when it came time to calculate taxes. The Internal Revenue Service considered dividends as earnings but permitted the deduction of interest on a loan as a cost of doing business. Thus, a company with earnings of $100 million and no debt would have to pay taxes on $100 million. By contrast, if the company borrowed money and used it to repurchase its common stock or to buy another company, and had to pay $100 million in interest, it would have no earnings to report—and no tax obligation. As Warren Buffett observed, the government is the not-so-silent partner in every profitable corporation—a situation that can be altered through the imaginative use of debt:

> . . . there is a certain rationale, of course, to corporate debt in that the federal government owns a very peculiar kind of what I call class A stock in American industry. This "stock" is entitled to 46% of the earnings and has no share in assets. It's a very unusual stock; it's an income stock. And you can get rid of it. I mean that by substituting debt, you can buy in the government's class A stock for nothing. I've always been intrigued by companies that buy in

stock. And when you can get rid of a 46% shareholder by reconstituting the capital structure with debt, that is tempting to people.[22]

One student of the subject put it this way:

The implication was startling. It suggested that if a firm had low debts and was paying a lot of corporate tax its managers were actually being incompetent: while proudly keeping their credit ratings high, they were handing their shareholders' money to the taxman. To do their shareholders a favor, they ought to borrow more. The value they were handing unnecessarily to the taxman offered a fine incentive to bidders to come along and do this for them.[23]

The lesson was clear. When the first Modigliani-Miller paper on the subject appeared, the effective corporate tax rate was 50 percent, and it would remain there until the Tax Reform Act of 1986 cut it back to 34 percent. Throughout the period, corporate managers, cognizant of Modigliani-Miller, preferred to attempt to issue debt rather than equities.

Almost every MBA student had been exposed to Modigliani-Miller, and Milken was no exception. He was not altogether convinced of the wisdom of debt financing, however. In his MBA thesis, the final form of which was written with James E. Walter and was entitled "Managing the Corporate Financial Structure," Milken argued for flexibility in determining a corporation's capitalization. Many factors have to be considered, including the business cycle, the nature of the industry, interest rates, and much more. Thus, Milken believed there was no hard and fast rule to be followed. At certain times, it made sense for a company to be highly leveraged, and at other times, debt should be avoided. This concept would suggest that corporate financial managers had to think like portfolio managers of mutual funds:

On the surface, financial-structure management appears to be a mirror reflection of portfolio management. Both managements are financially motivated to act in a manner that corrects temporary aberrations in the structure of market returns. The rational financial manager offers comparatively overpriced issues in exchange for relatively underpriced securities; whereas, the portfolio manager acquires underpriced issues and liquidates their overpriced counterparts.[24]

In Milken's view, then, debt itself was neither good nor bad. The real question for a company at a particular time was whether debt was appropriate. This was the germ of ideas that would be reexamined in the late 1980s, when Milken concluded that the time for junk might have passed.

In the 1970s, however, Milken was both surprised and frustrated by the inability of most investors to grasp the meaning of the data, and the unwillingness of portfolio managers to purchase high-yielding, low-rated bonds. The reasons were not difficult to find. By then, investors were purchasing stock when they offered rewards commensurate with risks. Most investors associated stocks with price risk and capital gains, while bonds were identified with safety and steady yields. Investors oscillated between one and the other. When the economic outlook was favorable, they demanded stocks, and when problems developed, they switched to bonds. So when stocks rose, bonds tended to fall, and vice versa.

Milken thought this approach was outworn. Investors would be better served by purchasing any instrument in which the potential rewards outweighed the risks. He argued that, in the case of low-rated bonds, the ratings did not reflect the true risks.[25] Rating agencies, analysts, and investors tended to look to the past rather than the future. A few years ago, Milken told a reporter:

> Traditionally, lenders have found the future more risky than the past. Future-oriented lenders, however, have a different perspective. For example, if you were considering buying a bond issue or making a new 25-year loan to the Singer company back in 1974, the fact that they had paid dividends for 100 years would not be the relevant issue. The only issue would be whether Singer could sell sewing machines or fabrics in the future. Future, not past, performance, after all, was going to pay off the loan. As it turned out, not enough women decided to continue sewing and making their own clothes and Singer lost millions in its fabric stores.[26]

Bond-rating methods in the 1970s were pretty much what they had been earlier and are still. The issuing company approached the agency and, in effect, engaged its services. For a fee, Standard & Poor's or Moody's— perhaps both—sent in teams of CPAs to gather and analyze information. The raters were concerned primarily with balance sheets and related data, and less with management talents, work in progress, research and development, and the like.

Moreover, the agencies' records on tracking changes at the client firms were (and are) spotty at best. For example, they moved sluggishly in both the Penn Central and New York City collapses. "Sometimes you miss these situations," conceded S&P President Brenton Harries in the aftermath of the New York City debacle.

Milken felt he was better equipped to establish the creditworthiness of firms than were those CPAs. As he later noted, the rating agencies liked the railroads long after the demise of their ability to generate substantial cash flows. They gave cable TV and cellular telephone companies, and child and nursing care companies, low ratings because they lacked track records and clean balance sheets. Milken would argue that a company's most important resources often do not appear on the ledger as assets.

The rating agencies were not completely blind to this; they recognized that brand names like Coca-Cola and IBM have intrinsic value. But what about a company's people? Milken noted that only the sports industry took the value of talent into consideration. In publishing, he observed, the real assets were the people who write and shape the information. Not so long ago, a Milken client, Steve Ross of Warner Communications, told a gathering at a Drexel convention, "Every afternoon I stand by my window and watch my inventory walk out the gate. I hope they return the next day."

A good deal of what Milken thought and said in those early years has been ignored. Much of this was his own fault. In his heyday as the pied piper of junk, when clearer statements of his position would not have harmed the market and might have made it more appealing, Milken refused to grant interviews.

Milken became a victim of his own success. By 1986—before any other prominent banker—he would realize that the time for most junk financings had passed and that having recourse to other instruments might be more sensible. But the bankers with whom he worked insisted on more underwritings. Milken might have stopped them by forcefully restating the ideas in his original thesis, but he never did that in a way to capture public attention.

THE EARLY YEARS AT DREXEL

Milken left the Wharton School in 1970, one paper short of the degree requirements (which he completed in 1974). In 1969, one of his professors had found him a summer job as an intern at the Philadelphia offices of Drexel Harriman Ripley, and he continued there on a part-time basis for the rest of his graduate school career. Now Milken joined the firm's New York headquarters as director of research for "low-grade bonds" at a salary of $25,000.

Drexel Harriman Ripley boasted a celebrated name and heritage, but little else. Its origins went back to the 1830s and included a close relationship with the great J. P. Morgan himself. Drexel & Co. had merged with Harriman, Ripley in 1965, in an effort to save both faltering concerns. People there liked to think of it as a "major-bracket" bank, but by the 1960s that was no longer true. By 1970, Drexel had only ten Fortune 500 clients, which put it in the same league as the stagnant Dillon Read and the smallish Hornblower & Weeks. Drexel was 18th in the industry in underwritings during the 1960s, sandwiched between Lazard Frères and Paine Webber.[27] Indeed, so unpromising were Drexel's fortunes that it had to solicit a $6 million capital infusion in exchange for 25 percent ownership, which came from the unlikely source of Firestone Tire & Rubber, whereupon the name of the firm was changed to Drexel Firestone.

Being director of research for low-grade bonds at Drexel Firestone was akin to being manager of a second-division minor-league baseball team— that is, it sounded fine unless you knew something about the game.

Milken lived modestly in suburban Cherry Hill, New Jersey, with Lori and his children. He didn't like it there at all. There was a two-hour bus commute to work, starting and ending in the dark. All his waking time was devoted to work, family, and travel. Later, when he was one of the acknowledged superstars of finance, Milken's habits would not change. Perhaps it was because of strong familial ties, or his relatively slower path to the top, or simply his character. Whatever the reason, even his detractors conceded that Milken was not one of those spoiled yuppie bankers caricatured so devilishly by critics and novelists in the late 1980s.

The bond business in the early 1970s was in the doldrums. Milken was probably pleased with this situation, since it might mean he was coming in at the bottom of the bond market cycle. Selling new offerings of investment grade bonds in this climate was not difficult. The asset manager at an institution could take the paper based on the S&P or Moody's rating, and put it away for 20 or so years, clipping coupons every six months. Even if rates rose or fell, the manager probably would hold till maturity, and so the fluctuations would cause him no problems. Or, so it appeared on the eve of the great upheaval in bond prices.

It was quite different with unrated or low-rated bonds. Milken had to convince the potential buyer that the rating was not reflective of their true value, and that the yield justified a purchase. Such bonds couldn't even be efficiently priced, since most had thin markets. Milken had to sweat out every sale in those days, while the gentlemen salesmen of highly rated bonds made their placements with ease. A Milken spiel must have sounded to them like the line of a tout at a bucket shop.

Milken's personality was suited for dealing with bankers, money managers, and other institutional customers, rather than with the high school teachers and plumbers Charles Merrill had courted. He was helped by the growth of private placements—the raising of funds by corporations by making direct sales of bonds to institutions. (By the late 1980s, the volume of private placements was almost as high at $200 billion as that of public debt offerings.[28])

Milken was given a pretty free hand at Drexel and, before long, was permitted to trade bonds for the firm, although with a capital base of only $500,000. To the disgust of the firm's salesmen and traders in highly rated paper, he soon made far more money for the firm than they did. This might have been tolerated, even admired, were it not for the fact that Milken and the business he brought in still were considered tainted.

Those who remember him from this period say Milken was intense and serious to a fault. Codirector of research Ernest Widemann recalled how

Milken would go to his office after the trading day to discuss junk bond theories. "He was very focussed. He was affable, but had his own agenda. There was no small talk."[29]

From his perch at Drexel, Milken witnessed two major market declines in the 1970s, during which widespread bankruptcies threatened but did not happen. Bond prices collapsed, only to rise again with recovery, and, as Hickman and Atkinson had suggested, the low-rated and unrated bonds did better than the investment grades. For several years, analysts and economists had warned of a higher default rate during such crises. When none occurred, it seemed to corroborate all that Milken had been saying about junk bonds.

If investors were reluctant to alter old perceptions in the face of empirical evidence, they were forced to recognize changes in the investment atmosphere. The experience of that decade demonstrated that in periods of high interest rate risk, it was possible to obtain strong capital gains (and losses) from bonds. If this were so, why weren't investors seeking capital gains drawn to bonds, which had the added merit of regular interest payments and a maturity date? And should they not want so much volatility, why not choose lower-rated and unrated bonds, which might be less unstable due to protection from down markets by their yield and low expectations?

Milken posed these questions to potential investors. He told them he would rather sell paper with a poor record that could be improved than equity in superb companies, whose prices reflected this circumstance but might fall sharply on the slightest hint of trouble. Further, bonds with high yields behaved more like stocks than bonds of very secure companies, in that their prices rose and fell in relation to the company's prospects, and not in relation to changes in interest rates, inflation, and the like. He startled an interviewer in 1977 by saying, "There is far less risk in LTV 5s at 57 cents on the dollar than there is in Polaroid, IBM, Xerox, you name it." He quickly added, "Obviously, I could be considered biased."[30]

Milken also told investors that effective control of a company belonged to those who owned debt, and not to the stockholders. He explained this to Meshulam Riklis, one of the first big businessmen to be drawn to him. At a breakfast meeting in the mid-1970s, Milken asserted that Drexel and its clients controlled Rapid-American, not Riklis, its biggest shareholder. "How can that be when I own 40 percent of the stock?" asked Riklis. Milken replied, "We own $100 million of your bonds, and if you miss one payment, we'll take your company away." If this was an exaggeration, it was not far off the mark. Milken claimed the bonds issued by MCI were safer than those issued by any sovereign government. "You can seize MCI for failure to pay interest," he said. "You can't seize Argentina."[31]

Some of the paper Milken sold and traded in those years were low-rated bonds issued by the conglomerates of the 1960s, securities of such firms as AVCO, City Investing, Gulf + Western, General Host, and, of course,

LTV. Whatever their pedigree, the possible returns on such bonds were much higher than those available from the higher-rated bonds. Consider the spreads on some representative issues. In 1970, the average yield on AAA-rated bonds was slightly more than 8 percent. The LTV 5s of 1988 were selling for 26 in late August 1970, for a current yield of 19 percent. In time, LTV would fall into bankruptcy, but had an investor purchased the bond then and held until the bottom fell out, the total return would have been higher than could have been obtained from AAA paper. Also in 1970, AVCO 5½ of 1993, which were convertible into common stock, sold for 55, for a current yield of close to 10 percent. Fuqua 7s of 1988 was at 57, yielding 12 percent. Whittaker convertible 4½ of 1985 were going to 35, yielding close to 13 percent. So it went. If an individual had purchased every bond yielding more than 12 percent listed on the NYSE—a fraction of the total outstanding, to be sure—and held to maturity, he or she would have surpassed the AAA bonds by far, even taking defaults into consideration.

Nor was this a fleeting phenomenon. In 1981, Chrysler Credit Corporation 7 percent bonds—backed by loans to auto purchasers, not by the company's own assets—would decline to the point where they were yielding 20 percent. While there remained a chance Chrysler might go bankrupt, this hardly would have triggered a wholesale refusal of owners of its cars to make their payments and so cause repossession. Yet, that was precisely the message that kind of yield was sending. It was reminiscent of the bond market panic of the early 1930s, and it was a prelude to the panic that would hit the junk market in 1988–1990. In both cases, the fears were exaggerated.

While Milken developed his client list, the company for which he worked remained at risk. Firestone's capital had rescued Drexel, but not for long. By 1973, more money was needed. This time it came from Burnham & Co., an unpretentious, generally conservative brokerage firm, which I. W. "Tubby" Burnham had founded in the improbable year of 1935, with $4,000 of his own money and a loan of $96,000 from his grandfather, the owner of I.W. Harper, a Kentucky distillery. Other brokerage firms were failing or merging in this period; Burnham had remained independent, and he was proud that the firm was always solvent and profitable.

Burnham could hope for little more than this, however. Not only were the times wrong for expansion, but he was a Jew and had arrived when only a small German Jewish group was able to enter the Street's inner circle. No less a personage than Otto Kahn was able to direct the fortunes of the Metropolitan Opera, but he still would be prevented from purchasing a box at the Metropolitan Opera House.[32]

Proud of his accomplishments but wanting more, Burnham was interested in acquiring Drexel. It would be his passport into both investment banking and the establishment—the means whereby he could acquire at least token special-bracket status. In 1973, they merged. Burnham became the firm's president, but in recognition of the power of the much older name, the firm became Drexel Burnham. Drexel's gentlemen bankers and salesmen did not welcome the Burnham brokers, who had attended less prestigious schools and were predominantly Jewish. But the atmosphere at the firm started to change.

Burnham retired soon after, to be succeeded by Mark Kaplan. Soon after, Drexel Burnham acquired Lambert Brussels Witter, an organization that specialized in research and was owned by the Belgian Compagnie Bruxelles Lambert, whereupon the firm became Drexel Burnham Lambert.[33]

The petroleum crisis of 1973 and the consequent market collapse that extended into 1974 led to red ink at many investment banks and brokerage firms. Not at Drexel, where profits generated by Milken's unit kept the firm afloat. Tubby Burnham relished these profits and set aside whatever doubts he had regarding junk. Milken asked for permission to organize a junk bond unit, composed of salesmen, traders, and researchers, to be recruited from within Drexel, but also open to outsiders. Burnham agreed, and Milken started organizing his operation and creating a company within the company.

According to Burnham, it was then that they worked out the compensation agreement that was to make Milken a billionaire. "Mike worked away trading securities no one was interested in. I offered him $28,000 a year and increased the position that he could handle from $500,000 to $2 million. I allowed him to keep a dollar for every three he made. He doubled the position's value in a year. Our deal never changed." Milken was to be given that amount to distribute as he saw fit to his unit. In addition, the Milken unit would receive fees for any new business it attracted. By 1976, Milken was making $5 million a year—not much considering what he would receive in the mid-1980s, but an enormous sum for Wall Street in this period.[34]

RELATIONSHIP TRADING

Milken was ever on the prowl for new customers. He hoped to woo small investors to junk bonds via mutual funds, which, of course, he expected to service. By the mid-1970s, there were a handful of high-yield mutual funds that, although not particularly popular, were growing in a period when the industry was being hit by massive redemptions. In 1974 and 1975, Keystone B4 and Lord Abbott Bond-Debenture Fund both reported good sales due to their high yields. In 1976, First Investors Fund for Income, one of Milken's important customers, was the nation's best-performing bond fund.

Here, too, the nature of the market worked in his favor. If a mutual fund wanted to establish or augment a position in equities, it would place an order at the exchange or market, or seek a block trader at one of the major houses. In either case, the manager would have an idea of price from the tape. It was different with junk bonds, where there was neither a liquid market nor a tape. Milken had tremendous leeway in setting prices for his clients at the high-yield mutuals. Since he knew far more about the companies behind those bonds than they did, the fund managers would have to rely upon him for advice on buys and sells.

Other changes were coming. Milken caught the attention of Frederick Joseph, an investment banker who had arrived at Drexel in 1974 from Shearson Hayden Stone, where, at the age of 36, he had been chief operating officer. Joseph was of the new generation coming to power at Drexel. His background was typical of those who were to flood Wall Street in the early 1980s, and not too different from Milken's.

Joseph had been raised in an Orthodox Jewish home in the Roxbury neighborhood of Boston, the son of a taxicab driver who worked until he was 71 years old. He attended the local public schools, then went to Harvard on a partial scholarship, and on to the Harvard Business School, from which he received his MBA in 1968. He went to work for Shearson that year.

Drexel was one of four firms that Joseph considered—the others were Reynolds, Wertheim, and Loeb, Rhoades. All were similar in lacking a strong investment banking operation, and all were in dire need of someone with his talents and ambitions. Joseph immediately saw a fit between Milken's operation and his. "He [Milken] was working 40 lines at once. I could see he had an incredible brain. He was making new markets for certain bonds, so I said, 'Let's do some deals together.'"[35]

In other words, Joseph wanted to take that next step—to create junk bond financing for clients unable to get an investment grade rating from the agencies. It was akin to a vertical merger in an industrial concern. Why sell someone else's product and give them a profit, or forgo one for yourself, when you were capable of turning out that very product? Especially when the fee structure made the business so lucrative. The nature and size of the fee was linked to whether the deal was completed; given Milken's customer base, Drexel not only could be confident of placement, but soon would have the reputation for being able to amass huge sums in short order for medium-sized, non-investment-grade companies with sales in the $25 million to $100 million range. Joseph recalled, "We knew they [clients] wanted to raise money, and we proposed the high-yield approach once we realized that was a market . . . . We found that Mike could sell them and that companies liked raising money that way."[36]

That Milken would have attempted to issue junk for corporate clients without prodding is probable, if only because of the additional fees to be earned by attracting new business. Besides that, a salesman has to have merchandise to offer. Riklis said, "Mike could sell it so well, he had to go out and create more of the product."[37]

In the investment atmosphere of the time, it seemed better for young, medium-sized companies, those in the process of reorganization or revival, or privately owned companies, to sell bonds rather than stock. Such firms might have trouble locating purchasers for stock and have to sell shares at low prices, relinquishing a large part of ownership and removing, or at least reducing, incentives. In the 1950s, the alternative had been bank loans. Now Milken offered another route: the issue of high-yielding bonds, whose interest and principal payout was structured through anticipated free cash flow. It was logical. ". . . we had a willingness to invest in the companies of the future—particularly on the equity side, but not on the debt side," Milken thought. "So I asked myself, why? Why—after factual information covering the entire century, showing that non-investment-grade bonds put out higher rates of returns, and showing they are less volatile, less risky— why does this skepticism still exist?"[38]

The structuring of a deal for a medium-sized company was different from raising capital for the likes of Exxon. Owners of junk had to know more about the company than did those who held investment grade bonds. Exxon bonds and those of other investment grade companies rise and fall on news of interest and money rates, approaching maturities, and changes in ratings. If the bonds of companies in the category of Exxon, Philip Morris, and General Motors were to bear the same coupon and maturity dates, their prices would be almost identical. Not so with the bonds of medium-sized companies, each of which faces a different business environment with different possibilities and risks. Owners of AAA-rated bonds don't have to pay much attention to earnings and dividends, except for unusually sharp degeneration in the former. Holders of junk bonds have to be concerned about such matters. If earnings increase sharply, the bond will bear less risk, and so its price might rise substantially. Poor earnings might not be reflected in major price declines, however, since the high yield already reflects the greater danger inherent in such paper. Should the company default on the bond, its price will decline, of course, but it still will be worth something, based on the underlying assets of the company.

Milken and the young traders and bankers he gathered around him had a different approach to their bonds than traders of investment grade issues. Most bond traders have extremely short time horizons. Not Milken. In his own idiosyncratic way, he had reinvented relationship banking, wedding it to what might be called "relationship trading." To most traders, bonds are paper; they have little interest in the companies behind them except for their ratings. Milken was different. He monitored activities at those firms for which he was a banker and in whose paper he traded. Actually, this wasn't old-fashioned interest; such care was necessary. A trader in Exxon bonds didn't have to worry about the company's creditworthiness. Sunshine Mining's trader did.

Both Milken and Joseph were supported by one of the comers at the company. Although he was of the older generation, Robert Linton (whose name was changed from Lichtenstein, and who also was Jewish), had a social background more in keeping with what one found in houses like Drexel in the 1970s. He was raised in a well-to-do atmosphere, but by the time his parents died, they had few assets. Years later, when he was quite wealthy, Linton admitted, "There is no amount of money that would make me feel secure."

After graduating from Phillips Exeter Academy, Linton went off to World War II. Upon his discharge, he took a job as a runner at Burnham & Co., delivering stock certificates and other papers. He rose slowly, becoming a floor trader, stockbroker, researcher, and, eventually, an investment banker. Linton would succeed Mark Kaplan in 1977. Yet, he always remained aware of his lack of the kind of education possessed by counterparts at Establishment banks. A close friend once said of him, "People who don't go to college overcompensate with determination, and Bob is a bulldog."

Linton also knew that no matter how powerful Drexel became, due to its heritage, it could not hope to be perceived as a member of the Wall Street club—the peer of a Morgan Stanley or a Goldman Sachs. In 1985, when Drexel was the most feared competitor in the industry, Linton told a reporter, "We want to be seen as a class act." Then he posed a rhetorical question: "Would we trade money for respect?" His answer, after a pregnant pause: "I don't know."[39] The following year, Linton said he wanted Drexel to be seen as the top investment bank "as measured by professionalism, integrity, and capability."[40]

INVADING THE MARKET

The first important original junk issues of the modern period were underwritten by Lehman Brothers and Goldman Sachs in early 1977, when they raised funds for LTV, Zapata, Fuqua, and Pan American World Airways.[41] Drexel now knew there was money to be made in such business. Milken's reputation within the industry had grown, and his influence within the firm was such that he could replicate Lehman's success with ease.

Drexel started small. In April 1977, it sold a $30 million issue of 11½ percent subordinated debentures for Texas International. Fearing it could not place the entire issue, Drexel syndicated it, taking $7.15 million for itself and allocating the rest to 59 other banks, earning a fee of $900,000. The success of this underwriting led to one for Michigan General. Others followed. In 1977, Drexel underwrote seven high-yield issues for a total of $124.5 million, which made it the second largest underwriter in that market, behind Lehman. There were 14 issues for $439.5 million the following year.

All this made Drexel one of the industry's rapidly rising investment banks. The old-timers there, thinking in conventional terms, still weren't impressed. Drexel still had only 12 Fortune 500 clients, and to them, this was the true measure of success or failure. Given the nature of investment banking in the late 1970s, the bank hadn't much of a chance to take clients away from the blue-chip houses like Morgan Stanley and Goldman Sachs. It also lacked the financial clout of a Merrill Lynch or a Salomon.

Milken and Joseph would respond that whatever hope there was for growth in areas of investment banking lay in new areas and new people. Let others cater to the needs of Ford, IBM, and GE, which seemed to Milken like dinosaurs. Drexel would serve the likes of Ted Turner, William McGowan, and Craig McCaw, who were building Turner Broadcasting, MCI, and McCaw Cellular, respectively. "There are really only two kinds of companies—the comers and the goers," said Drexel managing director, G. Christian Andersen. "We finance the comers." To this Joseph added, "Our business is not a social event. We don't want to forget who we are and where we come from."[42]

In other words, Drexel intended to finance companies for whom the debt market previously had been closed. Repeatedly, like a mantra, Milken would tell audiences around the country that the bonds of 95 percent of American corporations with revenues of over $35 million would be classified as junk, and there were only 800 or so corporations that merited investment grade status, adding that of the 22,000 or so companies with sales of over $35 million, only 5 percent were of investment grade. Moreover, those large, investment grade companies were employing fewer people each year, while the smaller, non-investment-grade concerns, were adding jobs. Yet, they could not easily raise capital.

Drexel would perform the task for them, not only to make money, said Milken, but also to revive American entrepreneurship. He truly believed in this, as much as Charles Merrill did in people's capitalism. Merrill had democratized shareholding. Milken hoped to do the same for financing. Without knowing it, Milken shared a vision originated by the Jacksonian Democrats of the 1830s in their fight against the Bank of the United States, and the Populists of the 1890s, who hoped to monetize silver and thus inflate the currency. Both fought against the "old money" in the name of those who hoped to benefit from a liberalized access to capital. The man who was to become notorious as an icon of unfeeling greed was in the liberal, even radical, tradition of American economic thought in this stage of his career.

Business was good, profits were being made, and Milken's remuneration was growing. There was only one problem. Milken still wasn't happy in New York. It bothered him that by the time he arrived home, the children were asleep. "I don't accept the change to a one-parent family," he told a reporter several years later. "I think a child should be raised by both parents, and that children should grow up with discipline, a love of knowledge, security and respect for their elders." Milken couldn't be as much of a father as he wanted in New York. In addition, two of the children had been diagnosed as epileptics, and Milken's father had cancer, which added to the desire to return to a familiar environment. Simply stated, the Milkens were homesick for California.

There were two other considerations. First, Milken continued to abhor the atmosphere of lower Manhattan, so different from that of Los Angeles. Ironically, Wall Street's symbol of the 1980s not only did not locate himself in the financial district, but he actually disliked the place. Second, when it was 9:00 A.M. in New York, it was 6:00 A.M. in California, which meant he could start the day earlier, and he could also contact Tokyo, Hong Kong, and London during business hours. In California, one could arrive at the office at 4:00 A.M., put in two hours of work before business opened in Manhattan, and then continue to work as late as one wanted. For Milken, it meant he could get in many more hours at the office and arrive home early enough to spend time with the children.

Milken told Drexel's leaders of his desire to move his operation to Los Angeles. At first Kantor, Linton, Joseph, and the others attempted to dissuade him. In the end, they had no choice but to accept his decision. Richard H. Jenrette, chairman of Donaldson, Lufkin & Jenrette, who attempted to lure Milken there in the early 1970s, thought this procedure somewhat odd. "We pride ourselves on being flexible," he told a reporter, "but we're not that flexible."[43] The move meant that Milken had become more important than anyone else at the firm—indeed, by himself, he was more than the rest of Drexel. So, in 1979, together with his salesmen, traders, researchers, and some others he carefully selected, Milken packed up and went home to Beverly Hills. For years, journalists and academics had been writing about the shift of the nation's center of gravity from New York to California. Now Milken was moving the most profitable part of the fastest-growing investment bank there. It was the kind of action to be expected of a revolutionary antiestablishment banker.

5

WEAVING THE
DREXEL NETWORK

On Monday, July 3, 1978, one day short of his 32nd birthday, Mike Milken set up shop in Century City.[1] Lori and he had purchased a $750,000 house within walking distance of his parents' home in nearby Encino, moved in, and enrolled their children in the local public school. Mike's brother Lowell, left his job at the Los Angeles law firm of Irell & Manella and joined the Drexel operation. The next phase of Milken's life, and of junk bond history, was underway.

Most of Wall Street's attention continued to be focused on Drexel's New York offices, where the investment bankers performed. And the media still seemed to believe this was the firm's hub. How could it be otherwise? How could a key part of a major investment bank operate from offices on the West Coast? As late as 1985, after Milken had participated in several spectacular deals, *Institutional Investor,* the most savvy Wall Street magazine, named Drexel CEO Robert Linton its "banker of the year," for "creating a new capital market and for demonstrating that creativity and opportunism—not sheer size—can propel a firm to prominence." The primary reason for Drexel's rise, the writer suggested, was Linton's leadership. "It's quite possible that Milken's brilliance would never have flowered if it weren't for the culture that Linton has fashioned at Drexel."[2] Even then, Wall Street didn't realize that Milken easily might have gone off on his own and succeeded admirably, while without him, Drexel would have been severely injured.

THE DEREGULATION EARTHQUAKE

The economy gave off mixed signals that summer and early autumn. Unemployment increased somewhat, but producer and consumer prices were rising. Alfred Kahn claimed that, in time, deregulation would increase productivity and employment while hindering inflation, but Paul Volcker, who became Federal Reserve Board Chairman on August 6, 1979, wasn't so sure and prepared to fight inflation with the weapons at his disposal.

One of these weapons was restricting money supply growth. The Federal Open Market Committee decided to set goals of from 1.5 to 4.5 percent growth for the year; until then, the rate had been more than 10 percent. Action on this front caused interest rates to rise in the late summer and early autumn. By September, mortgage rates were over 12 percent and rising, as investors purchased homes as an inflation hedge. Corporations borrowed even when they didn't need the money, stockpiling funds in anticipation of higher rates in the future and parking the cash in money market instruments.

On October 4, the Commerce Department announced that the Producer Price Index had risen by a whopping annualized 17 percent in September, the largest such increase in nearly five years. The following day, the Labor Department announced that unemployment had declined to 5.8 percent. It appeared that the economy was stronger than had previously been thought, and that inflation was accelerating.

At a press conference on Saturday, October 6, 1979, Volcker announced an increase in the discount rate by 1 percent to a record 12 percent. There would be stiff new reserve requirements on some bank accounts, which would discourage banks from making loans, and there would be credit controls.

This was heady stuff, meant to send the message that the Fed was declaring war on inflation. Even more important, however, was Volcker's announcement that, thenceforth, the money supply would increase at a steady—and even slower—pace. Interest rates would be permitted to fluctuate, which, in the context of the period, meant they would rise substantially and erratically. The timing of the announcement was no accident; Volcker wanted to give investors and bankers the weekend to digest the news before the opening of markets on Monday.

As anticipated, both stocks and bonds fell following Volcker's announcement, but not as sharply as they might have had the market not been given the chance to digest the news. The Dow Industrials had closed on Friday at 897; the index dropped to 883 in intraday trading on Monday, and closed at 884. Bonds declined only 9 basis points to end at 80.95 on the Dow Bond Index, hardly a serious sell-off. But the selling continued, and by the end of the month, stocks were at 816 and bonds at 76.55. Then stocks rallied; by December 1980, the Dow was once again flirting with 1000. But bonds had been savaged, with the index dipping below 61. Not since 1932 had the bond market been so critically injured.

This debacle resulted from the rapid rise in interest rates. The average Federal Funds rate for 1979 would come to 11.2 percent. It would go to 13.4 percent the following year, during which the Fed seemed uncertain and confused, and to 16.4 percent in 1981, peaking at a shade below 20 percent in June. The consequence was a short, brutal recession in 1980, followed by a recovery, which was followed by another recession during the

Table 5-1

BOND YIELDS, 1975-1982

Year	Corporate AAA	Bonds BAA	High-Grade Municipals
1975	8.83	10.61	6.89
1976	8.43	9.75	6.49
1977	8.02	8.97	5.56
1978	8.73	9.49	5.90
1979	9.63	10.69	6.39
1980	11.94	13.67	8.51
1981	14.17	16.04	11.23
1982	13.79	16.11	11.57

Source: The Economic Report of the President, 332.

early years of the Reagan administration. For the first time since the 1930s, the nation experienced double-digit unemployment.[3]

The deregulatory tone set by Carter and Kahn was continued with gusto by Reagan. Carter had accepted deregulation to fight stagflation. So did the Reaganites, but they also believed in it philosophically, with a firm faith that government intrusion into the marketplace was not only unwise but, in a sense, immoral.

This meant that the Glass-Steagall Act would become a dead letter—the regulatory wall between investment and commercial banking that had been created in 1933 would be ignored. So would the antitrust laws. The SEC would have its budget slashed annually. The Boeskys, Icahns, and Milkens of the world were given to know that, as far as Washington was concerned, almost anything was acceptable. The carefully regulated zoo of the 1950s was to be reconstituted as a jungle.

In time, inflation came under control, although the public's inflationary expectations remained high well into the 1980s. Investors refused to purchase common stock, keeping their funds in money market accounts, which rose from $45 billion to $207 billion between 1979 and 1982. This helped the junk market on the "sell side," meaning that in such a high rate environment, borrowers had to offer higher yields to obtain funds.

As the market held firm and interest rates started to slide, more companies came to market to borrow, and they found a situation somewhat similar to that of the late 1970s, when inflationary expectations obliged borrowers to pay higher rates to attract funds. Now the pressures were on the "buy side," as investors, accustomed to high rates, faced the choice of accepting smaller yields or lowering their quality preferences to obtain the same high yields. There were many who wanted those high yields in what was becoming a low-yield environment, and who were agreeable to taking lower-rated paper. There had been 161 new issues in 1981, bringing in net proceeds of $5.3 billion. The figures fell to 122 issues for $3.7 billion in the recession year of 1982, but they rose to 150 issues for $5.9 billion in 1982, and to a whopping 256 issues for $14.7 billion in 1983.

So the junk market had mutated. Initially, the borrowers had to scramble to find buyers. By 1983, they were swamped with demand from buyers. Nor was this the only change. Early in the 1980s, borrowers were troubled with the quality of the junk they took. Now, with the market having proved itself through a major downturn, they became more interested in yield.[4]

This was particularly true for the thrifts, which customarily borrowed short and lent long, which means they paid interest on deposits and granted mortgages. They were able to bundle new mortgages into Ginnie Maes, but, under the terms of Regulation Q, they were not permitted to pay competitive rates to attract deposits, which, instead, flowed into money market funds. In 1972, the thrifts had net assets of $16.7 billion; by 1980, they had a combined *negative* net worth of $17.5 billion, and 85 percent of them were losing money, as depositors withdrew funds to place them in money market funds. By 1982, close to one out of every five thrifts in operation in 1979 had failed.

To deal with this crisis, President Carter signed into law the Deregulation Act of 1980, which permitted the savings institutions to pay competitive interest rates to attract deposits. Then, in 1982, President Reagan signed the Garn-St. Germain Depository Institutions Act. Under one of its provisions, the thrifts were permitted to sell certificates of deposit at market rates to compete with the money market funds. Another section of the act permitted the thrifts to invest up to 40 percent of their assets in nonresidential real estate. In addition, they could invest in formerly forbidden instruments, like low-rated paper. This was the first legislative step toward the thrift debacle.

It didn't take Milken long to realize how the Garn-St. Germain bill would affect the junk bond business. The thrifts would compete with one another for deposits and CD customers, and they would have to seek higher-yielding investments than Ginnie Maes. Many thrifts preferred speculation in real estate, which promised even higher returns than junk, and this became their primary holding. Milken went after the others.

TOM SPIEGEL AND COLUMBIA S&L

Tom Spiegel, who, with Milken at his side, would make Columbia S&L a citadel of junk, became one of the biggest of Drexel's thrift clients. He, too, had been raised in Beverly Hills after World War II, the son of Holocaust survivors who had entered the home construction business. An indifferent student who was driven by his father to achieve, Spiegel rebelled by dropping out of law school in 1968. He held several jobs during the next nine years. For a while, Spiegel worked as a broker at Drexel, following that with a stint in Iran, where he tried to sell condominiums for Starrett Corp. In 1977, he reconciled with his father and became vice president at Columbia Savings & Loan, a small thrift operation that the senior Spiegel had acquired for a knockdown price at the bottom of the 1974 recession.

Columbia wasn't much of a holding. Like most thrifts, it had suffered grievously during the stagflation years, and it faced intense competition in its Beverly Hills home base. The Spiegels hoped to revive Columbia, but they lacked the financial clout to be anything but small players. Tom had another idea: the use of novel financial instruments to attract deposits. One of these was a five-year mortgage with no monthly payments. Rather, everything was to be repaid at maturity. Although Columbia charged higher fees and interest, these mortgages were attractive to people who hoped to purchase homes and sell quickly—hopefully, at a large profit.

The business was lucrative, and Spiegel might have gone on to create similar mortgages were it not for the golden opportunity presented by S&L deregulation. Spiegel might have turned to real estate, as so many others did, if he had not known Milken. As it was, Columbia opted for junk.

Milken tutored Spiegel on the intricacies of the market. "I needed a way to diversify our portfolio, and Mike needed a broader market for high-yield bonds," Spiegel later reminisced. "Working together made perfect sense. Purchasing junk bonds through Drexel allowed me to use Mike's expertise in evaluating these credits."[5] The trick was attracting deposits. This was done through the services of loan brokers, individuals, and institutions who would draw money through advertisements and then place it with an S&L for a fee. Columbia's chief source was Merrill Lynch, but there were others.

Columbia remained a thrift in name only. For all practical purposes, it became an investment trust. Depositors received a high yield and a guarantee of return of principal from the Federal Savings & Loan Insurance Corporation, while Columbia invested large amounts in junk bonds. The spread between the yield to the depositor and the return from the junk was far wider than would have been obtained from conventional thrift business. It showed in the bottom line: In 1981, Columbia reported a loss of $3.6 million. By 1984, after two years under Milken's tutelage, Columbia had earnings of $44 million; they rose to $122 million in 1985, and to $193 million in 1986.

By then, other high rollers had joined Riklis and Spiegel as Drexel clients, or, to be more precise, Milken clients, for it was he, not the firm, who counted with those concerned with investment in junk bonds. For the most part, these were individuals somewhat off the beaten path; they lacked establishment cachet and they certainly were not establishment types. With Milken's help, Saul Steinberg became a premier raider and also bought junk through Reliance Financial and other firms he controlled. Carl Lindner, of Cincinnati-based American Financial, did the same. Many more would follow, Charles Keating, the CEO of Lincoln S&L, was one of several industry figures who were Milken customers and who later faced disgrace and jail. But the most impressive performance was by Fred Carr, who, with Milken at his side, changed the sleepy First Executive Corp. into a major insurance company—becoming Milken's most important customer.

FRED CARR AND THE REVOLUTION IN INSURANCE

In the process of becoming the best known mutual fund manager, Fred Carr had garnered enemies, and the arrogance that came with success brought him more. In November 1969, he was forced from Enterprise and went off on his own. The market was topping out by then, and Enterprise collapsed. Some said it was Carr's fault for having loaded the portfolio with junk stocks. His defenders noted that the fund's failure came after he left, implying that if Carr had remained, all would have been well.

Carr, who at the time was only 38 years old, organized Carr Management & Research, a consultant operation. Although the bull market had ended, enough people were around who didn't realize it and still considered him a genius. Within months, he had more than $100 million under management and was seeking new challenges. He came across one in 1974, in the form of Executive Life of California, a smallish entity on the brink of bankruptcy. A member of the board, Al Handschumacher, knew Carr and, in early 1974, recruited him to the board. In July, Carr became the company's CEO.[6]

At the time, the insurance industry was somnolent. Agents would sell policies to customers to provide funds for survivors or for retirement. Premiums would be remitted each year, and in the case of the most familiar policy, whole life, the money would go for fees, commissions, and other charges, and into a reserve fund that was invested in securities and real estate, from whose earnings benefits would be paid. Policyholders would receive annual dividends, to be used to pay part of their premiums.

Although Carr had once sold insurance, he had little knowledge of the industry. What he understood best was investments, and almost from the first, his salvage operation at First Executive involved the creation of new products, which would be more attractive than conventional insurance due to their higher yields. In the 1960s, he had managed to extract high profits from capital gains on his junk stock portfolio. In the 1970s and 1980s, he would do it by using junk bonds.

As he worked, Carr transformed both the insurance industry and the way wealthy individuals viewed their policies. What once had been a way to provide for survivors became, for some, an investment vehicle. The assets in the reserve fund were free from taxes, while the proceeds from an insurance policy were not taxed either. This made insurance a perfect tax dodge. Barry Kaye Associates, whose offices were within hailing distance of those of Executive Life, concentrated on elderly, wealthy individuals afraid of what the Internal Revenue Service would do to their estates. Never fear, said Kaye. Make gifts of $10,000 a year ($20,000 in the case of married couples) to each of your heirs, who must use this money to purchase insurance policies on you, the benefactor. Then, when you die, the funds will go to the policyholders, tax-free, to be used to pay estate taxes. In the case of a very large estate, Kaye counseled more than $10,000 or $20,000 might be bequeathed; the donor would pay gift taxes, but these would be much lower than estate taxes later.

By the late 1980s, colleges and universities got into the act, urging alumni to make donations in the form of such insurance policies—in some cases, tying them to annuities. It was legal. It made sense financially. It worked.

First Executive's products became even more attractive as the tax reforms of the 1980s closed many other loopholes once available to high-income individuals. The once-small insurer, First Executive, was catapulted into the ranks of America's top 15 companies in terms of policies.[7] Other insurers followed suit. In the aggregate, insurance companies became the major holders of junk, owning some 30 percent of these bonds by the late 1980s.

One of the many new instruments devised by the insurance companies was the guaranteed investment contract (GIC), an annuity that resembled a certificate of deposit. GICs would accumulate interest and then offer high, regular payouts at some future time. How much would that be? It all depended on the earnings from the reserve. If the policyholder was to have a larger payout, to obtain it, the employer might be able to invest less funds with the junk-based First Executive Life than would be required at a more conservative firm.

Another new vehicle was the single-premium deferred annuity (SPDA). By investing a specific amount of money, the investor received, on retirement or any other date he or she wanted, a monthly, quarterly, or annual payout, the size of which was based on the interest rate earned. All of that interest was tax-deferred, so there was a double reason to want a high return. Many companies sold SPDAs, but First Executive had the most attractive interest rates, and so this vehicle became a major business for the firm.

Out of First Executive came a series of policies known as irreplaceable life. The firm also sold many single-premium deferred whole life and other related policies, in which the customer made a single payment, not unlike a mutual fund; in return, the customer received a policy with guaranteed minimum interest, which, in the case of Executive Life, was generally exceeded.

Executive Life pioneered and led the way with policies calling for structured settlements. Accident victims who successfully sued for compensation might receive income for life, and the insurance company involved might purchase an Executive Life policy rather than one of its own, since Carr's products cost so much less. By the late 1980s, single-premium policies accounted for the bulk of Executive's total undertakings. Again, this was not the historic role for insurance in the pre-Carr days.[8]

First Executive became involved in approximately 90 percent of Drexel underwritings, accounting for some $40 billion in bonds from 1982 and 1987 alone, and owning the world's largest junk portfolio.[9] Not surprisingly, First Executive underwent a transformation akin to that of Columbia S&L, coming to resemble less an insurance concern than a bank that offered a special variety of CDs, in the form of GICs, SPDAs, and similar policies.

First Executive had even closer ties to Drexel than had Columbia and the other thrifts, with some aspects of the dealings just this side of shady. It would purchase bonds issued by Drexel to finance takeovers and LBOs; once in control, using a policy called the customer-qualified retirement annuity, the new managements would switch the company's insurance and pension business to First Executive.

First Executive purchased the junk bonds that were used to enable Ron Perelman's Pantry Pride to acquire Revlon. After taking over, Perelman switched Revlon's $124 million pension plan to First Executive, where, due to the higher interest rates made possible by junk bonds, he obtained the same coverage for $85 million and was able to take $39 million out of the company.[10]

Meshulam Riklis was another Milken client on First Executive's buy list who transferred his company's insurance business there. David Murdock, CEO of Fieldcrest Cannon, also a Drexel client, did the same. When Murdock took control of the company, it had $102.8 million in its pension fund. Arguing that with a First Executive policy only $66.2 million was needed, Murdock removed $36.6 million from the fund.

In 1986, First Executive purchased $343 million in the junk bonds issued to finance a deal in which Pacific Lumber was acquired by Maxxam, whereupon Maxxam purchased annuities from First Executive Life to refinance Pacific Lumber's pension plan. This action raised a storm of questions. "As you know, our employees are vitally interested in the quality of the company selected for the annuity contracts," wrote Vincent C. Gardner, a Pacific Lumber executive, in a memo to Maxxam just before the award to First Executive. "If First Executive Life is selected, I believe its investment philosophy and the heavy concentration in junk bonds and its role in financing Drexel Burnham's deals, including the Pacific Lumber Company's purchase, will be major causes of concern to our employees." In 1989, Pacific Lumber would file a lawsuit charging that a quid pro quo existed between Maxxam and First Executive.

During the 1980s, more than 2,100 companies terminated their pension programs, transferring more than $27 billion of policies covering 2.4 million workers to insurers like First Executive, which offered lower-cost policies. These firms were able to take more than $21 billion in cash from their pension plans.[11]

For a while, it appeared that everyone benefitted. Later, when First Executive and several other insurance companies underwent stress and strain, owners of those policies and exotic instruments would also suffer. In some ways, the situation resembled that of the thrifts, and customers of both later were viewed as victims of the junk era. But there was a difference, in that thrift depositors were insured, and so they were saved by the federal bailout. There was no such guarantee for the owners of insurance policies, who lived with uncertainty until they were saved through restructurings.

Milken took personal charge of the Executive Life account, while others at Drexel's Beverly Hills office were assigned clients and encouraged to go into the field to find new ones. James Dahl became Milken's chief intermediary with the thrift industry, particularly with CenTrust, Columbia, and Lincoln, where he made certain that customers benefitted from the alliance and would remain loyal.

This was done through deals that skirted the law.[12] On one occasion, Dahl took some Caesar's World bonds, only to learn that they could not be purchased for the Drexel account due to restrictions. He telephoned Tom Spiegel and asked him to buy the bonds. Spiegel was a trifle reluctant, so Dahl threw in a bonus: If Spiegel took the bonds, Drexel would remove any downside risk and would split any profit realized from the sale. Spiegel accepted with alacrity.[13]

On one occasion, Dahl asked Keating to purchase Playtex bonds, throwing in shares of the company's common at a bargain price as a sweetener. Then he helped Keating transfer the shares from Lincoln to Keating's privately owned American Continental Corp (ACC) at a lowball price of $1 a share, when there was no market for the common. Eight months later, ACC sold 1.5 million of the shares through Drexel to CenTrust at $7.25 a share, and the remainder soon after. As a result, ACC—Keating, that is—reaped a profit of $12.5 million that the FSLIC later would claim was rightfully Lincoln's.

Whether Milken knew of such activities is moot, but given the intimacy of the Beverly Hills operation, it seems likely he did. In any case, Dahl hardly would have made such a move without his tacit approval.

Dahl generated new business through referrals and cold calls. This was the way he landed Prudential Insurance, which became one of his better clients, as he explained to the court at Milken's hearing:

> I made a cold call to Bob Angevine, who is a credit analyst in the Pru's work-out department. I had learned from a computer run that Drexel had available to it that the Pru was an owner of a distressed credit and I found out Bob Angevine was the fellow in charge of those bonds and I made a cold call, talked to him, flew to Newark, met with him and set up a meeting with some of the senior people at the Pru to meet with myself and Mike. Shortly thereafter Mike and I flew to Newark together, spent one day at the Pru meeting with a half dozen of the senior people, and shortly thereafter the Pru started buying high yield bonds from us.[14]

Some of the deals were, to say the least, suspect—flirting with the boundaries of acceptable behavior.

In this way, Milken created the most impressive client list in the industry. Like those who used Drexel's services to raise funds, most of his buyers were "new money." Both rosters were composed of outsiders, and, for the most part, they would remain so. As Dillon Read CEO Nick Brady, soon to become the scourge of junk, later remarked, "They were junk people buying junk bonds."

DOING DEALS

At the time, such critical remarks sounded like sour grapes. By the mid-1980s, junk had a track record, and it was a good one. Drexel asserted that in the 1970s, there had been average annual failures of 1.6 percent of all junk bonds (including fallen angels). The figure for 1980 was 1.5 percent, and dropped to 0.2 percent in 1981. More important, during the 1981–1982 recession, the failure rate for junk bonds rose only slightly; in 1982, it rose to 3.1 percent, then fell to 1.1 percent in 1983. Failures of original-issue junk bonds, which had been 0.9 percent in 1980 and 0.6 percent in 1981, went to 0.8 percent in 1982 and 0.7 percent in 1983.[15] Meanwhile, large, well-known firms with investment grade ratings, such as International Harvester and Ford, experienced financial difficulties. Chrysler barely escaped collapse. Confidence in junk soared.

By mid-decade, the mood was somewhat like the hectic days of the early 1960s, when initial public offerings were coming to market at a dizzying pace. In one 12-day period in 1983, Drexel sold 11 new issues worth $750 million in principal amount, for such companies as Kindercare, Petro-Lewis, Computer Consoles, and Sunshine Mining.

Milken later would declare that this was the part of the business he found the most appealing; if he never bankrolled a single leveraged buyout, he would have been quite content. In the 1960s, Milken might have entered the venture capital field or raised cash for young, small companies through equity offerings, for such were his interests. One easily can imagine him starting a firm like American Research & Development, taking equity interests in emerging companies like Digital Equipment. As it happened, circumstances of the market—what the buyer was prepared to take—dictated that it had to be done with bonds.

Venture capital operations continued in the 1970s, of course, but they were small, and the prices were high. Companies in the early stages of development could not hope for much from a venture capitalist; the average deal size for a new firm as late as 1989 was $1.9 million, and past the early stages, $2.5 million. For that sum, the company would have to give up a sizable amount of ownership. The zigzagging stock market frightened many investors and speculators from the initial public offerings arena, so that avenue was weak. The banks remained. The problem there was familiar: banks abhor risks; they will lend money to companies with secure assets but not to companies lacking them. Therefore, banks are prepared to lend money to companies whose need for it isn't that great, and they withhold it from those with less collateral, who need financing for expansion. Further, bank loans for smaller companies often are short-term and tied to the prime rate, leaving the borrower at the mercy of changes in interest rates if and when refinancing is necessary.

Milken thought long-term junk bond financing to be ideal for such companies. The beauty of such financing, he observed, was that the borrower knew just how much money he would need for interest payments and could schedule them accordingly. In time, Milken would refine this concept through a dazzling array of specially designed bond deals, for which he had scores of buyers who were willing to accept his products on faith. Carolco president Peter Hoffman conceded as much: "No one analyzes the credits that closely. You trust the Milkens to know what they're doing."[16]

One of the first companies Drexel helped finance was Comdisco, which was engaged in purchasing IBM mainframe computers from companies ready to upgrade, and then selling the reconditioned equipment to customers that didn't require the latest technology. Although not a pioneer in selling second-hand computers, Comdisco was one of the industry's fastest-growing entities. Initially, the company financed purchases through commercial bank borrowings and private placements, sources that were somewhat unreliable and short-term. While Comdisco had sales of more than $112 million in 1977, it could not hope for investment grade status.

CEO Kenneth Pontikas wanted to expand into computer leasing and required around $15 million to get started, more capital than he had in hand or could hope to obtain from the banks, even if he had been willing to pay their rates. What about raising capital through the sale of stock? This made little sense when P/E multiples had shrivelled, and the new-issue market was ailing. Pontikas thought he would have had to give up half the company.[17]

In 1977, Drexel underwrote its first Comdisco offering, an 11½ percent $15 million issue maturing in 1992, which had a B rating. Other underwritings followed. Within a year and a half, revenues had almost doubled while earnings had more than tripled. By 1989, Comdisco was nearly a $2 billion company whose senior notes were granted investment grade ratings, but even before then, it had become obvious that the company was growing strongly.

Other successful—and some unsuccessful—underwritings followed. From the start of Comdisco's operations in 1977 to September 30, 1983, a period of high inflation followed by severe recession, Drexel underwrote 276 high-yield issues worth $14.6 billion in principal amount. These issues outperformed Treasuries by 5.2 percent compounded annually; this meant that after eight years, a portfolio of junk bonds would be worth 50 percent more than perfectly safe Treasuries.

Of course, some of the issues rode a roller coaster, affected both by interest rate changes and the fortunes of the companies behind them. Documation, a manufacturer of high-speed printers, fell on hard times, and its bonds collapsed to 45, only to rise to 90 after a merger by the company with Storage Technology. The vast majority of bonds came out of the crises in good shape. According to one Milken analyst, Larry Post, "More than nine out of ten companies find ways to survive."[18]

In time, some Milken clients would become part of a community of interest, and here, too, he exercised his creativity. Often, one of them would be surprised to learn that not only would Milken be able to raise hundreds of millions of dollars in a short period but he also insisted on selling more of their bonds than they wanted sold. The extra money was to be used to purchase bonds of other companies Milken was financing. For example, Carolco Pictures, a Drexel client, took $5 million extra from one offering and purchased Memorex bonds with it. There was reciprocity in this practice; the beneficiary company would be purchasing some of the first company's bonds. Drexel managing director Chris Andersen estimated that, in 1986, the firm raised $2 billion or more by overfunding. "One thing we know for sure," he said by way of explanation, "is that companies don't go broke with too much cash."

These dealings were heady stuff, and Milken would have been unusual not to have been affected by all of his power. Here he was, a young outsider, summoning to his office CEOs of significant corporations for 5:00 A.M. meetings. Large institutional investors made themselves available, too, and they often purchased bonds on which they would have preferred to pass, for fear that they might be excluded from the next good deal.

Before his fall, this community arrangement seemed Milken's greatest accomplishment. Later, in an attempt to explain Milken's significance, John Gutfreund said, "It [Drexel] has created an investment banking syndicate that exists completely outside the traditional banking industry." Milken had developed a closed circle, a system to conduct financings and make markets that required no other player. On this account, Gutfreund considered Milken "a creative genius." Others noted a similarity to the Japanese *keiretsu*, that web of financial relationships with a bank at the center, feeding all members when needed by switching assets from one to another, and in which each unit is a potential or real customer of the others. In the *keiretsu*, however, there is interlocking equity ownership, with the bank as the largest owner of them all. Moreover, bank representatives sit on the boards of the member companies, which meet to plan common strategies. In the Milken web, the paper involved was bonds; there was no commonality, but, still, at the center was Drexel.

There had been something like this network close to a century ago. J. P. Morgan, with allies at First National Bank, Chase National, Bankers Trust, National Bank of Commerce, and others, as well as several insurance companies, commanded vast capital resources and sat on the boards of hundreds of corporations. There was a similar constellation commanded by John D. Rockefeller.

In modern times, Milken with his closed, self-contained system, came closest to them. In the early 1980s, he virtually owned the junk market, and anyone wanting to play there had to go through him. He not only bought and sold the bonds, but he also knew where they were. This meant that he could contact a customer and talk him into a buy, and then call the owner of the bond and invite him to sell. Milken could set prices within a very wide band, since buyer and seller would have had no precise idea of how much the bond was worth. Only Milken could know when to deal with those bonds, and only he had pricing power. His customers lacked this information and control.

THE MILKEN PARTNERSHIPS

With his associates and allies, Milken became the focus of what eventually became hundreds of partnerships—the government would later claim they numbered 415, while others set a figure of closer to 300—that dealt in the bonds, and at times skimmed deals of valuable paper. This was no small matter. By the mid-1980s, the network of partnerships had assets of more than $500 million, and their distributions were immense. According to a 1990 General Accounting Office report, from 1981 to 1988, the 25 largest Milken partnerships, led by Otter Creek Associates at $437 million, by themselves distributed $2 billion, with half of that going to Milken. Several Milken associates denied the amounts, but they conceded the partnerships did exist.[19]

One form of partnership was established to purchase bonds resold by clients to Drexel, hold them for a while, and then sell them to Drexel for placement with another client. So the first client might sell bonds to Drexel for $75, and Drexel would sell them to the partnership for $75.25. In time, the bonds might go back to Drexel at $77, whereupon they would go to the second client for $77.25. It was clean and usually riskless, since Drexel did the pricing.

The routine for a second kind of partnership also was quite simple. When Drexel financed a leveraged buyout, the client might be obliged to make warrants, rights, and other perquisites available to Drexel at low cost or no cost. Some partnerships combined these methods and others. There was nothing new in any of this; it had been done with stock in the 1960s. But when Dahl revealed the practices later, tremors went through the industry as Wall Street received a greater understanding of Milken's power.

James Dahl, who played hardball with the toughest and would come to embody the worst excesses of the junk decade, handled some of the disbursement of the paper, large amounts of which wound up in Milken partnerships. Dahl was involved in some 30 partnerships, and other salesmen were included. This was an important part of their remuneration. As he explained at Milken's hearing, "Once a year I would meet with Michael and we would go over the two components of the compensation package, which is what my salary would be for the coming year and a dollar amount that I would be allowed to invest in the partnerships in the aggregate for that year."[20] No one involved, except individuals who managed the funds, had a clear idea of what securities were being bought and sold.

Later, there would be allegations that several high-yield fund managers to whom Milken sold his securities were included in the partnerships, this being an implied or direct reward for purchasing bonds Drexel was having difficulty placing. One of these deals involved Patricia Ostrander, a fund manager at Fidelity. In 1985, Storer Communications was taken private by KKR through Drexel, which undertook to distribute $260 million of preferred stock. This was an ambitious underwriting, which helped make KKR's reputation, as well as Drexel's. To sweeten the deal, which appeared chancy, KKR provided 67.8 million warrants to purchase Storer common at $2.05 a share, and sold these at 7.4 cents apiece. The procedure itself was perfectly legal and conventional, and it is still being done. Under ordinary circumstances, the warrants would be sold to those who agreed to purchase the bonds or stock, and, in some cases, warrants would be distributed to salespeople as an incentive. On this occasion, however, some of the warrants went to MacPherson Investment Partners, which had been formed by the

Milken brothers, and which also included Ostrander and other fund managers. Milken later revealed that he provided $140 million of the funds needed, more than KKR, and perhaps he felt he merited such a reward. In 1988, the warrants were sold for a profit of $246 million.[21]

All of this made for comfortable and profitable work. Commissions and fees were substantial, a pleasing prospect in the age of deregulation when margins were tight.[22] Also, there were many more corporations without an investment grade rating than with that rating, which made Milken's potential universe larger than that of any other banker.

While Milken's financings and refinancings were spread over a wide number of industries, he had special interests in housing, health care, cable television, gambling casinos, cellular telephone, and entertainment. Within these special areas, he also excelled in nursing small clients into big ones. In 1979, Milken raised $20 million for Golden Nugget, then a rather small casino with assets of $35 million and less than $3 million in earnings. CEO Steve Wynn had to go on a road show with Drexel bankers, traveling from city to city, to get the $20 million. It was, said Wynn, "an exceedingly difficult sell." But the money was raised, and with the proceeds, Wynn was able to transform Golden Nugget into one of the most profitable enterprises in its industry. In the summer of 1983, he employed Drexel for a $250 million underwriting, which "came in on roller skates."[23] By then, Drexel had become the banker to most of the gambling companies, including Circus Circus, Bally's, Showboat, Caesar's Palace, and Harrah's, among others.

DREXEL'S FAILURES

Drexel had its share of embarrassments. In 1982, it comanaged and led an underwriting group in the sale of $25.6 million in stock and debentures for Flight Transportation, a firm that in three years had gone from its origins as a training school to a full-service carrier in the Caribbean, with projected revenues of $82 million. Flight Transportation reported strong operating results, with a 400 percent advance in earnings for the six months that ended March 31.[24]

Together with the law firm of Reavis & McGrath, the Drexel managers devoted the better part of ten weeks to due diligence work and found that all of Flight Transportation's figures jibed. After the underwriting was completed, allegations of false reporting surfaced. Further, it was learned that the FBI and U.S. Drug Enforcement Bureau had been investigating the company for months, suspecting its leaders, CEO William Rubin and first executive vice president Janet Karki, of smuggling gems on Caribbean flights. On June 18, the SEC suspended trading in Flight Transportation's stock and revealed that the company existed primarily on paper. Its cash position had been overstated by $3 million, the assets were worth around a quarter of what had been claimed, and a group charter service, presumed to be the company's jewel, didn't even exist. While all of this news was shocking, even more troubling was the quality of the due diligence work done by Drexel and Reavis & McGrath, which raised questions not only of competence but of possible collusion.[25]

Drexel sued Flight Transportation for a return of funds plus damages, and the firm promptly declared bankruptcy. Milken insisted on returning capital to his customers, even paying them accrued interest.[26] Whether this was done for matters of reputation or to avert litigation is not certain. There were scores of law suits in the wake of Flight Transportation's bankruptcy, but few came from Milken's clients.[27] Later, Drexel CEO Joseph claimed that investors would receive 95 percent of their money in a settlement, and that Drexel's costs would be between $3 million and $5 million.[28]

There were other failures. Drexel sold a $14 million issue of subordinated debt for motion picture producer American Communications in 1981, and soon after that, the company filed for Chapter 11 protection. The bank handled an $85 million underwriting for Grant Broadcasting, a newly formed television station operator. Drexel took 3 percent of the issue and 7 percent of the company's shares, and placed two nominees on the board. The rest of the issue was placed with Milken's corporate friends—First Executive took almost a quarter of the issue, and Lorimar, a relatively new arrival to the fold and a supplier of films to Grant, took a token 1 percent.

Grant had a short, unpleasant life. Seven months later, the firm stopped paying its suppliers, and a year after the underwriting, it was $25 million in debt and in bankruptcy. Creditors charged Drexel with self-dealing and related illegal activities.[29]

But these issues were the exception. From 1977 through mid-1984, Drexel underwrote 166 high-yield bond issues, and only five were for companies that went into bankruptcy.[30]

LEVERAGED BUYOUTS: THE EARLY DEALS

Drexel's New York investment bankers broke into the big leagues in 1983, when they underwrote their first billion dollar deal for MCI Communications, which was then in the midst of its titanic struggle with AT&T for a share of the long-distance telephony market. Joseph had made contact with the company during the late 1970s. At that time, he thought its bonds could not be sold, but circumstances changed for the better for both MCI and Drexel in 1981, and placement of a $125 million issue became possible. This was followed by a massive $1.1 billion placement of subordinated notes and warrants, the largest corporate underwriting until then.

The record was soon eclipsed. The following year, Drexel handled a leveraged buyout of Metromedia by its CEO, John Kluge. This was not the first publicly offered LBO, but it was the largest to date, and its complexity and size intrigued and troubled Wall Street.

Leveraged buyouts certainly weren't new or novel, or confined to business. Every time a person purchases a house by taking out a mortgage, he or she is performing an LBO. This is done by assuming ownership through borrowed money. When the proprietor of a small shop sells it to his or her managers, who raise the funds through a loan, they, too, have performed an LBO.

The more recent history of LBOs performed by Wall Street banks dates back to the early 1960s, when Laird & Co. and Bear Stearns acted to sell profitable, medium-sized companies, usually family-owned, to new owners. Stern Metals, LBOed in 1965 by Jerome Kohlberg of Bear Stearns, who later became a founder of Kohlberg, Kravis, Roberts, is generally considered the first of these. The first modern divestiture came seven years later, when Singer sold its Vapor subsidiary to its managers. In 1978, Congoleum became the first NYSE firm to go private through an LBO. Others followed. The practice was known, but it was not particularly popular at the time Drexel and Kluge came together.[31]

Metromedia was a large, diverse conglomerate, which owned television and radio stations, outdoor advertising, and other, nonrelated businesses like the Ice Capades and the Harlem Globetrotters. During the past four years, Kluge had bought or sold 13 television stations, purchased depreciation rights to $100 million of New York City buses and subway cars, invested $300 million in the nascent mobile telephone industry, and expended $400 million in a stock repurchase program. Part of the money came from transforming the outdoor-advertising business into a tax shelter and from financing arranged by Drexel. Kluge had borrowed heavily throughout—Metromedia had $550 million in long-term bonds outstanding—and, as a result, its debt-to-equity ratio in the spring of 1984 was 3:1.

Drexel's bankers, headed by 33-year-old Leon Black, presented Kluge with a plan whereby his former 26 percent stake in the company would become 75.5 percent through the transformation of equity into debt, much of the money coming from Prudential Insurance, which would receive short-term rates, plus a fee for initiation.

Drexel first offered shareholders $30 a share in cash, and bonds with a face value of $22.50, but with an actual value of more like $10. When hit by stockholder suits, Kluge added a half-warrant to purchase another bond, plus a 19 cents per share dividend before the buyout, which brought the package's value to around $41 per share.[32] The shareholders accepted the deal, but Moody's lowered the company's credit rating. "Metromedia's existing businesses remain sound and are strong cash-flow generators," it said, adding that "over the next few years, protection for fixed (interest) charges will be significantly reduced by the magnitude of new debt and associated interest expenses."[33]

Now Drexel had to arrange permanent financing. This was a key and questionable part of the deal. Metromedia's prior year cash flow would not cover interest on the debt, and its worth net of debt was negligible. But Milken and Joseph knew the company's intangibles were valuable and could be disposed of easily for high prices.

The financing took the form of a quite complex $1.9 billion offering. The composition was as follows: $960 million in six tranches of zero coupon bonds maturing from 1988 to 1993; $335 million in senior exchangeable variable-rate debentures due in 1996; $225 million of 15⅝ percent senior subordinated debentures of 1999; and $400 million in adjustable-rate participating subordinated debentures of 2002 offered at a discount, with interest payments to rise starting in 1988 should there be a specified amount of earnings from the radio and TV stations. It was an imaginative, bold, and puzzling offering. The entire underwriting was cohandled by Drexel and Bear Stearns. Most of the buyers were lined up by the Milken team before the offering, which sold out in less than two hours.

E. Theodore Stolberg, an LBO specialist at Weiss, Peck & Greer, analyzed the deal and pronounced it "prudent." But Keith A. Mulhare, one of Standard & Poor's rating officers, believed, "This is an enormous amount of debt even for those good cash-generating properties that Metromedia owns."[34] Jim Grant, a former *Barron's* journalist, who had left to organize *Grant's Interest Rate Observer,* was dubious regarding the Metromedia offerings, devoting the better part of an issue to an analysis of the prospectus. In his view, the business world was becoming overleveraged, and a day of reckoning was at hand. In September 1984, Grant pronounced, ". . . our hunch is that, in some basic way, junk has had its day." He would continue sounding alarms for the rest of the decade, making him a very premature bear.

In May 1985, Kluge sold Metromedia's TV stations to Rupert Murdoch for $2 billion, plus $650 million in debt. Other sales followed; by early 1987, Metromedia had raised close to $6 billion through asset sales. The company used this to repay debt, and Kluge became one of the nation's wealthiest men; the Drexel-Milken reputation was enhanced, while Grant and others—for the time being—ate crow.[35]

From 1984 through 1990, LBOs would account for $216 billion in financing, the peak year being 1989 at $54 billion, with Drexel the leader in this market most of the time. In this period, the debts of nonfinancial corporations advanced close to 12 percent annually, far more than the 8.3 percent of the period from 1950 through 1980. The debt service ratio soared to a record 20 percent by the end of the 1980s. Yet, given Modigliani-Miller, it did not appear all that troublesome. The implication of their theory was that the substitution of debt for equity would make otherwise chancy takeovers more secure. It was another rationale for takeovers. Finally, for doubters, Modigliani-Miller demonstrated that the level of corporate debt was still much lower than it had been before the Great Depression. That experience had frightened corporate managers into avoiding debt as much as possible. Modigliani-Miller suggested that irrational fears, not reality, were the source of rejection of more financial leverage. It made sense. The deals continued.[36]

The ability to sell, to convince others to share his vision, was Milken's greatest gift and talent. Drexel high-yield bond salesman Terren Piezer, who worked at his side, said, "I think Michael had an amazing ability, besides being an amazing salesman—that he had an amazing ability to create a belief that this security was more valuable than another security in the universe of high yield bonds and I think Mike, better than anyone, knew the relative values of high yield bonds."[37] "You should have heard Mike's speech at the junk bond seminar in the Beverly Hills Hotel," said a Drexel vice president based in New York, referring to the 1988 event. "It would have brought tears to your eyes."[38]

6

THE NEW BREED

Visitors to Mike Milken's Beverly Hills offices in the 1980s, or, for that matter, to investment banks and trading floors anywhere, might have been surprised to see so many alert young people, most in excellent physical condition, working two or three phones at a time, eyes fixed intently upon computer screens. What had happened to the older people, the previous generation? Where had they gone?

For one thing, there had been the weeding out during the 1970s, in which the number of brokers, bankers, and traders, as well as many banks, was cut back. Men and women who would have been in their 40s if they had remained in the industry had gone elsewhere and would not return. In addition, some simply couldn't deal with the pace of activity and the intellectual demands of the new era; they left for other pursuits, mumbling about "burnout." Others were dismissed.

In their place came a new breed of banker, trader, and salesman, who arrived with superb technical knowledge of markets and instruments, which had been acquired in MBA programs at the nation's top schools. They had the requisite intelligence and training, along with the burning desire to do deals and make fortunes. Never had investment banking attracted so many talented, remorseless, hardworking, and imaginative individuals. Investment banking was becoming professionalized.

THE B-SCHOOL BRIGADES

The change didn't happen all at once, or at the same rate at all banks. Later, it would seem that the beginning came at Salomon in the 1970s, which liked to boast that performance, not breeding, counted. This was not quite so, although the Salomon professionals of that period lacked pedigrees. Richard Rosenthal, the firm's crack arbitrageur, had quit high school at the age of 15 to take a job as a runner. Lew Ranieri, who popularized Ginnie Maes, had dropped out of St. John's University in New York, where he had been majoring in English. John Gutfreund had been an English major at Oberlin and originally wanted to be a theatrical producer. Bill Simon, the firm's top trader, had a BA from Lafayette, where, as he tells it, he had con-centrated on swimming and beer. "I never hired a B-school guy on my desk in my life," he told a reporter. "I used to tell my traders, 'If you guys weren't trading bonds, you'd be driving a truck. Don't try to get too intel-lectual in the marketplace. Just trade.'"

This attitude changed. No one would have suggested that the Salomon bankers of the 1980s, or those at other banks, would have made acceptable truck drivers. Many had spent the summer recess between the first and sec-ond years of graduate school interning at the firms where they eventually took their places.

This change accelerated as the investment banks became public corpora-tions. Before World War II and immediately afterward, it was common for firms to be run as family enclaves. Until it was close to half-a-century old, every partner at Kuhn Loeb was a family member, while Lehman Brothers got its first nonfamily member in 1924. The male offspring in the family of a senior partner usually would occupy an office at the firm 21 or so years later. This too, changed.

Samuel L. Hayes III observed all of this and, in his professorial manner, wrote, "The profile of the sought-after professional had changed over the years. An earlier interest in social and family background has given way to searches for the brightest, most articulate, and most attractive candidates available, regardless of background."[1]

There was more to it than that. The gyrating bond markets of the 1970s and beyond had placed a premium on skills in trading and sales. Tradition-ally, these areas had been the domain of street-tough individuals, while the aristocrats went into investment banking. Now the high remuneration of trading and sales would attract some of those who earlier wouldn't have considered such a career.

As we have seen, if one had gone to the graduate schools in the late 1940s and 1950s, and talked with the soon-to-be MBAs, one would have learned that most of them aspired to careers at corporations and hoped in time to become CEOs or, at least, presidents of divisions. A few had ambi-tions to start their own companies. Even fewer thought of consultantships. A goodly number would have had engineering and scientific backgrounds, or would be concerned with the creation of products. Not many would have opted for investment banking, a dull and even dismal profession, which, in any case, required the proper "connections" if one was to succeed. Invest-ment bankers existed to serve clients; those earlier MBAs intended to be clients, not bankers. Even so, there weren't many of them. Few top busi-nessmen of those years thought it necessary to have a professional degree—a BA would do. In 1948, the nation's graduate schools turned out 2,314 MBAs, and in 1965, the height of the conglomerate movement, the number was 8,648.

The alteration in personnel in the financial district began in the mid-1970s, as activity there picked up and markets became more complicated. More of the top business students were wooed to finance, and more of them were being produced. Each year the number rose, going to 50,331 in 1978. By the decade's end, the trickle had turned into a torrent, which would continue into the 1980s—there were 67,527 MBAs in 1985.[2] In the 1970s, one in seven Harvard MBAs became investment bankers, traders, and salesmen. By 1985, the figure had risen to more than one in four, and those with BAs also flocked to Wall Street. Fully one-third of Yale's undergraduates interviewed with one investment bank, First Boston, where Bruce Wasserstein had a reputation as the hottest merger-and-acquisitions operator in the field.[3]

Their goal was a desk at a major player, where starting salaries were in the high-five-figure neighborhood and could rise to the mid-six-figure level before one reached the age of 30. They earned their money. No longer did CEOs employ investment bankers for relatively mundane tasks; they were starting to look to them for creative concepts. Traders now were expected to turn in extraordinary results. Salesmen were required to place large blocks of bonds in a twinkling of a Rolodex.

Felix Rohatyn, of Lazard Frères, frowned upon such activity and was one of the harsher critics of junk financing. Earlier, Rohatyn had arranged takeovers for ITT's Harold Geneen and others of the conglomerate generation. Rohatyn became a Lazard partner in 1960 and a member of the ITT board in 1968, when fees from that acquisition-minded corporation accounted for almost 30 percent of Lazard's profits. In the 1980s, Rohatyn, by then an elder statesman of the industry, suggested that there existed a generation gap between the young bankers and salesmen and their predecessors, which was as great or greater than the one that supposedly existed between those who grew up in the 1960s and their parents. Rohatyn was one of the first to be troubled by the "epidemic of greed" on Wall Street.

It wasn't confined to banking. More young Americans during the 1980s appeared to be materialistic than their counterparts of earlier decades, and this characteristic showed up in many polls. An annual survey of college freshmen is conducted by the American Council on Education and UCLA; it was found in 1987 that "being very well off financially" was one of the most important personal goals for more than three out of four of the respondents, which was nearly twice the number who felt that way in 1970. The percentage of students concerned with developing a meaningful philosophy of life dropped from 83 percent to 39 percent between 1970 and 1987.[4]

THE RISE OF "ETHNICS" ON WALL STREET

Many of the new people bore surnames not usually found at old-line banks. At one time, being of East European Jewish background had excluded one from the district's leading firms. Of course, there were exceptions. Goldman Sachs, Lehman Brothers, Kuhn Loeb, and a handful of other Jewish-led banks were in the establishment. Sidney Weinberg became a powerful force. So did his successor, Gus Levy, also of Goldman Sachs. But young men whose parents or grandparents had arrived in this country from eastern Europe had a hard time cracking into other banks.

That earlier generation of newcomers had different expectations. Such was the case not only on Wall Street but in most sectors of American life. In the 1950s, anti-Semitism still was found in large corporations, government, and universities. Not only Jews but other "ethnics" were affected and had limited chances to rise in these areas, where, as the saying went, one had to be twice as smart, work twice as hard, for half the pay, to get ahead. Such individuals could find places in the community, however. There were several brokerage firms, such as Burnham, headed by Jews, who hired their coreligionists. Jews had no problem becoming specialists at the American Stock Exchange.

At the time, this exclusion didn't seem remarkable. Except for Sam Lesch and Warren Phillips, there were no Jews in visible positions at the *Wall Street Journal*. The staff had a decidedly midwestern flavor; virtually the entire management were graduates of Methodist-affiliated DePauw University in Indiana, and they exhibited something of a distrust of Easterners. Editor Barney Kilgore was not an anti-Semite, but, rather, he was convinced that American virtues were to be found in the nation's heartland.[5]

This circumstance in the district changed slowly after World War II, which made overt anti-Semitism decidedly unfashionable. In addition, the civil rights movement made racial and religious discrimination of all kinds objectionable. There were breakthroughs in government and business in the 1960s and after. Rohatyn's presence on the ITT board was one sign. Rohatyn said, "I always felt I owed Geneen a great deal. He put me on his board when that was a daring thing to do. In those days you didn't put a young, nonestablishment, Jewish investment banker on your board when you were a big white-shoe company, which ITT was at the time."[6]

At one time, Jews had found it difficult to find employment at such firms as DuPont, which elevated Irving Shapiro, the son of an immigrant Jewish pants presser, to the chairmanship in 1974. There were more visible signs of this in politics. In the Kennedy Cabinet were people with names like Goldberg and Ribicoff, and they were followed by Kissinger, Levi, and Klutznick in the Nixon, Ford, and Carter White Houses. Warren Phillips became managing editor at the *Wall Street Journal* in 1957. Brandeis University had been founded after World War II in the hope that it would become "the Jewish Harvard," since the Ivy League had a quota system. In the early 1990s, however, the presidents of Harvard, Princeton, and Dartmouth are named Rudenstine, Shapiro, and Freedman.[7] The closed system once was pervasive in show business, that most important mirror of American life. Artists of Jewish and other ethnic backgrounds used to change their names to "pass," but this no longer was the case after the 1960s.

And yet, given the long "old-boy" history, no one has tried to explain just how it came to be that, with the exceptions of T. Boone Pickens and Carl Lindner, none of the big players in the 1980s were Gentiles. That no reputable journal has dared to touch the subject is an indication of just how sensitive the issue was and is.

One reason for the presence of so many more Jews in visible positions on Wall Street was generational. The young people with Jewish backgrounds who began to appear on Wall Street in the late 1970s had become quite Americanized, and they did not fit the Jewish stereotypes prevalent even then.

The shift in access wasn't confined to Jews. This acceptance was extended to all groups that came over during the New Immigration of the 1890–1914 period. Consider that from 1865 to 1890, 262,000 immigrants arrived from eastern Europe, and from 1890 to 1914, 3.3 million came. Likewise, 409,000 came from southern Europe between 1865 and 1890, and 4.1 million between 1890 and 1914. The latter were also making their marks in areas of American life formerly closed to them. Grounouski, Celebrezze, Volpe, and Carlucci were in presidential cabinets. A man named Agnew became vice president. A man named Dukakis was a candidate for the White House. Consider show business. In a different age, Robert De Niro would have had to change his name, as would Danny Aiello, Danny DeVito, Rick Moranis, Joe Pesci, and Ray Liotta. No more.

This isn't to suggest that no East European Jews or Italian Catholics of the second generation made it big. Rather, the critical mass was reached in the third generation.

It had happened before. The grandchildren of Irish immigrants of the mid-19th century made their splash on Wall Street in the first two decades of the 20th century. The great bull market of the 1920s precipitated many interesting and astute characters, among them Mike Meehan, Esmonde O'Brian, Richard O'Brian, John Moyland, and J. P. McKenna. Allen Ryan cornered Stutz Motors in 1920, one of the more daring escapades of the decade. There was Joe Kennedy. Was it unusual for so many Irish-Americans to have become players in the 1920s? Of course not. When Al Smith received the Democratic presidential nomination in 1928, the Democratic national chairman was John J. Raskob, a Catholic and wet, prominent at DuPont and General Motors, and on Wall Street, too. When Franklin D. Roosevelt ran for the presidency four years later, among his closest advisers were Jim Farley and Ed Flynn. Again, there were important Irish-American businessmen, and especially politicians, in the second generation, but it was the third that made it to the top in significant numbers.

And yet, finance has always found a way to include individuals with financial clout. Bankers of different religions would cut deals when money and power were at stake. They might have been bigots, but a great many of them would suspend their animosities during working hours. It was so almost from the beginning. In the early 19th century, the ruling Dutch aristocrats weren't pleased with the Anglo-Saxons, but they formed partnerships with them. J. P. Morgan was anti-Semitic, but he respected Jacob Schiff of Kuhn Loeb. Why weren't there more Italian and Greek names in finance? Because in the 19th century, American Protestant banks formed alliances with London banks, in which Jews were prominent, and Jews of German ancestry came to represent European finance in New York. The Italian and Greek banks weren't represented, and so one found few with those ancestries in American finance. The Irish-Americans didn't have banks, so they made it in speculation, brokerage, and as specialists at the NYSE.

In the late 1970s and 1980s, as Peter Passell, of the *New York Times*, put it, "Sharp elbows and a working knowledge of spreadsheets suddenly counted more than a nose for sherry or membership in Skull and Bones." Refusing to hire people because of their religion was recognized as bad business, too. Milken's experience at Drexel was being replicated elsewhere on the Street. Alan "Ace" Greenberg, who rose to head Bear Stearns, said, "I look for PSD degrees—poor, smart, and a deep desire to be rich." Many of the new breed were smart and ambitious. Few were poor, however; rather, like Milken, they were solidly middle-class, and most of them had the ubiquitous MBA.

All of these factors contributed to opening the doors in all aspects of American life to the grandchildren of New Immigration Jews.

While recognizing the salutary nature of this change, one aspect of it troubled Felix Rohatyn. A refugee from Hitler's Germany, Rohatyn thought he saw some of the signs of a revived anti-Semitism, not only on Wall Street, but in the country at large, as old stereotypes of money-grasping Jews were coming out of the closet. Others felt the same way. In 1982, Laurence Tisch told one of Carl Icahn's associates that his raiding activities were causing problems. "Tell Carl to cut this out. It's not good for the Jews." Attorney Martin Lipton, who participated in some of the more spectacular deals, voiced his concerns regularly. One of Drexel's clients told Connie Bruck, then conducting research for her book on the bank:

> It used to be that the Jews would go into Manny Hanny, or Morgan Guaranty, and they'd *beg* for money, and they'd be rejected, while the Gentiles would come in and they'd all go out to lunch and smoke cigars. Now it's a shift of power to the Jews. Drexel is making these huge sums of money, and the banks comparatively little.[8]

Paul Levy, one of Drexel's investment bankers, put it bluntly. "There is a lot of anti-Semitism at work. People see Drexel as a bunch of Jewish guys who have been making too much money." Yet, such thoughts were rarely mentioned in polite company, and then only with some nervousness.

Try to imagine the impact of their success on the new ethnics of all religions. Most of the bright, young, middle-class members of minority groups had struggled through college and business school, and then they tumbled into opulence. Once, the decision whether to take a taxi or subway to an appointment had merited some thought, but now they now traveled in customized private limousines. First-class air travel was paid for by use of the bank's credit card, and they stayed at the best hotels and dined at celebrity restaurants. Their salaries enabled them to live in upper East Side duplexes, spending more to garage their sports cars than they used to pay for studio apartments. If they worked 12- and 16-hour days, there was a chauffeured limousine to take them home in the late evening or, on occasion, early morning.

It was heady stuff. Participation in a multibillion-dollar deal at that age, with that background, was like living in a fantasy. It was like playing basketball for a championship team, meshing with consummate professionals, and knowing not only that you were their equals but that they recognized you as such.

A few weeks of intense effort on a takeover or merger could result in the transfer of hundreds of millions of dollars—and a year-end bonus that, by the 1980s, could have six, seven, and even eight figures. It didn't require many such deals before an individual was written about, called upon by reporters for opinions, and noticed when entering a room. A merger-and-acquisitions star in his (occasionally, her) late 20s might be sought as a mentor by obviously very bright newcomers only half a dozen years younger, seeking to emulate his or her successes.

Isn't it logical that such movers would observe that Icahn and Pickens also came from comparatively modest backgrounds and conclude that, given time and opportunity, the new breed might rise to their level of prominence? These young people wanted excitement, power, and recognition, but, most of all, they wanted money. When Ivan Boesky told a graduating class at the University of California's business school that "Greed is all right, by the way. I want you to know that I think greed is healthy. You can be greedy and feel good about yourselves," he was greeted by applause and the nervous laughter of recognition. When the graduates later became stereotyped as yuppies, they seemed to glory in the label.

Ordinary Americans read about those who have immense wealth but know that, short of winning a lottery, they will never achieve it. They dream, which is what sells lottery tickets. It was different for that relatively small group of investment bankers from middle-class families. They were so close to great wealth; there were so many chances to achieve it, and so many temptations. In graduate school, they learned of the returns possible from investment banking. It was what brought them there. And they wanted the payoff as quickly as possible.

So, for that matter, did their clients.

INSIDER TRADING

Given this attitude among the new breed, ethical standards were decidedly lower than they had been in earlier decades. Take the matter of insider trading. This practice has appeared during every bull market; indeed, it existed at the very dawn of the nation's history. In 1790, Secretary of the Treasury Alexander Hamilton proposed that the new federal government assume the debts of the states and the old Articles of Confederation government at face value. Some of the state paper had fallen to as low as 10 percent of face value, so there was a possibility of a large profit for holders. Aware of the plan, several congressmen had their agents purchase the paper at the depressed price before the news became public. As a result, they made large profits. Thomas Jefferson and James Madison were outraged, but they could do nothing. This kind of activity may have been unethical, but it was not illegal.[9] Individuals traded on inside information legally until passage of the Securities Exchange Act in 1934, and illegally during the bull market of the 1960s. But it never was done on the scale of what transpired in the 1980s, when insider trading became a focal point for reform.

A minor, hastily written section of the 1934 Act dealt with such trading. This was supplemented in 1942 by Rule 10b-5, also vague on the issue. The rule made it unlawful "to engage in any act, practice, or course of business that operates or would operate as a fraud or deceit upon any person, in connection with the purchase or sale of any security."[10]

It is clear that the framers of Rule 10b-5 had in mind corporate executives who might be tempted to speculate in securities of their company, thus profiting from information unavailable to those outside the firm. The intent, in the antibusiness environment of the New Deal, was to place safeguards against corporate leaders who, in the view of the Roosevelt administration, had so misused their powers during the 1920s. Outside of that context, this particular section was regarded as more symbolic than anything else. The business scene and the securities markets were slack, and opportunities to profit from privileged information were virtually nil.

There were few market investigations during the moribund 1940s and 1950s. Not much by way of enforcement occurred even during the conglomerate period, when denizens of the financial district sought privileged information. The SEC did not see fit to pursue the topic, and there was little analysis in the press and law journals. Indeed, the term "insider trading" had not yet entered the lexicon, instead, it was called "a hot tip" from "a reliable source," presumably an officer of the company involved. This is what former SEC Chairman William L. Cary thought in 1962, when he stated the following: "When an insider has possession of facts which are known to him by virtue of his status and which, if known generally, would tend materially to affect the price of the security, the law requires that the insider disclose these facts to those with whom he deals or forgo the transaction."[13]

Rudolph Giuliani was aware that the lack of a definition deterred prosecutors from bringing charges regarding insider trading. The man whose reputation was to be based on prosecutions in this area has asserted that "In a 50-year period—from 1934 to 1984—the insider trading laws were rarely, if ever, used criminally. In fact, in the first 40 years or so of their presence on the books, no one was criminally prosecuted for violating federal insider trading laws." From 1966 to 1980, the SEC brought only 37 cases against insider traders, and only 11 were prosecutured. Those admitting guilt were required to sign a consent decree, disgorge profits and pay for damages, and pledge not to engage in such practices again.[12]

The situation changed in the 1980s. Insider trading became the subject of scores of articles. It now meant, in the words of one of the observers, "the buying or selling of securities on the basis of material, nonpublic information."[13] Yet, it remained a vague concept.

Addressing the matter in 1984, Congress passed and the President signed the Insider Trading Sanctions Act, which stiffened penalties to include treble damages, but still did not offer a precise definition. (To this day, insider trading has never been defined by the SEC with any precision.) Presumably, it involved trading on knowledge unavailable to others and gained in an illegal or underhanded way. In the 1980s, Drexel tried to resolve this dilemma through a statement all employees were required to sign:

Confidential Nature of Information

It is essential that all information concerning any business carried on in this office, whether security transactions or otherwise, should be kept completely confidential. The stock-in-trade of a banker is his integrity and his respect for the confidence that others place in him. There can be no excuse for failure to observe this fundamental principle.[14]

The courts performed where Congress did not. In general, case law offered two tests. First, had the person accused of obtaining inside information come into possession of material, nonpublic information? News that the firm intended to move its headquarters, for example, probably would not qualify, but a pending announcement of a significant takeover would. Next, who was the source of the information? It would have to be a person able to provide meaningful facts, whose disclosure could cause financial reverberations.[15] Clearly, if a person were to trade a stock on knowledge available only to that person and a few others sworn to secrecy, which would have caused the price to rise if the public knew of it, he or she would be trading on inside information and would be subject to legal penalties. If the trader passed on the knowledge to others, who then engaged in trading, and those people knew the information's origins, they, too, would be trading on inside information.

As takeovers grew in popularity, they attracted individuals who hoped to profit by taking positions in the stock that was about to be put into play. The possession of information available to those concocting the deal was a valuable commodity, a fact obvious to all involved. "Risk arbitrageurs" would take positions in likely takeover candidates, knowing they would profit should there be a contest for control. If an arbitrageur could be a fly on the wall at Drexel, Lehman, or Morgan Stanley, or at one of the major law firms involved in such activities, like Skadden Arps, Slate, Meagher & Flom; or Wachtel, Lipton, Rosen & Katz, he or she might make a fortune in a matter of days.

With so much money floating around, with so many deals to be done, the thought of utilizing inside knowledge was tempting. And this has been the case during every period when fortunes could be made quickly. No one seemed to care. The explanation was always the same: Everyone was doing it. What counted was making money and doing deals—little else.

For the better part of a decade, tales of multimillion-dollar salaries and huge profits on deals dazzled readers and viewers. To those with a knowledge of history, it seemed a replay of the Gilded Age of post–Civil War America, when corporations were milked or raped by voracious and amoral raiders, who hadn't a care regarding public welfare. No wonder those bankers and clients who were later charged with criminal violations earned slight compassion from the public. It is difficult to empathize with a Tom Spiegel, who took more than $20 million a year as remuneration for his efforts at Columbia Savings & Loan, and had a large expense account on top of that.

Moreover, when average Americans read of what Spiegel and others actually did to earn such sums, they were puzzled. What was being produced? Did Spiegel, who was in Milken's pocket, really have to understand the securities markets to say he was prepared to buy a few million dollars worth of bonds after a brief discussion? Where was the labor in all of this? The basic Drexel fee for assisting KKR in acquiring Storer Communications was around $55 million. But KKR, owned by its principals, did not pay that fee. Rather, it came from the shell company established to acquire Storer. So, the fee came from anticipated profits from the deal. In this sense, it wasn't "real money." None of it was, for that matter.

THE YUPPIE GENERATION

In many American homes during the late 1980s, working-class parents would listen with amazement to tales of wealth told by sons and daughters in their 20s and early 30s, whose yearly takes were in the hundreds of thousands of dollars. A plumber whose customers usually felt overcharged would hear that his son, with one telephone call, earned more than he did in several years—maybe a lifetime.

What the plumber may not have realized was that most of these young people felt they performed at the edge of a precipice. Always, there was the suspicion that this couldn't last, that others might do the job even better; there was the worry that all of those years studying and sharpening techniques had been unnecessary and all that was required was decent intelligence and a few weeks of apprenticeship. The key to success in this game was to make those who decided wages and bonuses believe you were someone special. This meant arguing with those who claimed to prize individualism and flatter those who preferred acolytes. When asked how compensation was decided, Drexel bond salesman Terren Piezer said:

> I think the environment was such that there was no direct way of compensation and to some extent the compensation was subjective and everyone it seems—well, there was like a competitive environment like look what I did and what kind of transaction I did and, you know, in a way it's like you do things to impress Michael. Everyone always tried to impress Michael.[16]

It was not surprising that Piezer would stand in awe of Milken, who wasn't that much older than he and received phenomenal income.

It is dangerous to generalize about an entire generation, but there was a core of truth in what the media wrote about the yuppie bankers. A few of the young people blamed the atmosphere for the excesses of the period, while others simply blamed a handful of bad apples. Whatever one thinks of the matter, it was difficult to defend such individuals, who not only were unapologetic regarding their single-minded quest for wealth but gloried in it, who tried to make a virtue out of being tough and merciless, and out of breaking rules and flaunting conventions.

Some apologists said that those who spoke of greed were inexact. What some call greed, others might label ambition. Everyone wants to get ahead, after all, it's the American way. The Texas tycoon, a cliché of an earlier time, often was portrayed as bumbling and crude, but he was also stereotypically endearing. T. Boone Pickens and Ross Perot, modern versions of the type, have been able to engage the public imagination to the point that leaders in both parties sought them as political candidates. "I don't want all the land in the world," goes an old Texas joke. "I just want what's next to mine."

Is this greed or ambition? It depends partly on whether you like or dislike the individuals involved, but also on the ethical price to be paid for wealth. The generalized view was that the earlier tycoons were unwilling, or at least reluctant, to sacrifice ethics and values for wealth. They saw wealth as the byproduct of making the world a better place. By contrast, the Wall Street generation of the 1980s appeared thoroughly amoral. These newcomers typically were devoted only to themselves and their careers. Lacking loyalties, they would move from firm to firm at the drop of a substantial raise or bonus, giving credence to the belief that, in the 1980s, everyone in the business had his or her price. Why not? They were talented, and they were making much more than their salaries and bonuses for their firms. At Drexel, which had among the highest remuneration levels in the industry, the moving was within the firm, with Milken's operation being the ambition of traders and salesmen.

In the last months of the 1980s, Michael Lewis' *Liar's Poker*, a memoir of his two years as a bond trader at Salomon, made its appearance on the best-seller list. The portraits he presented weren't wholesome. Lewis wrote of avarice, unethical behavior, back-stabbing, and vulgarity. Yet, this didn't seem to bother the players. Salomon bankers swore they saw people who performed as Lewis asserted, meaning that they misled clients, lied, and engaged in obscene behavior, while earning large salaries and bonuses without much of an idea of what they were doing. Of course, the ones verifying Lewis' portrait swore *they* weren't in that category; but they knew people who were. Nor did Lewis consider himself a betrayer of the confidence either of his former colleagues or his employer. It was merely a fact that he had been out to use Salomon, and it him.

Many have seen the motion picture *Wall Street* and reviled one of the main characters, Gordon Gekko. Gekko apparently was a composite of Boesky and other arbitrageurs, who prowled for takeover rumors, made purchases before the information became public, and profited when shares rose. In the most sensational novel of the decade, *The Bonfire of the Vanities* by Tom Wolfe, the yuppie hero, Sherman McCoy, couldn't make ends meet on a million dollars a year and was another of these amoral figures. When Wolfe was seeking a bank at which to conduct research, he decided on Salomon. He would appear on the floor to interview traders and spend days following the action. At least a dozen Salomon traders proudly claimed that Wolfe had modeled McCoy on them.

To those who were on the Street and inside the investment banks during the 1980s, *Wall Street* and *The Bonfire of the Vanities* rang true, and Michael Lewis' memoir, while exaggerated and embroidered, captured the flavor of the times. Recall the ethical ideals that existed at the top investment banks in the 1950s. By the mid-1980s, those ideals had pretty well disappeared in the scramble for business.

THE REBIRTH OF THE HOSTILE TAKEOVER

One indication of the prevalent attitude in the 1980s was the rebirth of the hostile takeover. Again, such moves were not new. As early as the 1860s, Cornelius Vanderbilt engaged in contests for the New York Central and Erie Railroads. We have seen how Lou Wolfson achieved fame in his hostile bid for Montgomery Ward in the 1950s, and how Jimmy Ling mounted hostile bids in the 1960s. There were many takeovers during the conglomerate period—approximately 280 of them between 1956 and 1966, according to Samuel Hayes III and Russell A. Taussig. As had been the case earlier and would be so afterward, these authors wrote, ". . . takeovers tended . . . to be utilized only by those on the outer fringes of the business fraternity."[17]

Such takeovers were the logical outgrowth of the thesis Adolph Berle and Gardner Means had set down in 1932, when they declared that ownership and management had been separated.[18] One consequence was that, as time passed, the owners had less and less loyalty to "their" companies, while managements used corporate assets for their own purposes.

Others took up the refrain over the years. In 1981, former SEC Chairman Harold Williams, in a speech before the Securities Regulation Institute suggested, ". . . the traditional concept of the investor is becoming obsolete. The linkage between ownership and participation in the equity markets is, to put it mildly, strained. Increasingly, the so-called investor is often nothing more than a short-term speculator in the company's income stream." The arbitrageurs, too, he said, were short-term investors. "Is an arb a shareholder in any traditional or meaningful sense? Who is left to discharge the responsibilities of ownership by thinking and caring about the corporation as an institution? No one is."[19]

This corporate side effect was the reason the Chance Vought and Wilson managements fought Ling's takeover of "their" companies in the 1960s. On the surface, the situation seemed outlandish. Ling offered to purchase the companies for a considerable advance over the current market prices of the stock. The managements replied that the offers were too low. If so, one would be justified to inquire, why were their stocks selling for the prices they did? The answer might be poor public perception of the firms' performances and promises, or it might be failures on the parts of management. Whatever the reason, a stockholder with shares selling for, say, 25, certainly would welcome the chance to sell them at 35. Yet, management urged rejection? Why? The Berle and Means theory. It was because management and ownership had separated and had different interests. The owners wanted dividends and capital gains. Managements sought to preserve their jobs.

The way it worked in the 1980s was this: the raider would make his bid. The arbitrageurs would come in, and the price of the stock would rise. In the end, management might buy off the raider with "greenmail," taking his shares at a high price, paying not from their own pockets but from the corporate treasury. Or they could use a "poison pill," taking steps to make the company less attractive—in effect, saying, "If you don't go away, we will harm the company to the point where you no longer will want it." Management would seek a "white knight," someone who would take the company over in a friendly fashion, meaning that the new management would take steps to ensure the comfort of the old. If all else failed, they would arrange for "golden parachutes," hefty severance pay in case of a takeover.

None of this would be in the interests of the shareholders. The old management would plead with them not to accept those higher bids, for the new management would ruin "their company." The trouble with this reasoning was that the company was not truly owned by the shareholders, who, in any case, would have no tie to it once the shares were sold.

Throughout the 1980s, these factors fueled the debate over the merits of takeovers. Raiders spoke of realizing the underlying value of companies they wanted to acquire; management spoke of how difficult it was to conduct long-term planning when one or two bad quarters might depress the price of a company's stock and invite a raid. Both arguments had their virtues. There were raids that could be defended and others that seemed frivolous, with the raider apparently out for greenmail. Some firms were better off for having been raided. Others were forced into bankruptcies. Some managements sought the best interests of shareholders, while many cared only for their own fortunes.

In neither era did raiders seem particularly concerned with the long-term performance of the American economy, although some gave lip service to the notion. Pickens posed as a savior of capitalism. Carl Icahn stated, "I'm no Robin Hood."

There were investment bankers who specialized in advising targets and others whose services were sought by raiders. The stakes were high, the fees immense. The country would be shocked to learn that Michael Milken earned $550 million in one year. The reason he could secure that much was that the people who paid Drexel for his services were getting the money from their companies. *They* had no complaints.

Besieged managements poured funds into lobbying, and had some success. In 1968, Congress passed the Williams Act, in order to put an end to the hostile takeovers of the conglomerate era. The act specified that when 10 percent of the targeted company's stock had been accumulated, the raider would have to disclose within ten days information regarding his background, the source of his funds, his intentions, and how many shares he and associates owned, in a form known as a 13-D. (Two years later the reporting threshold would be lowered to 5 percent.) This information had to be provided to the target, the SEC, and the market on which the stock was traded. No further open-market purchases would be permitted; any additional accumulation would have to be done through a tender offer. Thus, there could be no more surprise raids; there could be no accumulation of additional shares without public knowledge (which presumably would send their prices higher); and added shares would have to benefit all shareholders equally.[20]

Any shareholder who tendered shares would have the right to withdraw them within seven days after the tender was made public or 60 days from the time of the initial offer. This was done in case another raider appeared with a better offer, or a white knight came to the defense of the target. If the tender was for less than the entire capitalization, the raider would have to accept shares on a pro rata basis, rather than take those that were offered earliest. This stipulation was made to put an end of two-tier takeovers, in which the early sellers got a better deal than those who waited it out. Moreover, if the raider raised his price, he would have to pay it for all the stock accepted, even though some might have been tendered for a lower price.

On casual study, it would appear that the Williams Act had been designed to benefit shareholders, who now would profit from bidding wars. But consider that the act was passed in the atmosphere of the late 1960s, and not in that of the early 1980s. There were raids in the 1960s, but bidding contests were infrequent.[21] As it happened, the Williams Act became law when unwelcome bids by raiders were no longer threatening entrenched managements. In sum, Congress passed the law when it was no longer needed. It became significant only later.

The Williams Act had unanticipated consequences. Once the announcement of an accumulation of stock was made, others learned of what evidently was to be a takeover bid at a higher price and rushed to purchase the shares. Still others were willing to pay large sums to obtain such knowledge in advance of the announcement. The Williams Act of the conglomerate era invited the risk arbitrage and insider trading of the LBO period a generation later.

The first hostile takeover of the modern period occurred in 1974, after the first petroleum shock. At the time, there was much talk of the need for alternate energy sources. Many former opponents of atomic power now had second thoughts. Instant experts in the field spoke airily of windmills, solar power, geothermal projects, alternate fuels, and electric autos.

This last possibility intrigued the leaders of International Nickel. If electric autos were really in the future, manufacturers of batteries would profit largely. Informed by this vision, in July, International Nickel made a tender offer of $28 a share for ESB Inc., formerly known as Electric Storage Battery. This company was a declining but still important force in the auto battery market, best known for its Exide, Willard, and Ray-O-Vac brands. ESB rejected the price as "inadequate." But since the stock had been selling for $20 before the offer, how could they justify the claim? Within a month, more than 90 percent of the shares had been tendered, and the takeover was only a matter of time.

Robert F. Greenhill, who recently had been named as Morgan Stanley's head of mergers and acquisitions, managed the deal for International Nickel. This was surprising, since hostile takeovers weren't considered ethical or even gentlemanly, and firms of the caliber of Morgan Stanley were not expected to associate themselves with such business. By way of justification, the bank's CEO, Robert Baldwin, said the firm would only act for clients and would warn them of problems afoot; despite much anguish, he felt he had little choice in the matter: "There had been some hostile takeovers in London, and we saw that it was coming, whatever we did."[22] In other words, it wasn't a question of right or wrong. Profit was to be made, and Baldwin and Greenhill would have their company gather its share, no matter what the ethics of the situation. Unstated was the understanding that if Morgan Stanley did not adjust to the new rules being laid down by the new breed of bankers arriving from the business schools, they would take the business.

If so eminent a banker as Robert Baldwin could engage in situational ethics, how much more willing the newcomers would be to join the game. And nowhere was this more true than at Drexel Burnham Lambert. The young traders, salesmen, and investment bankers there defended their actions and activities. They also professed loyalty to Drexel. But why? Was it because of admiration for Milken, or their hope to emulate his successes while at his side? Did they genuinely buy his line that they were missionaries for capitalism, hoping to remake America and restore its competitive edge? Did they genuinely consider Drexel a capitalist version of the Peace Corps? It's not likely.

In time, Drexel would become the prototype of the insolent, arrogant, unfeeling company, its bankers setting new standards for toughness and brashness. Rumors circulated of broken promises, double-dealing, and shady operations, some of which turned out to be true. It did not play by the rules. For example, there was the practice of backing out of deals. Drexel might syndicate a large offering, only to learn that Milken had placed much of it on his own. Then the salesmen would have to telephone the members of the syndicate to cut back or eliminate their share. This simply hadn't been done before the 1980s, when a bank's word was its bond. Now this trust was eroding.[23]

Small wonder that Drexel didn't have many friends in the investment banking community, which would cost it dearly late in the decade. The firm preferred to handle major underwritings on its own, not spreading them out among several firms as was customary. "People get sore as hell about it," conceded a Drexel syndicate manager. But there was more to it than that. In the prejunk era, five investment banks—Morgan Stanley, Salomon,

First Boston, Merrill Lynch, and Goldman Sachs—had handled two-thirds of all American bond underwritings. It was a tightly knit club, and the members wanted no competition. Drexel not only contended for their old customers but, for a while, virtually owned the junk market, the most promising new area of the period. The other five tried to obtain business there, with only limited success. That they, and other banks, would have been pleased to see Drexel vanish might have seemed a given.

On the other hand, these banks received a good deal of business from Drexel-inspired hostile takeover attempts. For every attacker, there had to be a defender, and fees on both sides were immense. So the banks actually had mixed feelings regarding Drexel. The large increases in profits at most of them resulted in part from activities Drexel had popularized.

Still, Drexel's clout and arrogance alienated other investment banks. In 1981, for example, Drexel and Merrill Lynch were jointly underwriting an issue for Volt Information Services, with Drexel handling travel arrangements for the operation. Drexel booked its bankers and Volt's executives in first class, while the Merrill bankers traveled in coach. Without informing Merrill, Drexel changed the site of the meeting with Chicago investors. As a result, Drexel got the sales. Merrill later complained that disinformation like this was not in the interests of the client. Fred Joseph replied that when he heard about the situation, he ordered such practices stopped. But they continued. M. William Benedetto of Dean Witter put it mildly when he said, "Their [Drexel's] relationship with the Street leaves a lot to be desired."[24]

Joseph appeared genuinely disturbed by the attitude of Drexel's bankers, but he either could not or would not do anything to alter it materially. He said he refused to take on clients who felt threatened by Drexel. "We are not in the protection business," he told a reporter. "We're a big firm. We have a lot of very aggressive people here. Some departments are worse than others, some guys we've had to haul back, and [we] fired some for disciplinary reasons. It would be naive to say no one ever stepped over the ethical lines we set. But the guys knew what the lines were. I try to make our people understand that we don't want to be excessively aggressive."[25]

Through all of this, Joseph did little or nothing to curb abuses. Nor did Milken. Joseph had the authority but lacked the power. Milken had the power but rejected the notion that he had some obligation to manage. Drexel lurched from deal to deal, hauling in the profits, with little regard for limits.

BLACKMAIL

By middecade, some of Drexel's cocky young bankers had regularly transgressed the increasingly porous line between acceptable and unacceptable conduct. One of the more blatant instances of this began in late October

1986, when the Illinois-based food company, Staley Continental Corp., noted that its shares were unusually active, rising into the mid-30s. Management soon discovered what was afoot. James Bode, a Drexel banker, telephoned to say he wanted to establish an investment banking relationship with the firm, adding that a group headed by James Dahl, had purchased 1.5 million of Staley's 30 million shares. Dahl didn't bother filing the 13-D form notifying the SEC of his position, later remarking, "13-Ds are bad for business."[26]

Instead, Dahl contacted CEO Robert Hoffman, and said he was interested in creating a leveraged buyout for the firm, adding that with Drexel's clout, "We can take Staley private in 48 hours." Management would be left in place. All Dahl wanted to do was make money, by having management purchase his shares and paying large fees. Hoffman rejected the offer and told Dahl he would fight back by issuing additional shares through First Boston and Merrill Lynch. Perhaps taking his cue from a gangster film, Dahl said, "It is very important for us to sit down and talk before you do something that hurts me and I do something that hurts you." Hoffman wanted to know what Dahl had in mind. "The next thing happens," said Dahl, "is someone files a 13-D at $40 a share and management is thrown out," and he would "hate to see Drexel have to sell into the stock offering."[27]

Hoffman proceeded with the submission, but before First Boston and Merrill Lynch could put it together, the price of the stock started to slide and, within days, was under $28. Staley's attorney later claimed that Drexel and "associated parties" shorted the stock; Dahl had made good on his threat. Staley later charged Drexel with extortion and with not disclosing its position to the SEC.

Did Milken know what Dahl was doing? Considering the nature of the operation and his insistence on being informed of everything that was going on, it is likely that he not only knew but approved. Yet, when Dahl testified in Staley Continental v. Drexel Burnham Lambert on October 27, 1987, he indicated otherwise:

"Who gave you the authority to make the purchase and sale decisions with respect to the trading of Staley shares by the Beverly Hills office of Drexel?" Dahl was asked.

"I took it upon myself."

"Did you need any authority then?"

"It was my understanding I had the authority to trade in the stock if I chose to."

"That authority would relate to other securities, not just Staley. Am I assuming correctly?"

"Yes."[28]

Was Dahl covering for Milken? Or was he telling the truth, so that Milken was censurable only for his lack of oversight? Given Dahl's willingness to bend rules and his general approach to ethical matters, it seemed reasonable to assume that he would lie under oath if he thought he could get away with it, especially if doing so would earn him Milken's appreciation. The issue wasn't of major importance in Staley v. Drexel, but three years later, the testimony would be recalled in the far more consequential Milken hearing, when Dahl changed his statement.

Soon after the Staley affair, Drexel bankers approached another food company, CPC International, offering its services for a leveraged buyout. After CPC rejected the offer, long-time Drexel client Ron Perelman put together an 8.2 percent holding in the company and took greenmail to the tune of $94 million.[29] The CPC treasurer, Angelo S. Abdela, conceded that Drexel had approached the company but denied that pressure was exerted. Even so, it was generally known on the Street that Drexel played hardball as tough as any bank.[30] Later, Joseph wrote, "We refuse to represent someone when we think a major objective is greenmail. Sometimes they'll say it isn't, and the way to resolve that discussion is to say, 'Fine, we'll need a commitment from you not to accept greenmail.' We often do it when a raider's involved."[31] When confronted with evidence of greenmail, Joseph would reply that the raid had not been started with such profits in mind.

Joseph's position was not as altruistic as it sounded. The fees for deals that end in greenmail were minor compared with those in which the takeover was completed. Why waste time with greenmail operations when they lead to mistrust, while takeovers enhanced a firm's image?

There were other rough deals. Green Tree Acceptance, which financed mobile-home mortgages, learned the hard way just how trustworthy the firm was. In 1986, Midwest Federal, which owned 71 percent of Green Tree, decided to sell its holdings. Both Midwest and Green Tree were concerned that the shares be distributed so there would be no concentration; this was to avoid greenmail or a hostile takeover. In particular, Green Tree was troubled that Drexel had several well-known raiders as clients. Dahl assured the company that no Drexel client had ever raided another Drexel client and that using Drexel would actually be insurance against a raid. He gave repeated pledges that the shares would be widely distributed.

Dahl created units composed of a junk bond, plus 14 shares of common that he said would be priced as of the previous night's closing. He later said the price was $19.00, but Green Tree's attorney, Patrick McDavitt, claimed it was $19.50. The difference meant that Drexel was cheating Midwest Federal and benefitting the buyers, who, as it turned out, included Drexel clients Columbia, First Executive Life, Atlanta Sosnoff, and Saul Steinberg's Reliance Financial, plus others. The distribution was not widespread; 3.3 million of the 4 million shares were now in the hands of seven Drexel clients, and some of these were raiders and greenmailers or were associated with them. Drexel clients now owned a majority of Green Tree shares. In little more than three years, Steinberg had accumulated 25 percent of the stock, prompting the suspicion that this had been planned. Fearing a hostile bid, the following April, Green Tree purchased Steinberg's 1.6 million shares for $42 a share, some $12 above market price.

Green Tree sued. In his deposition, Milken said, "I would not consider it unusual to find six or seven institutions buying anywhere from 50 to 70 percent of the securities offered in an underwriting." Nor did he deny that he had used his connections with Executive Life and Columbia S&L in this deal, or that he and Spiegel were limited partners in Steinberg's Reliance Capital Group. Later, McDavitt explained how this kind of situation could have developed and why Dahl's promise to distribute the securities widely had been violated. Noting that the commitment had been made by the corporate finance department in New York, but the stock was sold from Milken's Beverly Hills offices, McDavitt said, "I think the emphasis in the California office is sell, sell, sell. I get the sense the [New York office] is intimidated by Milken."[32]

Even attempted bribery wasn't out of the question. Benalder Bayse managed high-yield funds at Mitchell Hutchins in 1985. He was contacted by Roy Johnson, a Drexel salesman at the Beverly Hills office with whom he had dealings, who asked whether Bayse would want to be recommended for a similar, but more responsible and lucrative, post at First Investors. Bayse was interested, and Johnson arranged an interview. Afterward, Johnson told Bayse that it looked as if he had the job and asked for a meeting. Bayse would later testify, "He explained to me that this in fact was a very important account for Drexel Burnham and that it had been a very profitable account for them and they wanted it to stay that way and, in fact, he wanted to make sure that I was going to continue the profitability for the account that they had had if they were going to endorse me for the job." Johnson went on to say that what he had in mind was control of the portfolios, meaning that Drexel could place new bond issues there at will.

Bayse could not provide such assurance, and if it came to that, he was prepared to stay at Mitchell Hutchins. Johnson then softened his stance and said he would have to think about it. A few days later, Johnson called Bayse and said he only meant that the old relationship—that of salesman and manager—should continue.

Bayse was offered the job, and Johnson urged him to talk with Milken, who might be able to help negotiate the compensation package. Bayse did, and Milken provided some advice, also suggesting that Bayse ask First Investors to spruce up their offices, which Milken thought were shabby. At no point did he bring up anything regarding the Drexel-First Investors relationship. But Bayse couldn't help feeling the implication was there that he owed his new job to Drexel, and it would be ungrateful of him not to show it some special attention.[33]

While Drexel was the prototypical yuppie firm, it was not the only one. Salesmen and bankers like Johnson and Dahl were to be found at practically all the big houses. Felix Rohatyn, who frowned on such antics, remarked, "A cancer has been spreading in our industry . . . . Too much money is coming together with too many young people who have little or no institutional memory, or sense of tradition, and who are under enormous economic pressure to perform in the glare of Hollywood-like publicity. The combination makes for speculative excesses at best, illegality at worst." To Rohatyn, these newcomers were akin to the rock stars of the 1980s.

When it was all over, outsiders had little sympathy for those who lost their jobs when Drexel collapsed. Talk show host Phil Donahue spoke for many when he told an audience of Drexel's former employees what many Americans thought of them:

> You not only were arrogant, you were snobbish, and in lots of ways, very impolite and mean . . . Nobody likes you. You're Wall Street yuppies, and you've got a bad image . . . I mean, mostly north-eastern, Yale, Harvard types. You are mostly Republican. You were raised in Connecticut. You never ride the subways. So who gives a damn about you guys?[34]

7
REINVENTING AMERICA

The economy was weak during the early 1980s, but it recovered steadily as the decade wore on. Except for the petroleum industry and a few special situations, corporate profits improved. When the public became convinced this performance was no fluke, it started nibbling at stocks. In August 1982, investors witnessed the beginning of what was to be a spectacular and highly unusual bull market.

THE BIRTH OF THE NEW BULL MARKET

In its early months, the new bull market was activated by the decline of inflation and the normal period of catching up after a long period of falling share prices. But after the initial recovery, takeover rumors became the engine that drove prices. Takeovers and potential takeovers became the subject of intense discussion at gatherings of investors; it was the topic at conferences costing audiences hundreds of dollars a day, at which they would hear from experts in the field and then rush to telephones to place orders for shares in companies they thought were about to be "put into play."

During the 1980s, more than a third of the Fortune 500 were acquired, merged, or taken private. Mergers and acquisitions were done at a $1.5 trillion clip. Bankers and their allies took in some $60 billion in fees, but stockholders did even better. According to Harvard Business School professor Michael Jensen, between 1976 and 1990, stockholders' gains due to takeovers and restructurings came to more than $650 billion.[1]

The Dow Industrials quadrupled in the 1980s, yet the stock market failed to produce glamorous figures or manipulators. Equity investing became more complicated and technology-oriented, leaving little room for gunslingers. Small investors took refuge in mutual funds managed by individuals of demonstrated ability. This time around, they shunned the go-go funds, concentrating instead upon those whose managers seemed able to perceive value in takeovers and special situations. The most celebrated person in equities was Peter Lynch, the manager of the Magellan Fund, who turned in an outstanding record before retiring in 1990.

The new Wall Street media stars were not plungers but, rather, journalists who ferreted out news of potential takeovers. The most prominent was Dan Dorfman, a reporter who became a much-watched personality on the Cable News Network's "Nightly Business News." Should Dorfman write or say that some raider was taking off after a company, its shares would rise sharply.

In those days, Dorfman rarely mentioned earnings growth, and he gave no evidence of knowing much about technical analysis. In earlier bull markets, these were the alternate methods of predicting stock movements. Such theories weren't dead, but they mattered much less than the takeover rumors. For this reason, inside information became more important than ever.

Another way this bull market differed from earlier ones was the close connection between stocks and bonds. The stock market was fueled by gossip about LBOs and restructurings, which were made possible by junk financing. The purchasers of stock were gambling on bonanzas that were activated by the Icahns and Pickenses of this world, who could not have performed as they did without junk financing.

But the general public gave little thought to such arcane matters as the structure of a deal, and they didn't yet know of Milken. The takeover movement was interesting, to be sure, but when most people thought of financial markets, they looked at stocks, not bonds. At the end of the day, when people asked, "What did the market do today?" they referred to the Dow Industrials, not to long-term Treasury bonds. To such people, takeovers were important because they affected the prices of stocks, and for no other reason.

There was no shortage of targets. During the 1970s, the book values of many large corporations had risen steadily, even as the prices of their stocks barely moved. The reason was inflation. Rising prices distorted corporate balance sheets and sharply altered the relationship between stock prices and the value of assets behind them. In 1966, the book value of corporate assets for the Standard & Poor's 500 was around half the price of their shares, and it actually fell somewhat by the end of the decade. As stock prices declined and the value of underlying assets rose, the direction was reversed. At the beginning of the 1980s, the S&P book value was 90 percent of market value. In July 1984, S&P estimated that nearly 30 percent of all industrial stocks listed on the NYSE were selling below tangible book value.[2] In a few cases, someone might have purchased all of a company's shares and, assuming this was done at market value, own a company whose treasury had more cash than was expended in the takeover.[3]

Another factor was a feature of the 1981 Economic Recovery Tax Law (ERTA) that made debt financing by corporations more attractive. Hoping to encourage greater investment, the government permitted corporations to accelerate their capital depreciation. This resulted in larger cash flows and earnings. SEC Chairman John Shad, a former banker at E.F. Hutton and Fred Joseph's mentor, noted that the ERTA-increased cash flow was not reflected in stock prices. As a result, many companies sold at "low multiples of their cash flow and their ability to service debt." Shad continued, "They have substantial untapped borrowing capacity, which allows acquirers to finance a substantial part of the acquisition price against the acquisition itself."[4]

This was not a novel insight. During the conglomerate era, George Selvage, of Selvage & Lee, had told a meeting of the American Management Association that takeover candidates shared several characteristics: They had large amounts of cash available; their stock would be selling for less than book value; they might have hidden tax credits and other assets; they had negligible stock ownership by the board members and management; and they had poor sales and earnings in relation to the rest of the industry.[5]

There were some similarities to the situation in which Wolfson made his plays for St. Johns River and Tampa Shipbuilding, and later for MC&S, Capital Transit, and Montgomery Ward, while Ling made his bid for Chance Vought. The difference was that now there were scores of sleepy companies with the kind of balance sheet that made them susceptible.

ATTACKING THE MISMANAGERS

The difficulties facing such vulnerable corporations were exacerbated by their leaderships' inability to respond imaginatively to challenges. Takeover practitioners thought they knew why. Sloan Wilson's "organization men," who had entered corporations by the droves in the 1940s and 1950s, were now CEOs and CEEs. An army of the timid had taken over at many of the old firms on the Fortune 500 list.

A generation earlier, Lou Wolfson had viewed his opponents as listless mismanagers: "We must revitalize a key American resource badly neglected—the individual in the business structure. We need to replace robot executives with constructive individualists."[6] In 1954, a reporter wrote, "Wolfson believes there are dozens of companies held prisoner by ultra conservative managements, like medieval maidens in a dragon's cave."[7]

In like fashion, during the mid-1980s, T. Boone Pickens would rake petroleum company CEOs over the coals for their sorry records: "Only a few chief executives have ever made money on their own. In fact most of them haven't made much money for their stockholders. They are bureaucrats and caretakers. They have learned to move up through the bureaucracy with a minimum of personal risk. It's a special talent."[8]

Pickens often attacked what he called the "Good Ol' Boys Club," which was "a loose network of chief executives who run large, publicly owned companies." These were bureaucratic types, timid to a fault, and not held responsible for their actions by the true owners of the firm—the shareholders.[9] This mantra was often voiced by raiders. Carl Icahn believed, "The takeover boom is a treatment for a disease that is destroying American productivity; gross and widespread incompetent management."[10] There was a gap between real value and market value, he asserted, because management had failed its duty and was "in the way." Icahn observed that at the turn of the century, when there were single owners of industrial companies, there was direct accountability of managers. "Today there is absolutely no accountability. We have built up a corporate welfare state that does not produce."[11]

Milken agreed with this analysis, although he was gentler in his criticism: "The value of a company and a business is the knowledge and wisdom and vision of its employees." Milken would ask businessmen seeking financing to "Tell me your hopes and dreams." Those dreams, he implied, could be realized through the intercession of a banker for whom raising money was not an obstacle. But Milken would not back just anyone who came along. He was seeking original thinkers with new products and services. Like Wolfson, Pickens, and Icahn, he disdained bureaucrats, incompetents, and robot executives.

In 1982, the government provided investment bankers having strong placement power with a rare prize in the form of another deregulatory reform. This one did for banks what negotiated commissions had done for the wire houses. In the new Rule 415, the SEC stated that qualifying corporations could register securities and then put them "on the shelf," not selling them until it felt the time was right, but within two years. Then it could utilize the services of any underwriter it wanted.

This move was a body blow to relationship banking, in which major clients traditionally utilized the services of the same investment bank for most of their financing. Such bankers were like old-fashioned family doctors, in that they knew the companies they served well, having been with them for many years, often generations.

This kind of banking had started to erode during the 1960s, when Salomon, Merrill Lynch, Lehman, and Blyth united in a casual affiliation known on the Street as the "Fearsome Foursome," and set out to take business from other banks by offering services at lower costs. As the decade wore on, more and more clients shopped around for advice and services, giving their business to the bank that came up with the best deal. These aggressive banks were doing quite well, leading others to emulate them.

All the while, the attacks on fixed commissions and fixed fees were having their effects. With Rule 415, the industry had to face what was known as "the bought deal," in which one firm would bid for the entire underwriting and then sell it through its distribution network.

Traditional bankers reacted to Rule 415 as to an electric shock. Frederick Friswold, of Dain Bosworth, told a reporter, "We're moving from the traditional concept of marriage to one-night stands." John Whitehead, the respected leader of Goldman Sachs, a quintessential establishment house, warned that the new rule "threatens to sweep away 50 years of investor protection and return the new issues market to the jungle environment of the 1920s."[12]

Under this new dispensation, there had to be close coordination between investment bankers and salesmen, since bidding on deals would require banks to know just where securities could be placed. Firms without strong sales contingents would be pressed to organize them in order to compete. The investment banker who offered advice had been prized during the conglomerate era, and he would remain important in the 1980s, but often only if he could place the securities he underwrote.

THE RISE OF THE TRADER

"Placement power" meant salesmen had to be able to place securities either with many small buyers or a few large ones. Given the evolution of the marketplace, clearly, the latter was the way to go. Banks also would have to provide an aftermarket. The need for placement power and aftermarkets meant that salesmen and traders would become the prized figures at investment banks.

In the 1950s, bond salesmen had resembled Willie Loman more than Mike Milken, in that they operated in an environment with meager action and poor remuneration. As for bond traders, they were a rare breed, since bond trading offered little action in a drowsy interest rate environment. Traders can make good money when prices are rising, and sometimes when they are falling, but not when prices are rock-steady. As has been seen, this changed in the 1970s. And the bond market of the 1980s was to be by far the most unstable in American history; 19 of the top 20 volatile months for Aaa rated bonds in the period from 1857 onward were in the 1980s.[13] This made trading a more appealing option and sales a rewarding occupation.

In addition, the customers had changed. Insurance companies and trust funds didn't trade bonds in the 1950s; rather, they accumulated them. Bond research was not required in those years. Standard & Poor's, Moody's, and a few smaller rating firms provided all the information required.

By the late 1970s, insurance companies were monitoring their holdings more carefully, and their managers now had more of a trading mentality. This was necessary, since prices rose and fell with the kind of volatility customarily expected of stocks. Insurance companies previously accustomed to buying and holding to maturity now had to trade, and they found they lacked the requisite talents in sales, trading, and research. New personnel in this area were needed, and they arrived from the graduate schools, from mutual funds, and from investment banks.

Unlike investment bankers, traders require large sums of money in their operations, which, after all, consist of the buying and selling of various kinds of investment paper. In this respect, they are acting as principals for their banks, and not as agents for a client. As the banks saw all those profits from trading rise, they came to understand that it made abundant sense for them to risk their own capital in deals. So they did. The combination of this new emphasis on trading and placement meant that those investment banks hoping to become major players had to enlarge their capital bases significantly and develop strong relationships with other pools of capital—banks, insurance companies, pension funds, and the like.

The rise of the salesman and trader did not mean the investment bankers would be relegated to a secondary role. Rather, they would have to become more cognizant of the nature of the markets for securities, and of the needs of both their clients *and* salesmen.

Therefore, the old notion of financing through ready-made instruments had to be rethought. Each deal required custom fitting and, often, the development of novel securities to satisfy the demands of both sellers and buyers. Just as Executive Life created new insurance vehicles to serve many different markets, so the bankers created new debt instruments in great abundance and variety. There were bonds with fixed yields that could be exchanged for other bonds on a specified date with coupons based upon one or another index. Dollar bonds paid interest in foreign currencies, and vice versa. Zero coupon bonds appeared, while old bonds were stripped of coupons and the corpus and coupons sold separately. Bonds were fashioned that paid varying rates depending on inflation statistics, which provided them with the pattern of returns generally associated with stocks.

In 1980, when there was much interest in precious metals, Milken and managing director Chris Andersen dreamed up silver-backed bonds for Sunshine Mining, payable upon maturity in 1995 at $1,000 a bond or 50 ounces of silver, and Drexel sold $25 million of them. Because of this twist, Sunshine paid $8\frac{1}{2}$ percent interest, half of what its credit rating might have suggested, which also was three percent below similar maturities of U.S. Treasuries. This was followed by two other issues for the company. In another such ploy, Drexel was able to sell $50 million of oil-indexed notes for Texas International, payable at $1,000 face value or the market price of 29 barrels of oil.

The corporations for whom these bonds were issued were more interested in selling bonds than in equity. There were many reasons. One was the debt lessons taught by Modigliani-Miller. Another was inflationary expectations; the corporations rushed to raise funds at interest rates that in a few months or years might seem quite low. Further, banks and insurance companies, traditional lenders to such customers, were reluctant to make long-term commitments for the same reason, and they had to be lured by higher coupons.

Investors who had become accustomed to high rates in the 1970s and saw them decline in the 1980s were faced with the choice of settling for

Table 7–1

SCOPE OF THE JUNK BOND
MARKET, 1970–1990

Year	Par Value Outstanding (millions of dollars)
1970	6,996
1971	6,643
1972	7,106
1973	8,082
1974	11,101
1975	7,720
1976	8,015
1977	8,479
1978	9,401
1979	10,675
1980	15,126
1981	17,362
1982	18,536
1983	28,233
1984	41,700
1985	59,078
1986	92,985
1987	136,952
1988	159,223
1989	201,000
1990	210,000

Source: Edward A. Altman, "Defaults and Returns on High Yield Bonds: An Update Through the First Half of 1991," in the Merrill Lynch magazine, *Extra Credit,* July/ August 1991, 19.

lower returns from high-rated bonds or increasing their level of risk and going into lower-rated issues. Many opted for the latter. This resulted in a veritable explosion in the junk bond market, which, until then, was known only to a relative handful of institutional investors. There was a new demand for Milken to satisfy—and with it, a new supply of clients wanting his brand of financing.

It all came together during the early 1980s. Small and medium-sized companies were prepared to pay high yields for financing. By then, too, some perceptive individuals recognized the possibility of unlocking unrealized values caused by market conditions, the law, and incompetent or inefficient managers. Large institutions were eager to purchase bonds issued for this function.[14]

THE USE OF JUNK IN CORPORATE CREATION AND TAKEOVERS

In the public mind, junk bonds came to be associated with hostile takeovers. The mention of one often led to the other. Yet, the hostile takeover movement was never as consequential or widespread as it was made out to be, nor were hostile takeovers a major market for junk. According to one study, during the peak year of 1986, there were 331 leveraged buyouts, which accounted for a quarter of the total mergers and acquisitions for the year. For the 1983–1988 period as a whole, close to three of four LBOs were friendly, and another 11 percent were unsolicited. The remaining had their origins in unfriendly approaches. Of these, 12 percent were carried out by white knights, called in to defend the target against hostile bids. Even some of these ended on an amicable note. Only 1 percent of all LBOs began and ended in an unfriendly fashion.[15]

The vast majority of junk underwritings were for restructurings and corporate growth. Of the 1,100 junk issues sold between 1980 and 1986, 22 percent were used in takeovers, and 3 percent were employed in hostile or unwelcome deals. A General Accounting Office study of the junk market at the height of the hostile-takeover movement, 1985–1986, indicated that slightly more than 15 percent of the high-yield issues of those years were used for such purposes.[16] Yet, the two remain linked in the public mind.

While each foray was different, the targets usually shared several characteristics. They were large, multidivisional firms that could be dissected easily and sold to others. Often, they were to be found in unglamorous industries with profitable but mundane products, with stocks at low P/E ratios. Raiders sought targets with swollen bureaucracies and wasteful methods of allocating funds. Once in control, they could introduce efficiencies. In these firms, business may have been competitive but not cyclical, so owners could expect a reliable cash flow. Such firms required little by way of research and development. It would be helpful if management didn't have much ownership.

By 1985, Milken had formed a strong alliance with several men who had been or were to become identified with raiding. In addition to customers like Fred Carr and Tom Spiegel, his clients included Henry Kravis, Ron Perelman, Saul Steinberg, Irwin Jacobs, Nelson Peltz, Victor Posner, and Carl Lindner. In time, there would be others, among them T. Boone Pickens and Carl Icahn. These men shared several characteristics, the most important being the ability to strike fear into the hearts of CEOs of large corporations. Their machinations were helping to fuel the bull market in stocks. They had become famous because of this. Eventually, Milken would achieve the fame he always disdained because he was perceived as the person behind the raiders.

The raiders were best known for financial legerdemain, not for managerial skills, and if they had limited themselves to raiding, one might have been able to make a case for their activities. But they intended to take an active role in management. Such was the hubris of the newcomers of the 1980s. The conglomerateurs had assumed that a good manager could lead any company—for example, they supposed the switch from lumber to car rentals to electronics at ITT could be made easily. The raiders of the 1980s took this idea one step further: Even a nonmanager could manage any kind of company. Perelman, Icahn, Peltz, and others seemed blithely confident of their abilities in this direction. In some cases, they proved capable, but their overall records were spotty at best.

The raiders and the bankers they employed made up the rules as they went along. This lack of standards in takeovers bothered some investment bankers. Fred Joseph went through the motions of arguing that Drexel had some hard and fast rules: "We have an absolute policy that when one of our clients attacks another client, we are opposed to the attack. If asked, we will defend the attacked company. We will never work with the attacker."[17]

After a while this became known as the "Joseph Doctrine." Few took it for anything more than image-making, something Joseph often attempted but, usually, with little success.

The reality was different, as was the rhetoric of others at Drexel. Chris Andersen, who was one of the more pugnacious Drexel bankers, was reported as telling an audience at a takeover seminar in 1985 that one of his effective ruses was to contact Company A and advise it to make a play for Company B, suggesting that if this was not done, he would call Company B and recommend an assault on Company A. Joseph all but conceded that such things occurred, but he charged that it happened elsewhere as well—another case of "everyone is doing it."[18]

RATIONALIZING TAKEOVERS

Seeking a rationale for its involvement in takeovers, Drexel hit upon Milken's earlier delight in helping to finance young, medium-sized companies in new industries or those run by members of minority groups. He had developed a warm relationship with Jesse Jackson, and he had attempted to help *Amsterdam News* publisher Bill Tatum when that black-owned newspaper tried to purchase the *New York Post*. Earlier, Drexel had said it was helping to build a new America. The bank now asserted that by enabling raiders to go after those indolent companies, it was assisting in rebuilding the old America.

Well-managed, profitable companies had no reason to fear raids from Drexel clients or those of any other bank. "If you take a list of the best-run companies, they typically make long-term commitments, and they'll sell as decent multiples," said Joseph in 1985. "IBM is not a target. ITT is a target, because it hasn't managed its businesses very well. So ITT is complaining that it can't plan long term because of the sharks." In any case, Joseph claimed the following year, publicity to the contrary, Drexel wasn't a major player in the hostile takeover game:

> Our association with raiders is overblown. The firm has 800-odd corporate finance clients, of whom a dozen are characterized as raiders by the press. From 1984 to 1986, Drexel served as financial advisor or arranged financing for 306 merger transactions, of which ten were hostile. And the fact is, in the last three years, Drexel has provided 10 percent of the funds for unfriendly and unsolicited takeovers; commercial banks have provided 58 percent.[19]

The first LBOs of the new era were friendly. In 1982, former secretary of the Treasury William Simon led in an amicable LBO of Gibson Greeting Cards, paying RCA $80 million for that unwanted operation. Simon and his group turned the company around and, a year and a half later, took it public for $290 million. It seemed so easy, so certain. Why hadn't someone thought of this earlier?

There were many stories, and each whetted the appetites of LBO practitioners. Leslie Fay was bought out for $58 million and, four years later, taken to market, fetching $360 million. KKR purchased Fred Meyer for $420 million and, five years later, took it public for more than $900 million. Better management, divestiture of undervalued assets, and some imagination—plus a compliant bank like Drexel—seemed all that was required.

Dozens of companies that had been cobbled together in the 1960s were disassembled in the 1980s. Some engaged in asset sales. Borg-Warner sold its financial operations, and Revlon sold its medical business and everything else unrelated to cosmetics. Hanson PLC purchased SCM for $930 million and proceeded to sell divisions—Glidden Paint, Allied Paper, Durkee Industrial Food, and Durkee Foods—for a total of $1.1 billion, retaining companies that in 1989 threw off more than $50 million in profits.

In time, the supply of corporations seeking to divest themselves of unwanted units was insufficient to meet the demands of those seeking to rejuvenate them, and this marked the beginning of the hostile-takeover mania.

The elemental technique of hostile takeovers is uncomplicated. After having identified a potential takeover, the raider accumulates just under 5 percent of its stock, to avoid having to report the position to the government under the terms of the Williams Act. Then he might drop a few hints regarding just how attractive the situation is, to stir the risk arbitrageurs into action. Let's assume he amasses shares at an average price of $20, and he doesn't intend paying more than $40 for the rest. By now, the price is around $25, and so he already has made an unrealized profit.

Next, with the assistance of a squad of lawyers, he organizes a company that exists only on paper, this being the vehicle to make the bid for the target. Now the new "shell" company announces a $35 per share tender for the rest of the stock.

Management likely will denounce the raider, claiming that the stock is worth far more than $35, to which he will reply that if this is so, why has it been trading at $20 so recently?

After some sparring, the raider might boost the bid to $40, and now there is a good chance he will get the company. What if he fails? He will walk off with a profit on the stock.

Should he succeed, the next step is to obtain financing, often through borrowing from banks and insurance companies, among others, or from his own coffers. He will sell bonds and use the proceeds to pay off part of the debt. Next, there will be sales of assets to get more funds for debt repayment.

This was the basic procedure in the mid-1980s. Much was added in the next few years by imaginative bankers and attorneys. There were defenses, counterdefenses, ruses, and diversionary tactics. At first, there were winners and losers, but after a while, there were only winners. Either greenmail was offered to the raiders by the old management, or the old management received a large cash settlement for stepping down peacefully, in that aforementioned golden parachute.

Lost in all of this maneuvering was the fiduciary responsibility of management. Was management acting in the best interests of the shareholders in refusing the takeover offer and paying greenmail? It might be argued that they genuinely believed the company to be worth more than that. But was it to serve the shareholders that they accepted their golden parachutes? Hardly.

BEATRICE AND ITT

Beatrice Companies was the subject of one of the more dramatic and successful LBOs. Beatrice was a food company that started making large scale acquisitions in the 1960s. At first, it concentrated on dairy products and then went on to other foods, but soon it decided to go further afield. Beatrice became a conglomerate through more than one hundred acquisitions, among them such well-known nonfood companies as Avis, Culligan, and Samsonite, as well as the food companies LaChoy, Tropicana, Dannon, and Hotel Bar.

CEO William Karnes ran a tight, lean ship, with a small office staff. There was no board room; large meetings were held in local restaurants. "You don't make any money at the General Office," said Karnes, "you only spend it; so keep it small and efficient." There were no corporate airplanes;

Karnes and the others traveled by coach on commercial airlines. For much of his time as CEO, Karnes didn't have a corporate limousine, or any kind of car for that matter. He considered these a waste. Karnes not only believed management was a trustee for the shareholders, but he behaved as though Beatrice truly was his company.

Much of this changed under Karnes' successors, especially James Dutt. There was a move to lavish quarters, a multiplication of staff, and purchases of corporate jets and limousines. Overhead rose to more than $220 million a year, quite high for a $12 billion business.

Dutt centralized operations, which demoralized managers in the field. He authorized the expenditure of close to $70 million a year on company-sponsored auto racing, and another $50 million a year to promote the name "Beatrice" for its already well-known branded items. Would victories in car races help sell Samsonite luggage? Would an auto renter choose Avis because he knew it was owned by Beatrice? Dutt seemed to think so.

Then came the purchase of Esmark by the newly renamed Beatrice Companies, which made it much larger but also saddled the company with debt. The market showed its opinion of Dutt's management in the usual way. In the midst of a bull market, the stock declined. By 1985, Beatrice was one of those companies worth far more than its market valuation, with dozens of businesses for which good prices might be obtained.

That Beatrice attracted KKR, which initiated a hostile takeover bid, came as little surprise. After protracted negotiations, KKR took it over in 1986, through a $6.2 billion LBO, with Drexel handling the banking end. Out went Avis ($250 million), Coca-Cola bottlers ($1 billion), Max Factor ($1.3 billion), and scores of other companies, all of which more than repaid the purchase price, leaving Beatrice as a profitable operation in foods.[20] This LBO was not as lucrative as John Kluge's Metromedia deal, but it did produce a profit of $1.7 billion. CEO Donald Kelly made more than $400 million on an investment of $5 million.[21]

For this deal, Drexel underwrote $2.5 billion in junk bonds, without which the LBO could not have succeeded. It was a hard sell, even for Milken, and he insisted on sweeteners in the form of 15-year warrants to purchase 33.4 million shares of Beatrice common at $5 a share, which would come to a 24 percent ownership of the firm. Drexel retained most of these warrants for in-house distribution. Two years later, Beatrice valued its common at $26 a share, providing the Drexel insiders with profits of hundreds of millions of dollars. Little wonder, bankers, traders, and salesmen fell over one another trying to gain positions at Drexel.[22]

Critics were horrified on learning of those "obscene" profits. Lost sight of was the fact that at the time of the takeover, Beatrice was a stagnant concern, its stock price not reflecting the underlying assets. KKR, Drexel, and others made enormous sums from the takeover and divestitures, but as a result of the restructuring, the component companies performed much better than the dissolved parent. There *was* a positive side of the deal.

There were negatives as well. If the stockholders and the major players benefitted, the bondholders suffered. The Beatrice LBO transformed a company with assets and a well-stocked treasury into one with the same assets but a large debt. This wreaked havoc with its credit rating. Beatrice bondholders had been owners of highly rated paper, which now was transformed into junk. It was a new experience for these bondholders. Those fallen angels of the past usually deteriorated slowly; with LBOs, a rating of AAA could become A or even BBB overnight.[23]

ITT was another of those companies that seemed nearly perfect for an LBO. In 1978, it posted earnings of $662 million on revenues of $15.3 billion; in 1983, the company earned $675 million on revenues of $14.2 billion. This was hardly a sparkling performance, for which CEO Rand Araskog offered no excuses. By then, ITT was also financially troubled, and Araskog slashed its dividend. The common had been selling in the mid-30s when Araskog took over in 1979; it now was in the low 20s.

Raiders Irving Jacobs, Jay Pritzker, and their allies and associates became interested in ITT. They hoped to perform a leveraged buyout of the firm with Araskog's help, but they would proceed without it, if necessary.

Araskog managed to fight them off. Yet, he recognized that the low regard ITT commanded on Wall Street would make it a likely candidate for other raiders, and he sought a suitable merger partner. Several were considered, but the company eventually divested itself of the large, troubled telecommunications unit, which was merged with France's CGE to form Alcatel, in which ITT received a minority position. The experience converted Araskog into one of the industry's bitterest opponents of takeovers and a lobbyist for legislation to prevent them. He received criticism from shareholder groups for taking large hikes in his compensation while the firm continued to languish, a splendid example of what happens when ownership and management are separated.

Some of the hostile takeovers of the late 1980s worked out poorly, while most of those earlier ones resulted in greater economies. There wasn't a single case in which shareholder values didn't rise on news that a campaign was being mounted. Eugene Fama, a professor of finance at the University of Chicago and one of the foremost authorities in the field, concluded that "The empirical evidence is clear. In mergers, tender offers, and proxy fights, stockholders of the attacked company almost always profit."[24]

PLUMS IN PETROLEUM

After the collapse of OPEC in the early 1980s, many petroleum companies shared those attributes perceived in Beatrice and ITT and became takeover targets. It began with a rudimentary exhibit of Adam Smith economics. As OPEC's power dissipated and the price of oil plunged, earnings fell at the major oil exploration companies and hundreds of wildcat operations failed. Exxon, which had earned $5.7 billion in 1980, posted just $4.1 billion in 1982. In the same time span, Texaco's earnings went from $2.2 billion to $1.3 billion, Occidental's from $711 million to $156 million, Phillips' from $1.1 billion to $646 million, and Gulf's from $1.4 billion to $900 million.

The reason was recognized by all within the industry: The elevated petroleum prices of the 1970s had encouraged companies to seek additional reserves in areas previously neglected due to the high costs of recovery. This worked fine when petroleum was at $30 or $40 a barrel but not when prices were falling steadily. Exploration became a losing game when the price of petroleum declined to the low $20s per barrel. It later was learned that during the first half of the 1980s, each dollar spent on exploration returned only 58 cents in reserves.[25] This made oil companies prime takeover candidates.

Recognizing this situation, several large oil companies diversified out of energy. It was a virtual admission of defeat, masked by talk of "new opportunities." In the 1970s, Standard of California made a $333 million investment in Amax; Atlantic Richfield purchased Anaconda for $784 million; Standard of Indiana acquired Cyprus Mines for $462 million; Exxon paid $1.5 billion for Reliance; and Standard of Ohio capped this trend in 1981 with the $1.7 billion purchase of Kennecott.[26] Each of these purchases proved disastrous.

The industry's hard times and unwise acquisitions caused the prices of oil shares to decline. Raiders hungrily eyed these companies. All they had to do was to take the reserves of any petroleum company, divide them by the price of the stock, and find out how many barrels were behind each share. The next step was to multiply the number of barrels per share by the price of oil. When this was done, one would have discovered that the companies' shares were underpriced in relation to those assets alone, and in many cases, sharply so.

In the summer of 1981, Getty, which had assets of $250 a share, was selling at $72. Marathon, with $210 a share in assets, sold for $68. Cities Service had $130 per share in reserves, and went for $56. In time, all these companies would disappear into the hands of a raider or white knight. What of the giants? Standard of Indiana had a market valuation of $15.2 billion, and its oil reserves alone were worth $30.3 billion at current prices. Exxon, the biggest of them all, was valued by the market at $33.5 billion, with reserves worth $41.7 billion.[27]

In 1983, the engineering firm of John Herold estimated that the shares of giant petroleum firms were selling for around 40 percent of their net worth.[28]

Why seek oil in the Gulf, which, if everything worked out well, would cost $12 to $15 a barrel and might be sold for little or no profit, when oil could be purchased at $3 or $4 a barrel by taking over a large company? In mid-decade, raiders liked to say that the cheapest place to locate oil was on the floor of the NYSE.

In this way, the stage was set for the next round in the decade's corporate takeovers and raids, which would take place within the petroleum industry. The mania within the industry began conventionally enough in 1979, when Shell purchased Belridge Oil for $3.6 billion. The following year, Sun bought Texas Pacific from Seagram for $2.3 billion. In 1981, DuPont acquired Conoco for $7.4 billion in cash and stocks, followed by the $6.5 billion purchase of Marathon by United States Steel (half cash and half notes). All of these deals were friendly and, despite their great size, conventional. The hostile takeovers came later, with T. Boone Pickens as the undisputed star of this phase of the movement, and Drexel as the most prominent banker.

Drexel came late to the takeover game. Indeed, Joseph was obliged to go into the market and raid other firms to obtain the expertise needed for such forays. Later, when Milken became celebrated, it would appear to some that he had started it all and had been the mastermind of the entire movement. This was not so. Pickens and others involved in hostile takeovers were the ones the establishment feared most—the ones they were out to destroy. When they couldn't get Pickens, and opportunity in the form of uncovered securities violations appeared, they went after others, particularly the largest targets of opportunity, Drexel and Milken.

8

T. BOONE PICKENS AND THE NEW CORPORATE RAIDERS

T. Boone Pickens got his start in 1951, as a geologist with Phillips Petroleum. He left five years later, at the age of 27, and with savings of $3,500, he founded Petroleum Exploration Inc., or PEI, which did exactly what the name indicated. Although Pickens had a bumpy time for a while, he survived in an industry in which failure is more common than success.

Pickens concentrated on exploring in the midcontinental United States, the Rockies, the Gulf Coast, and, later, in the Gulf of Mexico and North Sea. Even given this considerable geographic range, by 1968, the company was still small by industry standards; revenues in that year came to little more than $6 million. But Pickens was moving; like many CEOs of small concerns, he had decided that acquisitions were the best way to grow.

Pickens had made his first acquisition, Altair Oil & Gas, in 1959. PEI went public in 1964, and Pickens changed its name to Mesa Petroleum. Four years later, he located another likely (undervalued) acquisition candidate: Hugoton Production owned a portion of a large natural gas field in Kansas and, in Pickens' opinion, was inefficiently managed. He wanted Hugoton's gas reserves, which, given the price of Hugoton common, would come at a sharp discount to the market price of natural gas.

Pickens offered to buy Hugoton with an issue of Mesa preferred, but the offer was rejected. Management opted instead for a merger agreement with a white knight, Reserve Oil & Gas. Pickens refused to accept this rebuff and decided to pursue an unfriendly takeover.

It wasn't much different from what Ling had attempted in his forays. Pickens started by purchasing shares personally and through the Mesa treasury. By early 1969, Mesa had a third of the shares. In addition, Pickens believed he could count on the arbitrageurs for their votes. It worked. Hugoton's management bowed, and the takeover was voted on April 7,

1969. Thus, Mesa made its acquisition the old-fashioned way: through an exchange of corporate paper.

Little more than half a year later, Pickens lined up another property, Southland Royalty. He had learned that Gulf Oil held a large block of Southland stock and was willing to sell. But Southland's management, which owned 30 percent of the common, refused the Pickens offer of Mesa preferred for its common and filed a lawsuit to restrain him. Pickens was stopped on this one. Without missing a beat, however, he moved on to purchase a large interest in Pubco Petroleum, which came in without much difficulty.

Mesa was successful in North Sea drilling in this period, and it was able to benefit from the oil crisis of the late 1970s. But, like other firms, the company suffered during the price collapse that followed. Pickens did not think this would be permanent. One day, perhaps in the 1990s, the price of oil would rise to the point that drilling would once again be profitable. Until then, he would have to seek other opportunities.

In 1979, Pickens decided to restructure Mesa so as to maximize stockholder returns. "It was in March 1979 that I woke up suddenly one morning at three o'clock and said to myself, 'You could solve your problem by making Mesa smaller.' I went into the study. I thought, 'Why not spin off some of the reserves to the stockholders?'"

This would be done through the creation of a royalty trust, containing assets whose earnings would be paid directly to the owners of trust certificates. Under the laws of the period, companies paid taxes on earnings, and then shareholders paid taxes on dividends from these earnings. In a royalty trust, corporate earnings that were passed through directly to owners would not be taxed, and so the net return would be greater.

Champions of royalty trusts stressed the added income provided to owners, while critics argued that they were simply a clever way to liquidate a company.[1] Pickens wouldn't have disagreed. "Mesa is not going to hang around with a depleting reserve base. That would be unfair to the stockholders. If we fail to replace our reserves two years in a row, we'll either figure out something else to do or we'll get out of the business." Pickens started by organizing Mesa Royalty Trust on November 1, and into it he put around half of the company's natural gas reserves.

Mesa was one exception to the oil industry's general malaise. The company earned $95 million in 1980, a year in which Pickens paid himself $7.8 million and was the country's highest-paid executive. The shareholders also fared well. Mesa common, which sold as low as 39 in 1980, rose to just under 80, split two for one, and was back to 70 by the end of the year. There was another two-for-one split in 1981, and, after a pullback, a further advance.

Soon, however, earnings started an irregular decline. In early 1983, Mesa common was selling for 10, just about a quarter of where it had been three years earlier.

Mesa's problems were caused largely by a failed gamble on offshore drilling in the Gulf of Mexico. This operation was costing half a million dollars a day to keep going, and the outlook there was bleak. Pickens recalled a meeting of his company's leaders around this time, when he told them, "Boys, this is it. We've got to figure out a way to make $300 million, and we've got to make it fast."[2]

BOONE GOES HUNTING

Pickens would do it through raiding. When some critics asserted that, as an oil man, he should seek new petroleum deposits, he would reply, "That's ridiculous. I mean, if it isn't economically sound, you're a fool to do it. I'd be a sap to go out and try to find oil at $15 a barrel when I could buy three barrels for the same price. It didn't take a financial genius to figure that out."[3]

As noted, every major oil company had reserves not reflected in the prices of their stocks. This meant they had to worry about a quarter or two of poor earnings, which would further depress the prices of their shares so as to invite a raid. "When you're an ugly girl, no one pays attention to you," said John Norell of the Dutch electronics giant, Phillips. "Then she gets herself into shape . . . and the first thing that happens is, somebody rapes her."[4]

This kind of analogy did not sit well with Pickens. "I like to be identified as a large stockholder who sometimes becomes active," he once said, when the charges of corporate predation were made.[5]

His next target was Cities Service, which was selling in the low 30s and had assets Pickens thought were worth $90 a share. The initial plan, developed by Pickens' banker, Donaldson, Lufkin & Jenrette, was to find partners who would purchase stakes and then make a tender offer for the remaining shares. Pickens' intention was to offer $45 a share for 20 percent of Cities Service's outstanding shares. After some scouting, he was able to persuade some heavy hitters of the wisdom of his plan. Southland Corp., Davis Oil, Damson Oil, and the Madison Fund contributed to his war chest.

Pickens' objective was an amalgamation of Mesa and Cities, after which asset dispositions would be made to pay off part of the debt incurred to finance the purchase, while Pickens would set up another royalty trust.

This wasn't the first attempt at a hostile bid in an industry that soon became a major battlefield—a few months earlier, Dome Petroleum had made a pass at Conoco before it wound up with DuPont. But Dome and DuPont did not intend making a regular practice of raiding. Pickens did.

The news leaked. Before Pickens could act, Cities engaged in what was called a "Pac-Man defense," putting out its own tender at $17 for 51 percent of Mesa's shares. It wasn't a serious move—at the time, Mesa was selling for a fraction more than $16—but, rather, a shot across Pickens' bow. He responded with an offer of $50 a share for 51 percent of Cities' shares, which management rejected.

There was much parrying, and, in the end, Cities found a white knight in Gulf, which announced a tender at $63. The Pickens group sold its shares, enjoying a profit of around $45 million before deductions for costs. Pickens was disappointed but not discouraged. He told reporters, "We decided it was time to fold our tent and move on to another deal."

As it happened, the Gulf deal fell through, and Cities common fell from the high 40s to 32, causing massive pain among the arbitrageurs—it was thought that Ivan Boesky lost more than $52 million on this one. Eventually, Cities was sold to Occidental Petroleum for $53 a share. It was a sizable purchase for the time; Occidental paid $4 billion for the company.[6]

Other Mesa deals followed. A bid for Supron Energy fetched a profit of $22.2 million; General American Oil provided another $25.3 million; and Superior, more than $13 million. Each time Pickens lost, Mesa and its partners made millions, and then they sought other targets.[7] Always, he claimed to be sincere in his takeover offers, but the more money Pickens took from his raids, the more he seemed the highwayman of the American petroleum industry, looting executives at underperforming companies.

Pickens denied this, preferring to characterize himself as a tribune of the people. In the years that followed, he would speak out often on a variety of topics not related directly to oil but to the fundamental questions facing American capitalism. One of these was the purpose of the corporation. He stated repeatedly that "The basic principle of capitalism . . . is to create value for the owners." Given this concept, he would maintain that he was not a raider but a shareholder champion.[8] After his forays were over, Pickens remarked:

> When I first started talking about restructuring in the early '80s, some people called me a radical. They said I was really against traditional values and things like that, that I was fooling around with stuff that I had no business talking about. I saw undervalued assets in the public marketplace. My game plan wasn't to take on Big Oil. Hell, that's not my role. My role is to make money for the stockholders. I just saw that Big Oil's management had done a lousy job for the stockholders, leaving an opening to upgrade the value of those assets.[9]

Thus, Pickens cast himself as a crusader, a corporate Ralph Nader, exposing flaws in the American business system. It was a curious analogy, but Nader himself recognized the similarities. The two met in 1985, when Nader was preparing a book on major American businessmen, to be called *The Big Boys*. Pickens explained that once he threatened a corporation, other CEOs would unite to attack him. "So it's like the old-boy network," said Nader.

Pickens agreed. "Absolutely. Totally." Nader wrote, "The forces of opposition to Pickens are not unlike the corporate reaction to the rise of the consumer movement in the 1960s. The independent-minded oilman has been exposed to assaults on his motives and integrity . . . ."[10]

What Pickens and, apparently, Nader didn't know was that Louis Wolfson had adopted precisely the same crusading stance in the 1955 Montgomery Ward struggle. Pickens was more a reincarnation of Wolfson than he was a clone of Nader. Either way, Pickens was vulnerable to charges of hypocrisy. While denouncing managements' attempts to block hostile takeovers, he instituted staggered terms for directors at Mesa, required a supermajority to pass certain resolutions, and furnished himself with a handsome golden parachute should all of this fail to deter a raider.

THE GULF WAR

During the next two years, Pickens attempted to gain footholds at three substantial companies: Gulf, Phillips, and Unocal. Pickens selected Gulf because, of all the majors, it was selling at the largest discount to assets, at a price of just 2.2 times cash flow. The reason, Pickens said, was poor management. Gulf sat by doing little in the early 1970s, when the price of crude was rising, reaping fortunes from concessions in Kuwait. When that country nationalized its oil fields, Gulf was left short of reserves. In addition, there were failures in uranium. A contract to provide natural gas to Texas Eastern Transmission backfired when an expected find did not materialize. Yet, the dividends continued, as did the double taxation.

In 1983, Gulf had sales of $29 billion, making it the fifth largest firm in the industry. At the time, it was believed no one had the kind of money to acquire a major oil company like Gulf, especially in an unfriendly operation.

Mesa started picking up shares in August 1983, without creating much of a stir, and Pickens filed the necessary papers when his holdings reached 5 percent. His avowed objective was to persuade Gulf CEO James Lee to form a royalty trust, which would boost the value of the holdings, providing Mesa with a large profit. By early October, Mesa had 2.7 million Gulf shares, which were transferred to Mesa Asset Company, which, in turn, sold portions to Pickens' newly formed Gulf Investors Group (GIG). The buying continued.

Lee was not without resources and allies. Once he learned the company was under accumulation, Lee gathered 38 banks that provided credit lines of up to $4 billion.[11] Lee also had some unsolicited allies in the form of other large corporations prepared to assist Gulf, in whose problems they perceived potential difficulties for themselves. Pickens told Nader:

You won't even believe the pressures that are involved here. For instance, I knew I had a block of stock that was with us in the Gulf deal. And then there was pressure put on that particular investment advisor to [vote] with Gulf management. The pressure was totally removed from Gulf. It was another company. The CEO called the investment advisor up and said, "vote with Gulf management because we're thinking of putting some of our pension funds around and we're looking at your firm." That's the kind of pressure that is coming to bear on these money managers.[12]

For several years, Pickens had had a relationship with Lehman Brothers and Morgan Stanley. In the Gulf attempt, this created a conflict of interest for Morgan. "I wasn't surprised when I got a call from Joe Fogg, then head of [Morgan Stanley's] mergers and acquisitions department. 'We've got some problems,' he began. He didn't have to say anything more." (Later, it would be learned that Morgan received a fee of $16.5 million from Gulf for its assistance.) So, in the beginning, Pickens relied exclusively on Lehman.[13]

Most of the establishment banks would have nothing to do with so massive a raid, and Pickens had to settle for second-echelon and non-New York banks. He was able to line up a total of $325 million credit at 13 of them, including Texas Commerce, First City National of Houston, RepublicBank of Dallas, and Far West Financial. Appropriately, Monty Hall, host of the TV game show "Let's Make A Deal," was a director of Far West.[14] Pickens also brought into GIG such heavyweights as the Belzberg brothers (Hyman, Samuel, and William); Michael Boswell, of Sunshine Mining; Cyril Wagner, Jr., and Jack Brown, of Wagner & Brown; and John Harbert III, of Harbert International.

Mesa kicked in with $365 million and the others with an additional $135 million. The goal was for Mesa Asset to acquire another 6.3 million Gulf shares, which would give it 8.75 percent of the outstanding common. They did better. On October 24, Pickens revealed that his holdings were 17.9 million shares, or slightly less than 11 percent of Gulf common.

During the contest, Pickens had to cope with the same kind of harassment he had experienced during the Cities deal. Gulf hired private detectives to ferret out negative information on Pickens' operations and personal life. Pickens said he, too, had hired a detective—to keep tabs on the Gulf detectives.[15] Gulf denied all of this, but it did concede that its law firm was investigating Pickens.

Gulf had been incorporated in Pennsylvania, where state law required cumulative voting for directors. Since the board had 13 members, each owner of a single share either could vote once for 13 different candidates or cast all 13 votes for a single person. This meant that any owner of slightly more than 7 percent of the shares could place his or her representative on the board.

For this reason, on October 11, 1983, Gulf decided to reincorporate in Delaware, where there was no cumulative voting and state laws favored entrenched managements. A meeting was scheduled for December 30, at which time the shareholders would vote on the reincorporation, knowing that a Lee victory might end Pickens' plan for a royalty trust. Gulf management won 52.7 percent of the vote, and so the company was reincorporated.

Pickens concluded that a complete takeover of Gulf would be the only way he could manage a victory. At that point, he owned only 13 percent of the shares and had all but exhausted his financial resources. He would need a great deal of additional help to succeed.

William Belzberg suggested that Pickens see Milken, saying, "Milken has an uncanny ability to raise money." By then, Milken had essentially financed the reinvigoration of the Nevada gambling industry and had helped create such midsized firms as Kindercare, MCI, and CNN. One of Milken's core beliefs was, "Money is not the problem. Getting the right people is the problem." Talking to a reporter in 1987, he put it this way:

> In an industrial society, capital is a scarce resource, but in today's information society, there's plenty of capital. Energy companies have had $2 billion to $10 billion of cash for two decades. Everywhere you go people come up to you and say, "I have money to invest, what should I put it in?" There's $250 billion in money market funds. If people had something to invest in, a lot of that money wouldn't be in money funds.[16]

But up to that time, Drexel had not engaged in hostile takeovers. This was about to change. And with this change, Milken set out on the long, twisted path that would end in his incarceration.

A meeting between Pickens and Milken was arranged for January 6, 1984. Milken and his associates, Peter Ackerman, John Sorte, and Mike Brown, listened to the plan and discussed how much money would be needed. It was agreed that Brown and Sorte would go to Mesa headquarters in Amarillo on January 12, to meet with GIG members and discuss a banking deal. Thus, Drexel entered the game. Drexel hadn't been able to obtain the business of the nation's largest, most prestigious companies. Now, it would assist those who wanted to acquire them.

After reviewing the deal, Brown and Sorte told GIG that Drexel would try to raise $1.7 billion by selling senior preferred stock in Newco, a shell corporation into which Gulf would be placed, and $450 million worth of junk bonds. "Gulf was the first transaction where any investment banker was going to be arranging high-yield bonds to help support a tender offer," said Sorte. "We had a lot at stake."[17]

Backed by Drexel, and with 13.5 million Gulf shares already in his accounts, Pickens trumped a rival $65 a share offer from Atlantic Richfield.

That company's CEO, Robert Anderson, responded by offering Pickens $65 a share for his holdings, which Pickens rejected. Anderson next proposed to Lee that Atlantic Richfield acquire Gulf in a friendly $70 tender. Lee protested and said he would recommend that the offer be rejected. But to bolster his position against this new threat, he attempted to rid himself of an old one. Lee offered to purchase Mesa's Gulf shares owned by GIC, which would give the group a profit of $500 million or so. This offer would not be made to all shareholders, only to GIG, and Pickens later claimed he refused for that reason.[18]

Meanwhile, Drexel contacted its customers and confirmed that it would be possible to raise the $1.7 billion. Indeed, even more could be had if the terms were sufficiently attractive. Milken informed Pickens of his success. This communication was the forerunner of what soon would become known as the "highly confident letter," in which Milken would assure customers that a specified amount of money could be arranged for a particular deal. Some of the Milken clients came into GIG, with imaginative deals. One of these clients, Carl Lindner's Penn Central, arranged to purchase $220 million in newly issued Mesa 14.25 percent subordinated debentures and $50 million in $14.25 redeemable preferred stock, plus $30 million in eight-year warrants to purchase Mesa at $18 a share. Under the terms of the deal, Penn Central would be able to sell the options back to Mesa for a profit of $30 million, presumably after Pickens had cashed out of Gulf.

Later, those within the industry would recognize this interaction as a critical juncture in the history of the junk era—the moment Milken emerged as a superstar. Armed with such backing as Drexel could provide, raiders could go after just about any large, fat corporation. In his ability to raise enormous sums of money quickly, Milken had no peer—and major corporate targets had no greater adversary.

In early February, Pickens decided that GIG would purchase another 20 percent to 25 percent of Gulf stock. "If Pickens and the new partner can walk into Gulf's meeting in May with 35 percent to 40 percent of the stock, it'll be a lay-down hand," said one takeover stock trader, who, at the time, did not know of Milken's involvement. "He could have anything he wants—a royalty trust, or the whole company."[19]

Pickens and Milken had tried to act quietly, but on February 12, 1984, Gulf called a press conference: It had learned that GIG planned a tender through Drexel, which would eventually require $9.24 billion. The spokesman made it all sound mysterious and underhanded, but it really was a version of the Drexel offer to GIG involving Newco. Gulf warned that if the deal was implemented, some of its shareholders might be "forced to receive securities of questionable value," a euphemism for junk bonds.[20]

According to Gulf, it was to be a two-tier offer, of a kind not quite envisaged by the framers of the Williams Act.[21] In the first stage, GIG would raise $3.66 billion for a $55 a share tender for 61.3 million shares, which would give it more than half the shares. Then Drexel would form its shell, which would sell investment units composed of common and preferred stock for $1.73 billion, presumably to its list of Milken customers. Another $1 billion would come from bank borrowings, and $482 million would come from additional investments by GIG.

In the second stage, once in control, GIG would recommend the folding of Gulf into this new company, with remaining shareholders receiving paper with a face value of $55 a share, in the form of $3.07 billion in 20-year junior debentures paying 16 percent interest, and $1.5 billion of preferred stock paying a 15 percent dividend. Holders of the investment units also could exchange their preferred stock for a senior debenture paying 14 percent.

Everyone expected this new paper to sell at discounts. As can be seen, the amount was far less than what Robert Anderson and Pickens had offered earlier. The result would be that GIG participants would cash out handsomely, but the others would not do well at all.

GIG would then liquidate Gulf over a period as long as three years. If all went according to plan, GIG, plus the holders of shares from the unit sales, would have a profit of between $2.08 billion and $5.05 billion.[22]

All of this structuring was to be done through Drexel. Three years later, Pickens spoke of the bank's role. "They devised a plan that was very loose, and they explored some ideas, but nothing came of it. Even so, we said: 'Hey, these [Drexel] guys are not playing games. They're really seriously trying to figure out a way that could finance something.'"[23]

The plan was never implemented, but had it gone through it would have been the first classic Milken deal. Yet, Milken was not mentioned in the press reports at the time. As far as the *Wall Street Journal* was concerned, Mike Brown was Drexel's point man, and John Sorte, the firm's expert on oil and natural gas mergers, was the key player. For good reason. Traders and investment bankers were supposed to be separated by what was called a "Chinese Wall," to prevent conflicts of interest. With the Gulf deal, Drexel breached the wall.[24]

GIG, which now had 21.3 percent of Gulf common, made a $65 a share tender on February 22, 1984, which Gulf characterized as "unfair and inadequate." The board said it would explore "all alternatives," which was taken to mean it was prepared to be acquired by a third party rather than submit to Pickens. Gulf common, which had been selling in the mid-50s, moved higher on heavy volume.

Matters came to a climax on March 5, when, with the price of Gulf up to 69½, the company's directors met to consider several bids. Atlantic Richfield was there, with an offer of $72 a share. Newcomer Chevron held back for the moment, but was prepared to move if it saw an opening. Its

CEO, George Keller, would later confirm that he had been asked to be a white knight: "The main thing that made us decide to try the acquisition was that I got a call from Jimmy Lee saying, 'Help!'"[25] Kohlberg, Kravis, Roberts was prowling on the periphery, structuring a leveraged buyout for cash and debt with a face value of $87.50 a share.[26] In addition, a Gulf management team was attempting to put together an LBO of its own using junk bonds.

Chevron ultimately won the contest on March 5, with $80 per share in cash, which worked out to more than $13 billion. This gave credence to Pickens' contention that old business was united against new business, and to his claim of being the shareholders' friend. The movement that had begun with Pickens thinking about the establishment of a royalty trust ended by increasing the market value of Gulf shares by $6.5 billion. "That was $6.5 billion that would never have been made if Mesa and GIG hadn't come on the scene," said Pickens. There was more to come. According to one estimate, during the 1980s more than $100 billion went to petroleum company shareholders through major mergers, acquisitions, and recapitalizations.[27]

Taken together, Pickens' three major forays—against Cities Service, General American, and Gulf—had enriched shareholders by $9 billion. He had taken the risks, and while he did well in each case, others had made even more money.

Who were those others? GIG, which owned 21.7 million shares, of which Mesa had 14.5 million, took in $1.74 billion, which translated into a profit of $760 million.[28] Mesa's share was around $500 million, which, after taxes, took Pickens to that $300 million he had said the company needed back in 1983, before he started hunting.

Significantly, the largest single categories of Gulf stockholders after GIG were the arbitrageurs and the institutions. The former owned 20 million shares worth $1.6 billion, while the institutions, in the aggregate, owned more than 55 percent of the stock. The College Retirement Equity Fund (CREF), one of the biggest institutional holders, owned 1.7 million shares.[29]

Consider what this implied. While it had been distressing to management, Pickens' attempt to obtain control of Gulf cheered institutional and individual stockholders and the arbitrageurs, who delighted in seeing the price of their shares rise to new heights. Indeed, institutional investors, owners of high-yield mutual funds, owners of certificates of deposit issued by thrift institutions that were heavily invested in junk bonds, holders of insurance policies issued by Executive Life, and others invested in junk were among the chief beneficiaries of the takeovers of this period.

Pickens basked in the publicity his raids attracted, and he continued to swear that he never would accept greenmail. To do so, he said, would besmirch his reputation and trivialize the transcendent point he wanted to make regarding the management of dormant companies. Neither immodestly nor inaccurately, Pickens later wrote:

> My name became synonymous with the corporate takeover. There had never been anything like it in the annals of Wall Street. It made me a controversial figure in corporate America, and clearly changed my life. One oil company director told me not long afterwards, "We spend more time talking about Boone Pickens at our board meetings than anything else."[30]

Soon, there would be talk of Pickens running for governor of Texas, perhaps as a prelude to a shot at the presidency. He always derided such reports, but he took care to burnish his reputation. There were lectures, panel meetings, and after-dinner talks. A typical speech came after a dinner in Pickens' honor at the Regency Hotel in New York on June 5, when Mayor Edward Koch awarded him a crystal apple in recognition of the immense fees generated by the Gulf takeover for New York's financial community. Pickens then introduced a frisky monkey, saying, deadpan, "I'd like you to meet Jimmy Lee."[31]

DREXEL AS PREDATOR KING

As a result of the Gulf contest, Drexel became better known outside the investment banking community. With this, the first of its attempted hostile takeovers, it became the symbol for the movement. Drexel was to be the leading source for what Joe Perella, then a takeover specialist at First Boston, would call "the private pools of predatory capital."[32] If Milken could raise $1.7 billion quickly for Pickens in the Gulf deal, why couldn't he raise even more for others? No company would be safe. Suddenly, it had become imaginable for small players like Mesa to make bids for some of the nation's largest concerns. "Big companies used to worry only about takeover threats from other big companies," said Jay Higgins, head of Salomon's merger department. "But with Drexel doing the financing, anybody long on ideas and short on capital is a threat."[33]

In December 1984, the *Wall Street Journal* ran one of its increasingly frequent articles on the new finance, this a front-page piece entitled, "How 'Junk Financings' Aid Corporate Raiders in Hostile Acquisitions." Fred Joseph was quoted as saying, "There are very few companies too large for a takeover when our type of financing is used." Mike Brown noted that the firm was working on three deals—for $6 billion, $4 billion, and $600 million—implying that it wouldn't be difficult to raise that kind of money, or even more, if needed. "From a purely mechanical point of view, we could do any size acquisition," added David Kay, an investment banker who headed Drexel's mergers-and-acquisitions department. "But from the real world point of view, it wouldn't be appropriate to create the perception that our technique has the potential of toppling American institutions that are properly at the top of the pile. IBM isn't a candidate for takeover because it is an exquisitely run company."[34]

The article went on to discuss "Drexel's list of 400 corporate and individual investors," including "insurance companies like Equitable Life Assurance Society; wealthy individuals like the Bass brothers of Fort Worth, Texas; trust departments of banks; pension plans, and corporations like Penn Central. But savings and loan associations are the largest category of investors in Drexel advised financings."[35]

Not once in the article was any mention made of Michael Milken, who had made it all possible. He remained an invisible man, which is the way he wanted it to be.[36]

This would change, however. In 1986, Harvard Business School professor Samuel Hayes III told *Business Week,* "The only figure comparable to Milken who comes to mind is J. P. Morgan, Sr." Such hyperbole had its origins in the Gulf contest.

The takeover movement in petroleum companies was in full swing. Less than a month before the Gulf takeover, Texaco had purchased Getty for $10.1 billion in a hotly disputed contest that wound up in the courts, establishing a record that Gulf soon eclipsed.[37] Later, Mobil agreed to purchase Superior for $45 a share, a $5.7 billion transaction. Deals even bigger were on the way. In the seven years from Pickens' Gulf War to George Bush's, 657 American oil and natural gas companies were either merged or acquired.[38]

THE BUSINESS ROUNDTABLE BATTLES BACK

The activities Milken's financings made possible alarmed managements of large corporations. Calls for action to stop him were sounded in big business circles and transmitted to friends in Washington. The liaison between the two groups was the Business Roundtable, which became the most important lobbying organization against hostile takeovers.

Originated in 1972 through the efforts of Secretary of the Treasury John Connally and Federal Reserve Chairman Arthur Burns, the Business Roundtable was composed of the CEOs of 200 of the largest American corporations, whose combined revenues came to approximately half of the country's GNP. The Roundtable could be counted on to support a wide variety of measures to benefit big business. Its first crusade had been for lower corporate taxes, and others followed—*for* American retaliation against purportedly unfair foreign-trading practices, *against* government-mandated employee fringe benefits, *for* revision of the antitrust laws. The Roundtable opposed stronger clean-air legislation, helped defeat a proposed consumer protection agency, had a role in killing a bill to legalize secondary boycotts in the construction industry, and campaigned for a measure to make notifications of plant shutdowns voluntary.[39]

As the takeover movement gathered steam, it drew the Roundtable's attention. That the campaign against takeovers was self-serving was obvious. Pickens pointed out the hypocrisy: "Look at the Business Roundtable. They were lobbying on Capitol Hill in the '70s and the early '80s and saying, 'Leave us alone—acquisitions are just the free-enterprise system working at its best.'" (This, of course, was when large companies were acquiring smaller ones in friendly and occasionally unfriendly bids.) "Then along came Milken, and that's when those guys went back up on the Hill and said, 'The big one getting the little one is free enterprise; the little one getting the big one is un-American.'"[40] In Pickens' view, "They'll take stockholders' money and lobby in Congress to get legislation against stockholders."[41]

Later, Pickens learned that the Roundtable had actually called a special meeting to deal with him, and that General Motors CEO Roger Smith had asked each person attending to contribute $50,000 to create a fund to "get Boone Pickens to stop takeovers."[42]

Pickens' primary antagonist was the Roundtable's chairman, Andrew Sigler, CEO of Champion International. The two men had widely disparate views regarding corporate responsibility. Sigler often declared that the overriding concern of American corporations should be the public interest, and that shareholder rights were secondary. Sigler, who had been greenmailed on three occasions, considered raiders to be irresponsible rogues who poisoned the business atmosphere, and thought they had to be removed.[43]

Pickens shot back that Roundtable members weren't acting in the interests of the owners, simply because they were not owners of the companies they managed. "Individuals in Sigler's position might consider showing greater confidence in their companies by investing more of their own money in them," he said, adding that according to his calculations, the CEOs who composed the Roundtable owned less than 1/300 of 1 percent of the outstanding shares of the companies they managed.[44] "Believe it or not," Pickens said on another occasion, "9 percent of the CEOs from the Fortune 500 don't own a single share of stock in the companies they run. For all this, the typical CEO has absolute control of assets worth billions of dollars. I think they should have at least 75 percent of their net worth in their company's stock."[45]

Prompted by the Roundtable, during the spring and early summer of 1984, several congressional committees investigated takeovers. Senator J. Bennett Johnson (D. Louisiana) proposed a temporary ban of mergers among the top 50 petroleum companies. Johnson, from oil-rich Louisiana, might have been expected to come up with such a plan. "The attitude out there is eat or be eaten," said one of his aides, "and the companies we're hearing from are pretty much divided along those lines."[46] Unsurprisingly, the Johnson proposal won the quick approval of the American Petroleum

Institute and such firms as Unocal, Phillips, Ashland, and Sun, all considered prime takeover candidates.

"CAMEOMAIL" FROM PHILLIPS

Phillips' management recognized its vulnerabilities and prepared for an assault. In March 1984, the board asked shareholders to approve a charter amendment that would require any raider attempting a two-tier tender to obtain the approval either of the board or of the owners of 75 percent of the common stock. It was put into place the following month. In September, CEO William Douce announced that Phillips would purchase the energy operations of R. J. Reynolds for $1.7 billion, paying with cash and borrowings, thus leveraging the company and making it less attractive for takeover. He also lined up a defense fund of $5 billion from a consortium of banks headed by Morgan Stanley.

The following month, October 1984, Pickens announced that he had retained the services of the law firm of Skadden Arps, Slate, Meagher and Flom, which specialized in takeovers. Pickens played it coy when asked about targets, saying only that he was "always thinking about ways to enhance values for Mesa shareholders."[47] Rumor had it that he would soon go after either Unocal or Phillips. Some thought he might make bids for both simultaneously. The fact that the latter idea had credence demonstrated a growing confidence that Drexel could provide almost unlimited funds. That summer, Pickens had asked Drexel to raise $500 million to be used for the purchase of Mesa Royalty Trust shares, and it was done in a matter of days.

Pickens always enjoyed fooling the pundits. On this occasion, he opted to work on his own, without the aid of an investment bank. Pickens gathered a group not unlike GIG, as well as a consortium of commercial banks. Soon, a spokesman for Wagner & Brown, a member of the group, revealed that Pickens had $800 million in commitments lined up, which, taken with bank pledges, raised its total to more than $2 billion. With this takeover fund in hand, Pickens started making purchases of Phillips and Unocal shares. By the end of November, Mesa had accumulated close to 8 million shares of each company.

On December 2, Mesa Partners announced a tender for 23 million shares of Phillips' 118 million shares at $60 a share. As expected, Phillips announced that it would fight, and the contest began. Once again, it was a dirty campaign. Allegations of insider trading were planted through leaks to the press. In a repeat of the Cities Service and Gulf experiences, Pickens was put through the investigative wringer. Phillips hired private detectives to explore Pickens' past. Pickens promptly got an injunction to bring this to a halt. A Phillips representative asked a person he thought was a Pickens enemy, "Can you tell me where his children are located?" But the person told Pickens. "I really don't think they were going to do any harm to them," Pickens said. "I think what they were going to do was to harass them."[48] This information, which came from Pickens, was not challenged by management; if Pickens lacked proof, these charges would have opened the way for libel and slander suits. None were filed.

Phillips, based in the small town of Bartlesville, Oklahoma, played on fears of residents that Pickens would move the firm elsewhere and so destroy the local economy. Pickens' promise to move his own home to Bartlesville did not assuage local anxieties. TV newsmen rolled into town to interview residents, who looked like refugees from Norman Rockwell paintings and spoke in terms that recalled the Okies of the 1930s.

This time, Pickens had few institutional allies. Having been burned on the Cities deal when Pickens withdrew and share prices collapsed, some of the institutions were wary of him. Since they controlled approximately half of Phillips' stock, their attitude would be crucial. One shareholder, CREF energy analyst Philip P. Popkin, said he was likely to tender his shares because he doubted there would be a higher bid. But Robert Kirby, CEO of Capital Group, the largest owner of Phillips shares, with 4 percent of the common, said, "We've been investors in Phillips for four or five years. We feel management has done a good honest job." Kirby, who had also sided with management against Pickens in the Gulf deal, added that he believed Pickens might accept greenmail, and so leave the other shareholders in the lurch. Other large institutional owners refused to comment, suggesting that Pickens would have a tough selling job this time.[49]

The situation was further complicated by a long-anticipated institutional action, energized by the California state treasurer, Jesse Unruh. The state's pension fund was the largest owner of Texaco stock and had lost out when Texaco paid greenmail to the Bass brothers, who had attempted a raid. In January 1985, Unruh met with the New York City comptroller, Harrison J. Goldin and New Jersey's chief investment manager, Roland Machold. "Guys," said Unruh, "in this room we control the future of Phillips. We need only to vote the proxy."[50] He then brought together other interested parties to organize the Council of Institutional Investors, composed of 22 members with assets of more than $100 billion, hoping to harness the power of the institutions to help maximize values.

Pension plans of various kinds controlled half the nation's common stock. By the end of the decade, their assets would approach $2 trillion. The potential for a realization of Peter Drucker's pension plan socialism had arrived. Yet, it was only a potential. Unruh and the others were disturbed about greenmail, but, for the moment, they had no desire to proceed further than using their influence to discourage its use. Presumably, this meant they would pressure managements to accept a reasonable cash offer.

The council's first priority was to dissuade Phillips from paying greenmail. No attempt was made to contact Pickens. According to Pickens, Phillips *had* offered him greenmail, which he initially rejected. Then, perhaps realizing that he lacked adequate funding, he accepted. On December 21, Joe Flom, the Phillips lawyer, telephoned Pickens and offered him $53 a share, which would give the partners a profit of $89 million. He also had to agree never again to threaten Phillips. Pickens replied with an offer to sell half of his group's shares, on condition that the firm would commit $1 billion to repurchasing shares the following year and increase the dividend. He was to receive an additional $25 million for expenses. In this way, the group would have a profit, and Pickens could continue to claim a role as shareholder advocate.[51]

Was it truly greenmail? Pickens later claimed to have boosted shareholder values, since, on the day of the offer, Phillips common was trading $18 higher than it had been when he made the announcement of the raid. To this day, he denies having accepted greenmail, but, in fact, he did. Some on the Street dubbed the maneuver "cameomail," or disguised greenmail.[52]

Unruh certainly considered the payment to be greenmail. The Phillips deal energized the Council of Institutional Investors, as Unruh swore to play a greater role in such undertakings in the future. Pickens was irate at Unruh's allegations and, soon after, told the council, "We put 14 points in the Phillips stock, invested a billion dollars, fought the lawsuits, and took the heat. Did any of you help us? Hell no. When are some of you guys going to put some points in the stock? You haven't done a godamned thing but sit here and criticize me. And we helped make you millions of dollars."[53]

Pickens never discussed the reasons for his failure; yet, these were quite obvious. He had received little help from the institutions and not much more from the arbitrageurs, who wanted a higher price and so looked for the appearance of a rival raider. His group had raised a huge sum, but not enough for a two-tier offer. Had he employed Drexel's services, it might have gone differently. He knew this. So did Milken. It would be different the next time out.

Pickens left Phillips an exhausted company, obliged to take steps to restructure itself with a large debt-to-equity ratio, but one that also had attracted the attention of the Drexel bankers. Here was a situation that might interest a Drexel client. Several were approached. In the end, Carl Icahn decided to make a play for the company with Drexel's aid. To make certain of his intentions, Joseph entered into an agreement that Icahn would not seek merely to greenmail the company.[54]

In time, Icahn would become an even bigger player than Pickens, but in 1984, he was known as the man who had raided the likes of Bayswater, Tappan, Hammermill, and ACF—not the stuff of which legends are made.

Unlike Pickens, Icahn was concerned primarily with matters of efficiency and values, and he did not pretend to stand for any philosophical principle.

Like most raiders, Icahn generally had attacked on two fronts simultaneously, seeking proxies while making a tender offer with the backing of bank commitments. The problem with such tactics was that, more often than not, leaks developed from some of the banks, so the price of the stock would run up while the raider was accumulating shares. To prevent this, Drexel issued the first of its "highly confident" letters, saying it would be able to raise $4.05 billion for the undertaking, most of which were to be in the form of senior notes, senior subordinated notes, and preferred stock, to be sold to Milken's army of buyers. The idea, conceived by Leon Black, provided a short-cut for Milken and the New York-based investment bankers.

The Icahn foray was to follow the pattern of the Gulf deal. Icahn would form a shell company for which Drexel would sell junk bonds backed by Phillips' assets, which would be redeemed through the sale of parts of Phillips, plus the cash flow from what remained. All this would be done without participation of commercial banks or other investment banks. Milken's task force would orchestrate the deal.[55]

Drexel stood to garner large profits from the operation. There was $1 million up front for the letter, plus $\frac{1}{8}$ of 1 percent of the commitments obtained if the deal did not go through, or 20 percent of Icahn's profits if he sold the stock obtained through the tender. In addition, those clients who made the commitments were to receive from Icahn a fee of $\frac{3}{8}$ of 1 percent. When Icahn realized just how high the fees would be, he decided to raise only $1.5 billion (after all, the fees would cut into his profits). The price for the Drexel commitment was $7.5 million.[56]

Milken had no trouble lining up buyers, including the Belzbergs and others from his inner group. Icahn purchased 7.5 million Phillips shares in preparation for the contest. In response, Phillips hired attorney Martin Lipton, famous for having designed the poison-pill defense, which triggered a recapitalization, making life miserable for a takeover artist once he spun into action. Phillips adopted its poison-pill resolution, designed to be set off when a raider gathered 30 percent of the stock, which would have to be voted on by the stockholders.

The Phillips meeting to consider recapitalization took place on February 22, 1985, and, for two reasons, it was one of the more significant moments of the junk decade. First, the highly confident letter, and its implementation, was an awesome display of Drexel's power. From then on, raiders could rely completely on Drexel. Second, and perhaps even more portentous over the long run, was the role played by the institutions. Thomas Acietuno, who led the California State Teachers Retirement System, voted its 124,000 shares against recapitalization, saying, "There are certain aspects of the recap plan we don't approve . . . the staggered board, the poison pill . . . ." He added, "We're opposed to greenmail, and we think the payment to T. Boone Pickens *was* greenmail. We are voting in opposition to the recapitalization."[57]

The takeover failed, in the most impressive display of shareholder power to that time. Yet, the institutions didn't win ultimately, since Phillips was forced to pay Icahn greenmail to the tune of $25 million. The real winner was Milken, who had again demonstrated his ability to raise large sums on short notice.

DON'T GO HUNTING WITHOUT IT

The following month, March of 1985, Drexel assisted Coastal Corp. in its $2.46 billion takeover of American Natural Resources, a deal that began as hostile but ended on a relatively friendly basis. On this occasion, banks provided most of the required funds, with Milken selling $600 million of junk notes and preferred stock. It was the first large, successful takeover by a Drexel client, and it seemed clear there would be many more.

It was an active season. Sir James Goldsmith was seeking Crown Zellerbach, after greenmail expeditions against St. Regis Paper and the Continental Group, and he was accumulating shares in Colgate. Scarcely pausing after Phillips, Icahn made a bid for Uniroyal. Ted Turner was after CBS. Drexel was in the midst of all these deals. Other banks participated, but none had as much exposure and press coverage as Drexel.

The firm relished its new reputation. At Drexel's 1986 Institutional Research Conference in Beverly Hills that spring, a specially made film was shown. It began with a shot of a limousine pulling in front of "The Fat and Lethargic Corp." Out stepped a raider waving a credit card. Sweeping past the guards, he headed toward the boardroom, where an executive meeting was taking place. The chairman accepted the card, and as he placed it in an imprinter, the other members strapped on golden parachutes and jumped out the window. Next, there was a close-up of the credit card: It said "Drexel Titanium," with a credit line of $10 billion. It was waved by none other than Larry Hagman, the unscrupulous J. R. Ewing of TV's "Dallas." With a wicked grin, Hagman advised the audience, which contained many raiders, "Don't go hunting without it." Everyone roared.[58]

III

DEBACLE

9

THE COUNTERATTACK

Even while attempting the Phillips takeover, Pickens prepared for his next target, Los Angeles-based Unocal. This was no fat, sluggish concern. "Its oil replacement rate had consistently been among the highest in the industry, and its findings and development costs among the lowest," said Dillard Spriggs, president of New York consulting firm, Petroleum Analysis. Unocal had pioneered in such alternate energy sources as shale oil and thermal energy. It was soundly and conservatively managed. At the end of 1984, Unocal had $5.7 billion in cash and equivalents against $1.1 billion in long-term debt. With 173 million shares outstanding, selling in the mid-30s, it was a $6 billion-plus company.[1]

THE ANTITAKEOVER ALLIANCE

Unocal CEO Fred Hartley was aware of the possibility of a raid on the firm. Assistant general counsel Sam Snyder began monitoring raiding activities in 1983. That year, the board applied "shark repellent" by creating Unocal as the parent for Union Oil of California. It also instituted staggered elections for the board and a requirement of a supermajority of 80 percent to approve bylaw-change proposals from insurgent shareholders.

Hartley enlisted support in Washington, including the services of former Senate majority leader Howard Baker. Like other CEOs of petroleum companies, he lobbied for legislation favorable to industry interests, but, unlike the others, he wanted legislative action to halt takeovers. This emphasis on Washington wasn't original. DuPont CEO Irving Shapiro, one of the Business Roundtable's prime movers during its early years, favored a continuing and developing alliance between business and government. He believed "the only practical course [for businessmen] is to regard as essentially permanent the system that has evolved. Call it what you will—'quasi-public', 'half-free enterprise', 'the mixed economy'. By any name, it is a system in which heavy government involvement with business will remain a fact of life for business."[2]

Such had been the goal of some businessmen since the nation's founding, and, of course, many other special interest groups use political action committees to exert influence in Washington. In the past, each industry had used its own PAC. Now, the Business Roundtable hoped to present a united view of big business, a more formal voice for ideas generated at Bohemian Grove and other places where corporate leaders gathered. Pickens described the old-boy atmosphere succinctly: "It's all done at lunch."[3]

Later, it would be realized that Hartley had found the winning combination to thwart Pickens. Together with the Business Roundtable and other allies, including the American Petroleum Institute, he had fashioned the same kind of alliance of political liberals and economic and business conservatives that had stopped James Ling in the late 1960s.

Dillon Read Chairman, Nicholas Brady, whose firm had conducted investment banking business for Union Oil since the 1920s, was a key figure in the new alliance. Even before the Unocal contest, Brady had become a critical player in the antiraider movement. Dillon Read refused to work for raiders and firmly opposed what Brady termed "this junk bond takeover binge": "Busting up corporations for the sake of a few extra dollars for shareholders is a very short term view. We ought to be a little careful in allowing a system that dismembers corporations."

Brady had undisguised contempt for those who were attempting to disrupt the neat, well-organized universe of relationship banking, in which he had grown up and now embodied. When a journalist suggested that, given their intelligence and drive, the bright, aggressive yuppies might be better employed in some other line of work, he seemed astonished. "These aren't the best," he retorted. "This is all they can do. These are the people you want to keep off the streets . . . the best you can say about them is that they are gamblers and hustlers."[4]

Brady was a product of an earlier generation of Wall Streeters, with a vastly different background from that of Milken, Joseph, and the others at Drexel. Brady's forebears had been major figures in the creation of the electrical utility industry and had played a role in the founding of the automobile industry. By American standards, the Bradys were "old money," among the largest landholders in New Jersey, associated with the DuPonts, the Rockefellers, and the Mellons. Brady had been chairman of the Jockey Club! One does not rise much higher among American aristocrats than that.

Few on the Street were as well connected politically as Brady. From spring 1982 to January 1983, he had served as Senator from New Jersey, selected by Governor Thomas Kean to fill out the term of Harrison Williams, who had been forced to step down due to criminal charges. Brady was a member of the National Bipartisan Committee on Central America in 1983 and, in 1985, was chairman of the Commission on Executive, Legislative, and Executive Salaries.

Thus, Brady was a splendid example of the old order, which Milken, Pickens, and others of the new order threatened. How would Brady and his kind endure if those who scorned relationship banking prevailed? No less than Hartley, Brady wanted to see Pickens defeated. The threat to the old boys concerned money and power, but on another level, it actually was cultural.

Throughout the spring of 1984, Brady shuttled between New York and Washington speaking out against the raiders. In testimony before a congressional committee, Brady spoke of abuses in takeovers and strongly urged passage of legislation to hinder them. Fred Joseph tried to retaliate: "He was being paid $5–20 million by Unocal, and that was not revealed," noted Joseph. "I thought this was unusual and so I followed him on the next panel and I said, 'I think we need to get this record straight, that Nick Brady is working for Unocal.'"[5]

THE CONTEST FOR UNOCAL BEGINS

In November 1984, the proxy firm of D.F. King placed Unocal on its "stock watch." Soon after, Brady telephoned Hartley to say "Fred, you're under accumulation." Who could be responsible? The betting was that one of the giants would move in, the best guess being Standard Oil of Indiana. Pickens was another suspect, but, at the time, he was deeply involved with Phillips, so attention turned elsewhere. By the end of February 1985, however, it had become evident that Pickens was the one, with Drexel as his lead bank.

Pickens began his campaign by lining up a consortium of lenders, including Texas Commerce, Mellon, and the Security Pacific National, which happened to be Unocal's primary bank, to create a fund of $1.2 billion, to be employed in the bid by Mesa Partners II. By midmonth, Pickens had filed with the SEC, disclosing his ownership of 5 percent of Unocal, and then increased his stake to close to 10 percent, or 15 million shares. The total cost was some $645 million. When asked about his intentions, Pickens drawled that all he was after was a good investment.

On February 28, Unocal's board adopted another shark repellent in the form of a requirement that anyone seeking to nominate a director or bring up business at the annual meetings had to give the board at least 30 days notice. The next annual meeting was scheduled for April 29, so Pickens wouldn't have much time to act.

On learning of Pickens' accumulation, Hartley opted to play it cool. "We agree that our shares are a good investment," he wrote to shareholders.[6] He also started to retaliate. Hartley flew to New York to meet with bankers from Dillon Read and Goldman Sachs and executives from the public relations firm of Hill & Knowlton. Others would come in later, including veteran Washington lobbyist Charls Walker and the former assistant secretary of the Treasury for tax policy, John Chapoton.

None of these would lead the counterattack, however. Unocal's assistant general counsel, Sam Snyder had concluded that target companies had been mistaken in using outsiders. The company's best defenders, he wrote in a 1983 memo to Hartley, were its own management people. "Nobody calls the shots at Union Oil Co. except the Union Oil Co." Hartley would be the point man. He took to the road to deliver what one Mesa official would call "sassy speeches" about corporate raiders.[7] "We must eliminate the legal fictions, tax code twists, the easy money, and the speculative mania that's making it so simple to destroy productive companies," he told a refiners group in Chicago on March 26.[8] He spoke of "the shadow world of the arbitrageurs," whose activities were ravaging corporate America, and he told another industry group, "We must close the door on those who seek only short-term profit without contributing to our industry and the economy as a whole."

Hartley usually included personal attacks against Pickens. "Clearly he's not buying into Unocal because it's a good long-term investment (which it is), or because he's the friend of small shareholders. He's doing it for personal gain." Hartley observed that Pickens had received bonuses of some $27 million from Mesa, largely from profits from the Gulf and Phillips deals, which was twice the total dividend amount paid to Mesa shareholders in 1984. Thus, Pickens was using Mesa as a vehicle for raids and taking the lion's share of the profits for himself.[9] Others had said the same, but none as insistently as Hartley. Pressure for action against hostile takeovers had been building before the Unocal contest, but Hartley provided the actual spark.

While Brady and Milken were cultural antithetical, Hartley and Pickens were diametric opposites in personality. Pickens was droll, engaging, and soft-spoken. Hartley had become known for his blunt, unsentimental style. After an oil spill from a Unocal rig had gushed 20,000 barrels of oil into the Santa Barbara Channel in 1969, Hartley was quoted in the *Wall Street Journal* as having said, "I'm amazed at the publicity for the loss of a few birds." When a Unocal shareholder at the 1984 annual meeting complained about the stock's price action, Hartley replied, "You look like an elderly fellow. Why don't you sell your stock and have a good time?" In 1985, a reporter asked when the 67-year-old Hartley would retire. Hartley roared, "It's none of your damn business." His power cruiser was fittingly named "My Way."

Pickens, for his part, used to tell these stories and others to depict Hartley as a blustering, insensitive bully. He might have exaggerated, but his barbs had some truth.[10]

The two men's plans for Unocal were also different. Pickens estimated that Unocal had around $80 per share in oil reserves. He would sell most of it and distribute the proceeds to the shareholders. Hartley thought of the company as a self-regenerating entity that existed for its officers and employees, and he was convinced that the way to increase earnings was to accelerate exploration.

In one of the many articles Pickens wrote in this period, he recalled a remark made to him by a Unocal director in 1982, which he felt illustrated the way Hartley thought. "He said that he told CEO Fred Hartley 'Fred, we're making a lot of money, why don't we raise the dividend?' And [Hartley] said, 'You're crazy. Why would we want to give a bunch of money to people we don't even know?'"[11] To this attitude, Pickens countered:

> Shareholders own the company. If shareholders do well, the employees of the company do well, as does the community in which the company operates and, in turn, the general economy. But the shareholders are at the top of the list. Otherwise the foundation of our economy weakens, the system falls apart, and the public interest is not served.[12]

On another occasion, he wrote, "Management's attitude is, 'We're going to take our salary and our bonus, and the shareholders are going to take the risks . . . .' This is absurd. These people have no ownership. They are actually dealing with other people's money."[13]

In early March, Hartley sued the Security Pacific Bank for breach of its fiduciary responsibilities; it was lending money to Pickens for the raid while still acting for Unocal, which meant that information about Unocal the bank had gathered over many years might now be used in support of the takeover. Pickens responded by charging Hartley with using "heavy-handed, bludgeoning tactics" to undermine Mesa's position with its banks.[14] "I am the champion of the small stockholder," declared Pickens. "Many American companies are heavily undervalued, and I blame their managements entirely." Among the worst were the oil companies. "I get letters every day that start, "Mr. Pickens, have you thought about our company?"[15]

Unocal's legal team also designed new shark repellents. Ricardo Mestres of Sullivan & Cromwell came up with an elaborate plan, given the code name of "Onion," under which Unocal would have created an intermediate holding company between itself and Union Oil. Pickens might eventually acquire a Unocal that would immediately be transformed into an empty shell packed with "every shark repellent known to man." If he succeeded in penetrating that shell's defenses, he would come upon another holding company, and then another, like the layers of an onion. And there were other plans, prepared in case of need.[16]

FRED HARTLEY GOES TO WASHINGTON

In one of several letters he wrote to Federal Reserve Board Chairman Volcker in the winter of 1985, Hartley asked for an investigation of the role of financial institutions in the wave of takeover attempts in the petroleum industry. "Through the threat of junk financing and loans to raiders and arbitragers, the banks and investment bankers are playing both sides of the game. . . . Abuses by some banks and financiers are feeding the takeover frenzy that strikes at the economic well-being of this country," he wrote, comparing their activities to the "stock and bond and credit schemes . . . of the 1920s—but on a multibillion dollar scale."

Volcker was favorably inclined toward this analysis. He thought that whenever a financial structure favored debt rather than equity, it became more vulnerable. "More cash flow must be dedicated to debt servicing, exposure to short-run increases in interest rates is magnified, and cushions against adverse economic or financial developments are reduced." Volcker acted by recommending that Regulation G, which limited margin requirements on stocks to a minimum of 50 percent, be applied to bonds as well.

In reporting the story the following December, the *Financial Times* said that Hartley's letter "may be remembered as the turning point in the current U.S. takeover boom."[17] Hartley had shifted the terms of the debate.

Hartley's major Washington target was Congress, where his lobbying efforts had won many supporters. He appeared before the Subcommittee on Securities of the Senate Banking, Housing, and Urban Affairs Committee, which was holding hearings on one of several measures to curb hostile takeovers. On April 3, Hartley implored the subcommittee to amend the tax laws to impede junk bond financing of takeovers and institute a moratorium on them.

> Clearly, the immediate need is for a congressional moratorium on hostile takeovers—a sort of "cooling off" period while the nation has a chance to realize that this speculative chain letter can't go on forever, and Congress has a chance to make needed changes in the tax code and elsewhere . . . . If the Russians had somehow quietly managed to murder five of the nation's leading oil companies—and were stalking the rest—surely I'm certain that Congress would be in an uproar, demanding action . . . . You may be looking at a target right now—you may be looking at the next guy to be murdered.[18]

Pickens bumped into Hartley after he testified. "Hi, Fred, how ya doing," he drawled when he saw Hartley approach. Hartley replied by growling, "Go away." "Be careful," countered the smiling Pickens. "You're talking to your largest shareholder now." "Isn't it a shame," snapped Hartley, and he turned aside.[19]

The subcommittee was chaired by Senator Alphonse D'Amato (R. New York), while its most knowledgeable and outspoken member was Senator William Proxmire (D. Wisconsin). Proxmire, who had always refused to accept campaign contributions, was viewed as a maverick—politically unpredictable, although usually voting liberal. So it came as something of a surprise when he opposed junk financing. "Everyone has his price but an honest man," said one businessman, referring to Proxmire. "You get him for nothing."

Proxmire was one of many legislators concerned about the intensity of the takeover movement, which, by then, had reached a frenzy point. He was adamantly opposed to the raiders. During the hearings, he said, "The rising tide of hostile takeovers threaten the very foundations of the American business system. In theory, hostile takeovers are supposed to increase efficiency by ousting inept corporate managers. In reality, they serve little purpose but to make millions for the professional raiders, their lawyers, and investment bankers."[20] Proxmire already had introduced a measure called the Corporate Productivity Act of 1985. He linked this measure to the growing federal deficit and debt in general. His speech on that occasion might have been written by Hartley:

> Corporate executives have argued for years that hostile takeovers loot corporate treasuries; undermine our ability to compete in world markets; force managements to sacrifice long-term strategy and the development of new products and services for short-term gains; inhibit innovation; lead to the misuse of capital; cheat shareholders; and cause job losses and economic upheaval that disrupt the lives of communities and employers. I agree and as a result believe that such takeover activity should be tempered, but not prohibited."[21]

Proxmire noted that there were three methods to curb takeovers. First, Congress could end the deductibility of interest paid on bonds used in hostile takeovers. Second, it might ask bank regulatory agencies to "jawbone and discourage banks and other financial depository institutions from making loans to finance unfriendly takeover bids."

The third approach would be to amend the Williams Act to forbid anyone owning more than 15 percent of a company's shares from acquiring more except through a tender offer, which would have to be submitted to the board of directors. If accepted, the offer then might be presented to the shareholders. To be approved, the bid would have to be approved by a two-thirds vote of shareholders of record on the date of the offer, the vote taking place within 60 business days of that offer. Finally, the independent members of the board would determine what was and was not a hostile takeover.

In effect, the Proxmire proposal would have ended hostile takeovers. It favored managers over owners and would have diluted ownership rights. Was this wise or fair? When a company is worth more dead than alive, it is usually a sign of management failure to serve shareholder interests. Was it in anyone's best interest to protect inefficient or inept managements?[22]

FUELING THE REGULATORY FIRES

Regulation was in the Washington air, and corporation lobbyists were bringing matters to a boil. While the D'Amato subcommittee held its hearings, Representative Peter Rodino (D. New Jersey), chairman of the House Judiciary Committee, introduced a measure to require investigation of the possible social and economic side effects of takeovers. Unocal had a major molybdenum mining subsidiary in New Mexico, and Atlantic Richfield's Robert Anderson was its leading landowner. One of New Mexico's senators, Peter Domenici, was chairman of the Senate Budget Committee. "I'm not an antitakeover Senator," said Domenici in a speech attacking junk financing. "I'm not even against hostile takeovers. But the get-rich-quick crowd has just gone too far."[23]

Fred Joseph approached Domenici after one of the early hearings and asked, "Do you know what a junk bond is?" "Nope," he replied, "But I bet you I am going to learn now."[24] So he did. In April 1985, Domenici introduced a bill to establish a temporary ban, until the end of the year, on hostile takeovers that were at least 20 percent financed through junk bonds. The measure also would have prohibited federally insured banks from purchasing more junk bonds. The Senator thought this would "buy time" to examine junk financing. The measure failed in committee. Several other bills were introduced in the House that would have ended tax deductions for interest on junk, which also failed to reach the floor.

Senator Timothy E. Wirth (D. Colorado), Chairman of the Subcommittee on Telecommunications, Consumer Protection, and Finance of the Senate Energy and Commerce Committee, prepared legislation that summer to require raiders to have financing in place before making bids. His draft would have restricted the takeover involvement of federally insured lending institutions, cut back on the 10-day period investors have before disclosing ownership of 5 percent of shares of a company, and obliged raiders to study and reveal the impact of their actions on communities involved.[25]

Joseph Perella, of First Boston, was troubled by these varied legislative activities and feared that Congress would hastily pass laws that could cripple beneficial takeovers and raids. "Congressmen don't understand the takeover game," he said. "But they have to get reelected and they need campaign contributions, and they understand that game very well."[26] Robert Linton agreed. When asked about the possibilities of restrictive legislation, he said, "There are all sorts of politicians getting up and talking about junk bonds that don't have the slightest idea of what they are." Joseph appeared in Washington to testify in defense of junk. By May, the *Washington Post* was reporting that "Today Joseph and other Drexel officials find themselves commuting to Washington to try to quell the anxiety of Congress over junk-bond financing."[27]

As the debate raged, Hartley again wrote to Volcker, urging him to "act now to curb this abusive use of credit." Sigler traveled to Washington to second the recommendation. They were persuasive. The powerful Fed Chairman announced an increase in the margin requirements for junk financing in hostile takeovers.

UNOCAL BEATS BACK THE RAIDERS

Throughout the counterattack by big business, Boone Pickens continued to accumulate Unocal shares. On March 27, 1985, Mesa purchased a block of 6.7 million shares for $322 million, giving Pickens' company a total of 23.6 million shares, or 13.6 percent of those outstanding. The stock rose $7/8$ of a point to close at $47^5/8$, making the holdings worth more than $1.1 billion.[28]

At the time, Pickens was in Beverly Hills to deliver a speech at the annual Drexel Institutional Research Conference and to confer with Milken and Joseph. He dismissed questions regarding his intentions for Unocal with a smile and a wink, but the following day, he said he would consider forcing a restructuring plan or a takeover, presumably through a proxy contest. Pickens had reason to believe he might win. During the past three months, more than 40 percent of the outstanding shares had been traded. Most appeared to have wound up in the accounts of arbs, who would favor a Pickens victory, or into accounts of rival raiders or white knights, who would have to come through with better offers. More to the point, he had received assurances from Joseph and Milken that the campaign was proceeding smoothly, with all of the needed financing falling into place.[29]

With all of this activity, one would have expected pressure to be exerted on the institutions by both sides. In late March, some institutions volunteered that they had not been contacted by either Hartley or Pickens, indicating, perhaps, that Pickens still hoped to obtain a royalty trust at Unocal, while management believed in the efficacy of its defenses. "I have given up trying to read Mr. Pickens' mind," said AmeriTrust executive vice president Richard C. Hyde. AmeriTrust owned some 500,000 Unocal shares, and Hyde indicated that he intended to sell some of them "from time to time." Some institutions were selling to lock in profits because if Pickens accepted greenmail, the stock would decline sharply. In addition, as a result of Pickens' activities, Unocal common had risen to the low 50s, and one institutional holder told the *Wall Street Journal* that he doubted the price would go over 55. At Unocal's current range, he said, "a lot of joy has gone out of the stock."[30]

Goldman Sachs partner Peter Sachs analyzed the takeover situation for Hartley. In his view, despite the action in Washington, Pickens had a good chance of carrying it off. "The most dangerous step [Mesa] can take is a two-pronged attack: commence a proxy fight and tender offer for at least half the stock, with financing from Drexel. If you do nothing, on May 3, Pickens will have maybe 80% or 90% of the stock because you can expect that many shares to be tendered. By June 15, he owns the company and you guys are in Paducah."[31]

As part of his strategy, Pickens asked for a delay in the company's annual meeting, still scheduled for April 29. He must have known he had no chance of this. On March 31, Hartley fired back, "Unocal doesn't intend to inconvenience its shareholders just because T. Boone Pickens wants a delay."[32] He also reduced the quorum required, to thwart any idea by Pickens to stay away from the meeting and withhold his shares. Hartley raised the quarterly dividend by 20 percent to 20 cents a share, the first time this had been done since 1981, and charged that Pickens had violated the securities law by telling the SEC that his intention in accumulating shares was for investment purposes only. But Hartley was defeated on a key element of his plan. Judge A. Wallace Tashima ordered Unocal to delay its meeting for two weeks, to May 13, so both sides could correct misstatements in their filings.

Pickens took little of this seriously. Over one weekend, claimed Drexel's John Sorte, the Milken group raised $3 billion from 140 sources, and other group banks chipped in another $500 million, for a tender offer for 64 million Unocal shares at $54 in cash. On April 8, the tombstone advertisements appeared in the *New York Times* and the *Wall Street Journal*.

This was to be a two-tier offer like the Gulf deal, in which the first to arrive would get cash and the second, $54 a share in junk paper that clearly would be worth less than that. If those who did not come in on the first half protested and refused to tender, the Pickens group could depose management, though, due to the staggered board, they would not gain control for two years. But if they had 90 percent of the proxies, Pickens could merge Unocal into Mesa without the consent of the board.

Hartley's initial response was to declare the offer "grossly inadequate," followed by a plea to shareholders not to act hastily. He then filed an antitrust suit against Mesa, Pickens, and others of the Mesa II group, in which he alleged that they had acted to limit petroleum exploration by their pursuit of takeovers and restructuring.[33] "I was prepared for a battle," he later recalled. "A very barbaric-type situation."[34]

Dillon Read and Goldman Sachs came up with a tender plan of their own, a poison pill that was revealed on April 17. Unocal's offer would be $72 in paper for 49 percent of the shares, to go into effect only upon the successful completion of the Mesa Partners II bid. It would include $20 of 14 percent senior-secured five-year notes; $32 of floating-rate 13½ percent notes, adjusted every three months to be 3¼ percent above the LIBOR rate; and $20 of senior-secured extendable 13½ percent notes due in 1997. This package would add more than $5.8 billion to Unocal's debt. The offer also contained a provision raising all the rates by 1 3/4 to 2 percent in case of a merger with another company.[35]

The tender excluded Pickens from the deal. Since the Unocal treasury shares would be canceled, Pickens would own 100 percent of the company, while the old shareholders would have received a package better than the one he had proposed. Therefore, Pickens would own a company with such a large debt that its viability would be questionable. The press dubbed this move a "Boone Bomb." Pickens characterized it as "a highly conditional poison pill," adding, "This latest proposal is a sick joke on Unocal shareholders," because it offered them "virtually nothing." All of that junk paper could bury the company, he seemed to be saying. He also sued to obtain permission to tender Mesa Partners II shares into the Unocal offer.[36]

At the time, the stock was trading at 48, but on the poison-pill news, it dropped to 46 5/8, showing that the investing public looked upon the Unocal offer as tantamount to an unattractive, partial-liquidating dividend.

The matter went before Judge Tashima, who, on April 29, denied Mesa Partners II a temporary restraining order. But on the same day, in a court in Delaware where Unocal was incorporated, Judge Carolyn Berger ordered the company to include Pickens in its buyback.[37] Unocal appealed to the state supreme court, where, on May 13, Justice G. T. Moore II decided in Unocal's favor. Mesa Partners II need not be included in the $72 tender.

The annual meeting was held at Unocal headquarters the same day, Tuesday, May 13, and during the session, those present learned of the Moore decision. Weary and fearful of what might come next, both Pickens and Hartley had reason to compromise. Shortly after the meeting, the two contestants agreed to parley in a neutral place, nearby New Otani. The conference got off to a bad start, when Hartley crudely tried to kid Pickens about having arrived in "your goddamned stretch limo." Nonetheless, a deal was struck. Mesa Partners II would be allowed to tender close to a third of its shares at $72 a share and would not sell the rest of its holdings for another year. Unocal would establish a royalty trust such as Pickens had first proposed, and it agreed to maintain the dividend.

The settlement was announced on May 20. Pickens showed grace. "Some you win, and some you lose, and some get rained out. This one we lost."[38] According to financial writers Allan Sloan and Jack Willoughby, Mesa Partners apparently lost $143 million in the contest. The stock and expenses had cost the group $1.16 billion, and the paper and remaining Unocal stock was worth $1.017 billion. But due to the vagaries of the tax code, Pickens would be able to claim a tax loss of $600 million. "Combine the $198 million refund with the $50 million Mesa saves because its Unocal expenses are tax-deductible, and you have a cool quarter billion-dollar gift from the public to T. Boone & Co."[39] Pickens later would claim that Mesa made a profit of $83 million on the deal because of this tax break.[40]

The Unocal War was a watershed event. A triumphant Hartley told reporters, "I'll be giving lectures on this for the next 20 years," and he started promptly before a senatorial subcommittee the following week:

> Corporate raiders and bust-up takeovers have not inspired one new technological innovation; they have just drained off investment capital. They have not strengthened companies: they have weakened them, loading surviving firms with onerous debt. They have not strengthened the nation's economy: they have weakened it . . . . While we may be able to compete with each other at home if all companies are similarly debt-ridden and weakened, certainly we can no longer succeed in the international markets where we once were world leaders. The whole world is laughing at us—especially the Japanese.

As expected, Pickens took a different view. "Fred Hartley took on $4 billion of debt just to keep his job. Where did Unocal's $4 billion dollars go? It went directly into the pockets of the shareholders and straight back into the U.S. economy."[41]

Pickens had failed to get seats on the board, and, while the royalty trust had been created, the remaining Unocal shareholders could not have been pleased. Later that year, the stock fell to $26, half of what it had been only a few months earlier and below where it had been before Pickens had taken an interest in the company. Unocal would decline even further the following year, hitting a low of $15.50 before rebounding. In all probability, Pickens had hedged his position, and whether he suffered a major loss is not known.

Once again, Pickens had accepted greenmail, although, as in the case of Phillips, it was not pure and simple greenmail. Since he was obliged to hold onto the Unocal shares for a year, his days of raiding were over, at least until then. While he would make plays for other companies, the Unocal battle was to be his last major foray. Pickens turned increasingly testy, rejecting assertions that he had accepted greenmail. He also resented what he perceived as ingratitude on the part of those he had enriched. "Eight hundred thousand stockholders made $13 billion [in the Unocal contest] . . . . We took all the risk, paid all the money, did all the work, and got less than 5 percent of the profit."[42] On another occasion, he said, somewhat bitterly, "We've put up 100 percent of the money and taken 100 percent of the risk and 100 percent of the heat, and had about 10 percent or 15 percent of the profit. The sad part of it was 85 percent or 90 percent of the other stockholders were being helped by our efforts and half of them didn't even realize it." Pickens felt he could have taken a much larger profit and just "let the stockholders hang," but he had rejected this notion.[43]

One might understand his position, but Pickens was a no philanthropist—that 10 percent to 15 percent of the profit was a handsome reward for his efforts.

THE TAKEOVER DEBATES

The Unocal War was over, but the debate regarding junk continued. On December 6, 1985, the Fed curbed the use of junk bonds in acquisitions. Senator Domenici called the move "a welcome step," while Pickens characterized it as "another move against stockholders," and Drexel's Jim Balog warned that the rule change could have both "intended and unintended effects."[44] The Fed's action was contentious, and defenders of junk took some solace in an SEC report on financing that concluded, "We argue that there is no cause for excessive concern about current levels of junk bond financing in takeovers. Nor is there justification for new regulatory initiatives aimed at curbing the use of this kind of debt issuance in takeover bids or indeed as it relates to any other aspect of corporate financing activity."[45]

Knowing that one of its core businesses was in danger, Drexel stepped up efforts at damage control. Drexel executives made contributions to the campaign war chests of senators and congressmen who would have input into any legislation dealing with junk bonds. Senators Bill Bradley (D. New Jersey), Frank Lautenberg (D. New Jersey), and Alan Cranston (D. California), would all be paid speakers at the 1986 Drexel Institutional Research Conference. Representative Wirth also was courted with donations, and his zeal for a strong anti-junk measure waned. Senator D'Amato had made it known during the hearings he chaired that he supported legislation to restrict thrift institutions from investing in junk and to limit the use of junk in takeovers.[46] Drexel hosted a fund-raiser for him in Beverly Hills, at which $33,000 was raised for his campaign account, and other banks held fund-raisers for him. In all, the investment community raised half a million dollars for D'Amato, whose attitude toward junk underwent a remarkable transformation. "The fact is that junk bonds have produced millions of jobs," he said with a straight face.[47] So it went. In 1984 and 1985, 31 measures were introduced to limit takeover activities, and none passed.

In late January 1986, Senator John Chafee (R. Rhode Island) addressed the "Stakeholders in America" about the chances for passage of legislation limiting takeovers. "Our menu is so full. I don't see anything taking place this year." The author of a proposal to eliminate the tax advantages of borrowing to finance certain takeovers, Chafee still believed some takeovers to be worthwhile. "American corporate management had to get its act in shape too. The picture isn't clear-cut." He commended Pickens and fellow raider, Irwin Jacobs, for forcing managements to be more responsive to shareholder rights, adding, "I've never been one of the world's great admirers of boards of directors. I think the behavior of directors in some of these things has been shocking."[48]

Nonetheless, pressure for legislation continued, and Milken still considered the situation dangerous. On November 16, he met with Fred Joseph,

Peter Ackerman, and Leon Black. Among other topics discussed was legislation pending before Congress regarding the barring of hostile takeovers via
junk financing. Milken later asserted that, at that meeting, he told his colleagues the string had run out on such deals. Troubled by the debates in
Washington, Milken requested that the firm stop engaging in takeovers on
behalf of acquirers, but he was unable to win the others' support.[49]

For a while, nothing consequential happened, as congressional committee
and subcommittee staffs investigated the impact of junk. One of the first reports came out of the House Energy and Commerce Committee's Subcommittee on Telecommunications, Consumer Protection, and Finance, which,
in December 1986, concluded:

> There is . . . no evidence to date that high yield bonds represent more than
> a small percentage of merger and acquisition financing. Moreover, given
> highly flexible innovations that traditionally characterize the securities mar-
> kets, there is no evidence to suggest that restricting high yield financing used
> in takeovers will stem the tide of overall merger and acquisition activity.[50]

At the time, Representative Dan Rostenkowski (D. Illinois), chairman of
the House Ways and Means Committee, had united with the Reagan administration in an effort at tax reform. Rostenkowski had no interest in
Hartley's agenda, but what emerged suited Hartley's purposes. Under the
terms of the Tax Reform Act that passed Congress on October 24, 1986,
marginal tax rates for individuals were lowered and simplified. While the
basic corporate rate also was lowered, the effective marginal rate for corporations was upped from 37.2 percent to 42.1 percent. More important,
scores of tax loopholes were closed. The investment tax credit was eliminated, and an alternate minimum tax was passed to prevent some forms of
tax avoidance. While there was no connection between the Act and the on-
going debate on junk financing, the changes made debt less attractive than
previously had been the case. This was not the death knell for the theory of
Modigliani-Miller, but the Act did make it less relevant.[51]

In April 1987, Representative Edward Markey (D. Massachusetts), chairman of the House Subcommittee on Telecommunications and Finance, introduced the Tender Offer Reform Act. It was discussed during the next few
months, and on the morning of October 19, the subcommittee worked out
final details. That day the stock market crashed. Markey commented, "Well,
the events of October 19 caused us to defer further legislative action on tender offers."[52]

Unable to obtain satisfactory federal legislation, the Business Roundtable and its allies took their campaign to states where large firms were
domiciled and were under threat of takeovers, and they succeeded beyond

expectations. In August 1987, the state of Washington passed a tough anti-takeover law, primarily to protect its largest company, Boeing, from a threatened raid by Pickens. Indiana passed a similar law when Dynamics Corp. of America threatened CTS. Minnesota acted to protect Dayton Hudson from the Dart Group. Arizona did the same when it appeared that Greyhound was under attack. Massachusetts enacted an anti-takeover law when Revlon went after Gillette. North Carolina, Florida, Louisiana, and Nevada passed laws under similar circumstances. In time, 21 states passed legislation limiting the holding of junk by certain institutions.[53]

Absent anything else, legislative action, coupled with opposition from the executive branch and the regulatory agencies, would have sufficed to prevent Pickens, Icahn, and other raiders from making further forays. It wouldn't have happened suddenly or dramatically, but there would have been fewer takeovers.

Even so, the raiders had one more major battle to fight, and the public had one more landmark contest to marvel at. In late 1988, Wall Street and much of the rest of the nation witnessed the making of the largest LBO of them all. Ross Johnson, CEO of RJR Nabisco, set it off with a stab at taking the company private through a tender offer that would require $17 billion. The price clearly was quite low, and other players soon entered the arena. Kohlberg, Karvis, Roberts, backed by Drexel, ultimately won the contest with an offer that worked out to $31 billion, which required it to raise $25 billion quickly.

The financing, which came in several tiers, made some of James Ling's pioneer efforts look like child's play. At the senior level, approximately $13 billion was in bank debt, more than half of which was taken by foreign institutions. It came in three tranches—a $5.25 billion term loan, a $6 billion sale-of-assets bridge loan, and a $1.5 billion bridge refinancing facility. The bridges would be retired once KKR placed new RJR bonds. Once again, it appeared that Drexel had the power to help raid just about any company. However, the RJR Nabisco contest would come to be seen as the last successful, large-scale takeover.

On September 15, 1988, outgoing President Reagan named Nick Brady secretary of the Treasury, and Brady continued in that role in the new Bush Administration. Now, one of Wall Street's most prominent opponents of junk financing would be in a position of enormous power. "More than anyone else, he [Brady] put T. Boone Pickens out of power," said Dillon Read's new chairman, John Birkelund. "Pickens hasn't made a move since he lost Unocal."[54]

10

THE GREAT DEBACLE

In the autumn of 1985, a delegation from the Business Roundtable called on Representative John Dingell (D. Michigan), Chairman of the Subcommittee on Oversight and Investigations of the House Committee on Energy and Commerce, and one of the most powerful members of Congress. Dingell was known as a forthright opponent of hostile takeovers. His district was heavily industrialized, and Dingell was on a first-name basis with many CEOs of large companies. Big business was a family affair; Dingell's wife worked in public relations at General Motors.

Dingell was also strongly pro-union. For the previous year, "National Journal" had gauged his votes on social issues and economic matters as 77 percent and 76 percent liberal respectively. Dingell had voted *for* the Equal Rights Amendment, *against* restrictions on abortions, *against* the MX missile, *against* increased aid to El Salvador, and *for* the nuclear freeze.[1]

The purpose of the Business Roundtable's meeting with Dingell was a discussion of antitakeover activities. Dingell assured the deputation that the matter was being studied. Further, an investment banker, a risk arbitrageur, and a corporate raider were being investigated and soon would be indicted.[2]

THE TWO-PRONGED ASSAULT

The first major opposition to takeovers had come from threatened businessmen like Fred Hartley. Traditional bankers, like Nick Brady, sometimes had been enlisted in their cause. As has been discussed, these businessmen lobbied for legislation and won support in Congress. When the alliance of old-line businessmen and liberal legislators came up with programs to hinder the efforts of takeover players like Pickens and Milken, it seemed a reprise of the Ling experience.

In both instances, a second front developed. In Ling's case, it was action from the Justice Department, which eventually brought him down. With Milken, the challenge would be a development out of the SEC, unrelated to the outcry in Washington; this first led to prosecution of some minor players in the takeover contests and then went up the ladder to end with Milken.

On May 12, 1986, while Congress debated several antitakeover bills, Drexel investment banker Dennis Levine was arrested on charges of insider trading in 54 stocks. His take had come to $12.6 million. This was hardly big money for people in his position during the junk era; it was small next to what Milken received, but impressive by the standards of ordinary mortals.

That Levine was unethical was obvious—his was a case of out-and-out avarice—but he also was foolish and shortsighted. Attempting to explain himself later, Levine said, "At the root of my compulsive trading was an inability to set limits. Perhaps it's worth noting that my legitimate success stemmed from the same root. My ambition was so strong it went beyond rationality, and I gradually lost sight of what constitutes ethical behavior."[3]

Two months later, on July 17, LTV filed for bankruptcy under Chapter 11, defaulting on more than $1.7 billion in debt in the form of junk bonds issued in the 1960s for some of James Ling's large takeovers. It was the biggest junk default to that time. There was no connection between the Levine indictment and the LTV failure, but, in retrospect, they may be viewed together as preludes to the end of the junk decade.

SEC Chief of Enforcement Gary Lynch and U.S. Attorney Rudolph Giuliani offered Levine a plea bargain on condition that he name his accomplices. Levine accepted, and, on February 20, 1987, he was sentenced to only two years in prison, plus a fine of $362,000. Levine seemed little different from scores of other errant bankers. His transgressions would not have been front-page news, except for Rudolph Giuliani.

The Levine indictment was only the first step in what Giuliani expected to be the most sensational criminal disclosures in Wall Street history. He had positioned himself for this mission by stepping down as the number-three person in the Justice Department, to become a U.S. attorney in 1983. During the next two years, he had refused offers to become SEC chairman or to be considered for the top job at the FBI.

Many wondered whether Giuliani had a political agenda. As the prosecutions rolled in, his critics claimed he was willing to use any tactics toward that end. His admirers denied this, picturing him as a crusader for honesty in an industry permeated with greed, corruption, and lies.

Giuliani accomplished his objectives through a combination of dogged work and shrewd insights into the mentality of his prey. Early on, he realized that those apparently powerful, arrogant young men of Wall Street had more than their share of insecurities, fostered by middle-class origins, cravings for respectability, and terror at the thought of being found out and disgraced. To capitalize on the latter, especially, Giuliani cultivated the media, staged well-attended press conferences, and provided selected reporters with a steady stream of leaks, knowing the effect news and rumors would have on his targets. Each time a wrongdoing was uncovered, there was a barrage of press and television coverage, along with predictions that more was to come. As it did.

BOESKY TALKS

Ivan Boesky was one of those fingered by Levine. On November 14, 1986, Boesky pleaded guilty to securities fraud and agreed to assist in cornering other malefactors. In asking for leniency in sentencing, Giuliani said Boesky had "revealed that criminal conduct is at the heart of [a] substantial amount of market activity by established securities industry professionals." He added that only a portion of the "rampant criminal conduct" Boesky had disclosed had been made public, and that this was minor considering what was still to be learned.

On April 23, 1987, Boesky received a sentence of three years in prison, of which he would serve slightly more than half. He also would pay $100 million, half in fines, the rest in return of illegal profits—the latter portion being deductible from his income taxes! Boesky was treated generously throughout by Giuliani and the SEC's Lynch, to the point of being permitted to dump the $500 million holdings of one of his arbitrage funds before the indictment was announced, an action *Barron's* writer Kathryn M. Welling suggested might be viewed as "the ultimate inside trade."[4]

After Boesky's plea bargain, Lynch issued subpoenas to Milken, Icahn, Victor Posner, and several others. It was reported that Boesky had implicated all of them in his activities.

One of the better leads Boesky provided regarded Martin Siegel, an expert in takeover defenses, who had moved to Drexel from Kidder Peabody in 1986. Giuliani went after Siegel, who, on February 13, 1987, pleaded guilty to illegal stock trading and tax evasion while at Kidder. Siegel was sentenced to two months in prison, plus 3,000 hours of community service. He also had to return $9 million to settle civil charges related to complaints that he had engaged in insider trading with Boesky while at Kidder. Kidder Peabody agreed to pay a $25 million fine to settle civil charges of insider trading and stock parking. Judge Robert Ward said this was a reward for "cooperation, contrition, and candor." Success in the Siegel affair further encouraged Lynch and Giuliani.[5]

Siegel had told Giuliani that while at Kidder, he had instructed Goldman Sachs partner Timothy Tabor and Kidder Peabody vice president Richard Wigton to trade on information provided by Goldman Sachs partner Robert Freeman. The next month, Giuliani ordered their arrests. They were confronted in their offices and, with cameras clicking, handcuffed, taken away, and charged with insider trading. In April, the three were indicted for conspiracy to violate federal securities statutes and mail and wire fraud by a federal grand jury, to which they pleaded not guilty.

In this expedition, Giuliani has his greatest embarrassment. In May, due to lack of evidence, he had to drop charges against all three bankers. Flustered, Giuliani hinted that a broader indictment against the three would soon be handed down. No new charges were brought against Tabor and Wigton, who, as it turned out, did not know that Siegel was acting on inside information and merely had carried out his orders. Nonetheless, Tabor was unemployable, while Wigton was told he would be fired if and when he was reindicted.

Robert Freeman, of Goldman Sachs, was another matter. He had plunged heavily into Beatrice, wagering that KKR would successfully acquire the company. Soon after, he had received a call from Bernard "Bunny" Lasker, a prominent NYSE floor trader, who told him of problems with the deal. Freeman then called Siegel, who was handling matters for KKR, to make further inquiries. When told of Lasker's comment, Siegel replied, "Your bunny has a good nose." Freeman sold out his position, avoiding close to $1 million in losses when the deal ran into a temporary snag. Freeman received a sentence of four months in jail for the technical crime of mail fraud.[6]

Boyd Jefferies, founder and CEO of his own powerful Los Angeles brokerage firm, was next. He pleaded guilty to two charges of securities fraud, including an arrangement that enabled Boesky to falsify his stock holdings. He was fined $250,000 and received a five-year probationary sentence.

When it was all over, it seemed clear that Boesky had been the shrewdest player. He received much from Lynch and Giuliani, who had become convinced Boesky could uncover a widespread conspiracy. But he gave little, and some of that turned out to have been fabricated.

All who had been indicted so far, including Wigton, Freeman, and Tabor, were pawns as far as Giuliani was concerned. Few even knew who they were. Michael Milken was Giuliani's ultimate target. He would be the end of the line, and Giuliani vowed there would be no deal. Milken's trial and conviction would enhance Giuliani's image as a fearless prosecutor. Such a reputation had elevated Thomas E. Dewey from Manhattan district attorney to Governor of New York and two presidential nominations. It could happen again.

Associate Justice Robert Jackson remarked on this kind of behavior in 1940. "If a prosecutor is obliged to choose his case, it follows he can choose his defendants. Therein is the most dangerous power of the prosecutor: that he will pick the people he thinks he should get, rather than cases that need to be prosecuted.[7] In 1987, some thought that this was the case with Giuliani, including Fred Joseph, who said:

> I tend to be nonparanoid, but a lot of people whose judgment I respect have told me that there really are significant elements of social revolution vendetta in some of the legislative proposals, press coverage, responses by Wall Street

competitors, and maybe in the enthusiasm of the prosecutors because we are a politically attractive target.[8]

Joseph knew that Giuliani was armed with a powerful weapon—one that could destroy Drexel before prosecution or even indictment: the Racketeer-Influenced and Corrupt Organizations statute, known as RICO.

GIULIANI AND RICO

RICO's origins are murky and contentious. In 1970 Congress was winding up debates on what appeared to be a simple piece of legislation but, as the financial community would learn, turned out to be multifarious in its application. The RICO name was evocative, since its intended target was the Mafia.[9]

G. Robert Blakey, who drafted the law as a Senate committee counsel in 1969, later would claim that it "makes fair the fight between the Davids of this world and the twin Goliaths of organized crime and white collar crime."[10] Did the legislators consider white-collar crime to be a target of RICO? In the definitions section of the initial measure, "racketeering activity" included "any offense involving fraud under title 11, fraud in the sale of securities, or the felonious manufacture, importation, receiving, concealment, buying, selling, or otherwise dealing in narcotic or other dangerous drugs, punishable under any law of the United States."

What generally goes under the rubric of white-collar crime did not appear to come under the statute. Indeed, one of the few moments of levity during the debates on RICO came from a congressman who voiced objection to the measure because "whatever its motives to begin with, we will end up with cases involving all kinds of things not intended to be covered, and a potpourri of language by which you can parade all kinds of horribles of overreach." For example, he suggested, suppose several members of Congress played a marathon game of poker. This could mean that they "have been running an organized gambling business and can get 20 years, and the federal government can grab off the pot besides." Such a scenario would not seem preposterous by the late 1980s.

The legislators debating the issue indicated that their intention was to provide more severe penalties for gangsters. Senator Robert Dole (R. Kansas) said, "It is impossible to overstress the importance of S. 30's legislative attack on organized crime . . . Title IX of the Organized Crime Control Act . . . contains a proposal designed to curtail—and eventually eradicate—the vast expansion of organized crime's economic power."

The term "organized crime" did not appear in the final version, partly in deference to the sensibilities of the Italian-American community, as expressed by Representative Mario Biaggi (D. New York) and others. Some doubted that a precise definition of organized crime was possible. Instead, the term employed was "racketeering activities," which was now defined as "(1) a pattern of racketeering activity or the collection of an unlawful debt, (2) the establishment or operation of any enterprise that is engaged in, or the activities of which affect, interstate or foreign commerce."[11] Included were "acts or threats of murder, kidnapping, gambling, arson, robbery, bribery, extortion, or dealing in narcotics or other dangerous drugs." In addition, bribery, counterfeiting, embezzlement from pension and welfare funds, extortionate credit transactions, obstruction of criminal investigations, and certain dealings with labor unions were listed as coming under RICO. All were the purview of criminal elements. As late as 1980, a reporter could write, "RICO [is] a federal law enacted in 1970 that gave the government a powerful new weapon in its fight against organized crime's takeover of legitimate businesses . . . . The purpose, as the Justice Department put it in a training memo to its lawyers and agents, is 'to hit organized crime in the pocketbook.'"[12]

The penalties provided were harsh. Even if a business were run legitimately, it could be confiscated if it had been purchased with illegally obtained money, and in civil cases, treble damages could be levied. Funds and property could be seized before the trial, presumably to prevent them from being hidden. The punishment was so severe that, even as the measure was being approved and signed into law, attorneys doubted its constitutionality.

Casting about for means to thwart raiders, target companies turned to the civil side of RICO. One of its first uses in this area came two years after the law's passage, when Carl Icahn was attempting to raid Marshall Field. Attorneys for the store alleged that Icahn had violated securities law and invoked RICO provisions, charging that he had obtained some of the funds for the raid from a "pattern of racketeering." This "pattern" was reflected in a consent order from the New Jersey Bureau of Securities, an NYSE censure, four fines from the Chicago Board of Trade Options Exchange, and other minor charges.[13] Nothing came to this charge, as Marshall Field entered into a merger with Batus and the matter was dropped. There was talk of using RICO against Boone Pickens during the Unocal contest. Again, nothing materialized, although at least one Justice Department official thought it was possible. "Isn't putting a company in play criminal and an act of racketeering?" he asked, somewhat disingenuously.[14]

In the late 1980s, RICO was invoked against a small investment bank, Princeton/Newport Partners L.P. Boesky had fingered John Mulheren, who ran a risk arbitrage operation and supposedly manipulated the shares of Gulf+Western for him. Mulheren conducted his business through Princeton/Newport, which had made purchases and sales through Drexel's Bruce Newberg. On August 4, 1988, together with five Princeton/Newport executives, Newberg was charged with having engaged in illegal trading. Specifically, the government alleged that the firm had parked securities with Drexel in order to hide transactions from SEC scrutiny. Princeton/Newport was charged with tax fraud, securities violations, and racketeering under RICO. The bank collapsed in December, and all the defendants were convicted on August 2, 1989.

This was not the end of the affair, however. It turned out that the allegations against Princeton/Newport were deeply flawed. The following June, the Court of Appeals reversed all the convictions centering around racketeering, but left standing convictions against two of the officers for conspiracy and securities violations. The court went so far as to assert that the prosecution hadn't even produced evidence that a crime had been committed. In January 1992, the government quietly dropped all its charges against those in the firm. Mulheren also went to trial, was found guilty, appealed, and won a reversal.[15] Little was accomplished except the destruction of what turned out to have been an innocent bank.

TARGETING MILKEN

Interested bystanders were already wondering what kind of relationship Boesky might have had with Milken, since their businesses were quite different. Boesky was an arbitrageur, not a major buyer of junk bonds like Fred Carr and Tom Spiegel, or a Milken client like Boone Pickens and Carl Icahn. It was Levine, not Milken, who had provided inside information to Boesky. Indeed, Boesky turned down Levine's suggestion that Levine leave Drexel and join him. Levine simply was too valuable where he was. If Boesky had conspired with Milken, he hardly would have needed Levine.

Yet, there was some evidence of collusion. Setrag Mooradian, once Boesky's accountant, agreed to cooperate with the investigation in return for immunity from prosecution. He provided the government with a document he had prepared, which listed funds owed in secret deals by Boesky to Milken and vice versa. But this was a Boesky document, and Mooradian later said he had no direct knowledge of Milken's involvement with Boesky, so it could not be used in court. At the time, however, it enabled Giuliani to move closer to a Milken indictment.[16]

Since leaks from Giuliani's office continued to appear regularly in the press, Milken had a good idea what was happening. While appearing calm and continuing his work, he was worried. On the surface, Milken's situation appeared solid. Given that Boesky was an admitted felon, Milken's credibility would be the greater, if it were only Boesky's word against his. But evidence might be uncovered to alter this situation.

What followed the Boesky indictment was the stuff of cloak-and-dagger novels. On the morning after Boesky's guilty plea, Milken had a strange conversation with salesman Terren Peizer. Peizer spoke of wagers he had placed for Milken, who had never gambled in his life. Milken concluded that either Peizer had gone crazy or was wired to a tape recorder, and was trying to signal this to him. Immediately, Milken became suspicious.

Peizer later testified that he had gone into the office kitchenette with Lorraine Spurge, one of Milken's closest confidants, turned on the faucet, and given her records of trading arrangements with David Solomon, the manager of Finsbury Fund and Solomon Assets Management, the latter a fund created by Milken. "Michael asked me to give this to you," he said.[17]

When Cary Maultasch, a Drexel trader operating out of New York, who earlier had been at the Beverly Hills office, learned that Boesky had agreed to inform on his associates, he took a sedative and then booked a seat on the next flight to Los Angeles. The next day, he met with Milken who wrote questions and answers on a yellow pad, always erasing them afterwards. "I assume there are no records," was one of Milken's statements. Was Milken referring to records of insider trading? His critics believe this was the case, but defenders respond that no evidence has ever been presented on the matter. When Maultasch left the building, the guard tore up the slip he had signed on entering. "Don't worry. You weren't here," he assured him. So the word was out.[18]

James Dahl was called to the Beverly Hills offices. According to his later testimony, after a two-hour wait, Milken beckoned him to the men's room, where he turned on a faucet and started washing his hands. "There haven't been any subpoenas issued," Milken said. "Whatever you need to do, do it." "He spoke in hushed tones," Dahl testified, asserting that he didn't understand what Milken was trying to convey. The government later would claim that Milken wanted Dahl to destroy any records that might embarrass them. Milken denied this.

It appeared from these actions that Milken was attempting to cover his tracks. But Milken knew Giuliani had targeted him and, given the power and resources of government, was capable of conducting a vendetta lasting years. A degree of anxiety, distrust, and paranoia on Milken's part can be understood.

THE WAR ON DREXEL

Meanwhile, Representative Dingell had scheduled hearings on "Securities Markets Oversight and Drexel Burnham Lambert." He started by conceding the value of junk financing for midsized companies, but he was troubled about raids on larger concerns:

> . . . companies which have existed for decades, which have carried the brunt of our national defense through two World Wars, which have provided employment in the heartland of America, no longer exist. They have

been victims of takeovers, financed through the junk bond market. Research and development budgets have suffered as millions of dollars have been diverted to pay high interest rates on junk bonds. In short, the competitiveness of the United States in the international market, indeed, our balance of trade and the future of this country, is impacted by junk bonds.

Another subcommittee member, Representative Michael Bilirakis (R. Florida), was equally stern:

My interest also stems from the fact that there is a company in my district that is a major employer. This company has recently filed suit in the U.S. District Court alleging that Drexel and its so-called junk bond network manipulated its stock downward. Many of my constituents are investors in this company.

The stock in question had declined from 47 to 5, said Bilirakis, who wanted a full investigation of Drexel's role.[19] Thus, the pressure was on in Washington as well as New York. While Giuliani cast his net, Congress was acting to impede the issuance of junk bonds.

True to the plea bargain agreement, Boesky told the Justice Department about his dealings with Milken. In September 1988, the SEC accused Drexel of 21 violations of the securities laws, of which two concerned insider trading. Almost immediately, leaks surfaced regarding deals struck with Giuliani by Drexel insiders. Giuliani turned up the heat, and the Milken lines started to crack. Some former associates agreed to testify against Milken. In fact, they had no choice. Giuliani granted them immunity, which meant they couldn't plead the Fifth Amendment, and so, if they were going to be loyal to Milken, they could either risk contempt charges or commit perjury.

Dahl was one of the first to turn. When colleagues wondered how he could testify against the man who had made him so wealthy, he disdainfully replied, "I don't have to worry. I've got $50 million and immunity."[20]

Dahl's defection was followed by those of Maultasch and Peizer. Rumors were floated that Giuliani would gain cooperation from half a dozen others, possibly among them Lowell Milken. In an affidavit, Lowell's attorney, Michael Armstrong, charged that the prosecutors "in the course of threatening people with indictments unless they gave satisfactory information, indicated that testimony against Lowell Milken was a requirement of any such deal."[21]

By now, the government's campaign of trial by leaks had come under fire. "What the government wanted was publicity," said Armstrong. "A confidential SEC report was leaked in its entirety to the press," which often attributed information to "sources familiar with the investigation."[21]

Milken's attorneys filed a brief calling for contempt citations against government officials for "numerous unlawful leaks to the press." There was a cursory investigation, and the leaks persisted. On February 5, 1987, for example, the *Wall Street Journal* reported: "People familiar with the investigation said that Mr. Milken is the official that evidence suggests was most directly involved with Mr. Boesky in the suspected scheme [to profit illegally from takeovers]." The leaks continued throughout the year and into 1988, when a steady flow of such articles appeared, many by James B. Stewart, the *Journal's* page-one editor. On February 4, came "Boesky and Drexel Aides Joined in Illicit Scheme, Records Suggest." An April 8 headline was "U.S. Accumulates Evidence Supporting Case Against Milken, Sources Say." On September 24, the *Journal* ran "Boesky Ex-Aide Could Provide Data on Milken." So it went.

At the time, Stewart was writing *Den of Thieves,* released in 1991, and an immediate best-seller. A reading of the book suggests that the major sources of those leaks were Giuliani, Lynch, Boesky, and Siegel.

Interestingly, the newspaper's editorial page, whose editor was Robert L. Bartley, consistently criticized the government for its actions against Milken, while the *Journal's* "Rule of Law" columnist, L. Gordon Crovitz, was one of Milken's biggest boosters.

The *Journal* wasn't the only newspaper to receive the leaks. On April 24, 1987, the *Washington Post* reported, "Boesky paid Drexel $5.3 million in 1986. Boesky has said that his payment to Drexel reconciled accounts in a secret arrangement he had with Milken, according to sources familiar with the case." There were similar articles in the *New York Times, Los Angeles Times,* and other major newspapers.[22]

The government exerted other forms of coercion and harassment, among them rumors of a superceding indictment of 160 charges. Milken's 92-year-old grandfather, Louis Zax, was subjected to Justice Department questioning.

All this occurred before a trial or even an indictment. With RICO, Giuliani had the power to smash Drexel before any further legal steps were taken. In mid-December 1988, he told Drexel that he would indict on RICO charges unless it agreed to a settlement on his terms. As one Drexel banker characterized it, "Giuliani put the gun on the table and said to us, Either you will pick it up and use it on yourself or I will."[23]

Within Drexel, some, including Peter Ackerman, John Kissick, and Leon Black, wanted to fight. Others, like I. W. Burnham, Robert Linton, and the management of Bruxelles Lambert, all of whom had equity interests in the firm, were prepared to abandon Milken to safeguard Drexel's future and their stakes. When the time came, the 22-member board elected to cooperate with the government, with Joseph joining with five others to vote in the negative. In his opinion, however, "The settlement was the only survivable alternative." So he had it both ways.

Milken was sold out. In a period when loyalty in investment banking had all but disappeared, Milken had been true to Drexel. Scores of other firms would have paid handsomely to have him on their team, or he could have left

Drexel to form his own operation, taking clients with him. Milken never considered these options. Now, Drexel had turned on him, and despite Joseph's vote, Milken held him responsible. These men, who once were in contact many times each day, now drew apart.

CAPITULATION

On December 21, Drexel agreed not to contest six charges and to pay $650 million in fines and restitution. The firm would add three outside directors to serve as eyes and ears of the SEC: John Shad, who replaced Linton as chairman, Ralph Saul, and former investment banker Roderick Hills. Shad had become one of the more vocal critics of the use of junk bonds. "The greater the leverage, the greater the risks to the company, its shareholders, creditors, officers, employees, suppliers, customers and others," he had said. "The more leveraged takeovers and buyouts today, the more bankruptcies tomorrow . . . . The leveraging-up of American enterprise will magnify the adverse consequences of the next recession, or significant rise in interest rates."[24]

As part of the arrangement, Joseph placed Milken on a leave of absence, and Drexel officials agreed not to contact or speak with him. A portion of his earnings—$200 million—was withheld. Drexel also agreed to assist in the government's investigation of Milken.

Some believe Joseph had a deal with Giuliani in which he abandoned Milken to save himself. At the time, however, it appeared that Joseph himself might go, with his rumored replacement being former Senator Howard Baker. But Joseph held on, cooperating fully with Giuliani's office, while Ackerman temporarily assumed Milken's place.

Wall Street was not caught off guard by the move. Many saw it as only another step in a drive to indict Milken. But why move against Drexel then, given the shaky nature of the markets after the October 19, 1987, crash? Did the government really know what it was doing? How might a "junk panic," triggered by Giuliani's actions, affect the pension and mutual funds and insurance companies with sizable junk portfolios? Thomas Donlan of *Barron's* thought "all of this suggests serious trouble ahead if Milken disappears from the picture." He wondered what would happen to the prices of junk bonds if Milken "were not there to create the market and keep it going on his terms."[24]

Milken's departure was untimely for other reasons. The battle for RJR Nabisco had begun, and Drexel was in the middle of it, committed to raise funds for KKR. Without Milken and his web of contacts, could the firm carry it off? Not only did the underwriting succeed, but Drexel's salesmen oversold the issue and had to allocate portions. Drexel's fee for the deal was $250 million. Merrill Lynch, the comanager, was left in the cold and was irate. Thus, Drexel demonstrated that its abilities at placement had survived Milken's departure, and, once more, the firm earned the enmity and envy of other banks.[26]

Although it appeared that Drexel would be able to endure its travails, it cut back on operations. Joseph announced a restructuring in which Drexel reduced commitments and abandoned an expensive plan for relocating its Manhattan offices. John Kissick, who had arrived from Shearson in 1975, now became the permanent head of the high-yield department. While no one could accomplish what Milken had done, the firm still had a corporate finance department in New York with 265 professionals, plus the Milken-trained Beverly Hills staff of 84 more. Even so, matters continued to unravel, and the market for junk continued to decline.

FIRREA: CONGRESS PILES ON JUNK

The beginning of the end for Drexel came in June 1989, when it was unable to roll over a mere $40 million of commercial paper for Integrated Resources. In Milken's day, some rescue would have been fashioned, if only to maintain Drexel's reputation for supporting clients. Indeed, Milken once had saved the day for IR through an equity infusion from another client. Not now. Its back to the wall, on June 15, Integrated Resources defaulted on $1 billion of debt, most of it held by Drexel customers like Perelman ($24 million) and First Executive ($49 million), which had guarantees on their investment from Drexel, which itself owned $41 million of the paper.[27] Said one banker, "As far as many buyers were concerned, [Joseph] threw away the franchise," while another remarked, "When Drexel didn't stand behind Integrated, there was a sea change. Other companies said, 'They won't stand behind us, either.'"[28] Now there was a whiff of panic in the air.

Narrowly focused on its goal, the government again compounded the problem. Continuing its crusade against junk in the face of an imminent collapse of the market, Congress passed the Financial Institutions Reform, Recovery, and Enforcement Act (FIRREA). Signed into law in August 1989, FIRREA required the thrifts to mark their junk bonds to market. Some would have to show large losses. In addition, they would have to sell their junk portfolios by August 1994, which meant that 6 percent of all junk would come to market around the same time. Moreover, the thrifts were prohibited from purchasing new junk issues, and that restriction effectively removed a major player from the market. Almost at once, the thrifts started liquidating their portfolios. This caused deep distress for several of the institutions, which promptly filed for bankruptcy.

Later it was asserted junk caused the S&L debacle. Public opinion to the contrary, junk was *not* a major contributor to the downfall of most thrifts, although it certainly played a role in some of the more dramatic failures. One report indicated that, of the $200 billion of junk outstanding by the end of 1988, some $70 billion was owned by mutual and pension funds, $62 billion by insurance companies, another $20 billion by individuals, and only $12 billion by thrifts, with the remainder owned by foreigners and others.[29] Further, relatively few thrifts had much exposure to junk. As of March 31, 1988, 55 percent of thrift junk was owned by four institutions. The book value of defaulted junk bonds at these thrifts was $184 million, or 2 percent of their portfolios. Another report, by the General Accounting Office (GAO), indicated that, as of September 30, 1988, 161 of the country's approximately 2,000 thrifts had invested $13.2 billion in junk bonds, with 25 owning 91 percent of the total.[30]

Also contrary to conventional wisdom, junk bonds had performed well for the thrifts. In March 1989, the GAO found that the returns on these bonds exceeded risks and that "high yield bonds have not caused the current thrift industry problems."

> High yield bonds have been good investments in relation to other investments for thrifts during a period of unprecedented peacetime economic expansion. So far, the returns on an actively managed and diversified portfolio of high yield bonds have been higher than returns on most alternative investments, after accounting for comparative risk.

This was not to say there were no dangers. "Whether this will continue to be the case is uncertain," said the authors of the report. "The dramatic recent increase in the size of the market and the increasing debt levels of some of the companies issuing bonds causes concern about how these bonds would fare in a recession."[31]

FIRREA exacerbated an already troublesome situation at the thrifts. As recently as 1987, only 47 thrifts had failed. Failures the following year came to 223, and in 1989, when FIRREA went into effect, there were 328 failures. Yet, until then, not a single thrift had failed due to its junk holdings. A year later, when there were 217 failures, a *Fortune* writer estimated that losses related to junk bonds accounted for 2 percent of total thrift losses.[32] What the government had done with FIRREA was to set off a junk-selling panic at the thrifts, which rippled through the market, impacting on existing issues and holding up pending financing.

Other measures were debated in Congress. Representative Markey introduced a measure to require that financing for takeovers be in place before a raider mounted an LBO. In addition, the raider would have to file an impact statement, indicating the harm his move might cause. Several other legislators proposed bills that would hamper takeovers made possible through junk. None got far beyond committee hearings, but the assault triggered by Hartley and Proxmire accelerated.

All the while, there were failures of junk issuers and weakness in the market. On July 14, 1989, Southmark filed for bankruptcy. Seaman's Furniture missed a debt payment. Ramada Inc. scrapped a $400 million offering. Resorts International defaulted on its $325 million in debt in late August. On September 13, Robert Campeau, who had gobbled up Allied Stores and Federated Department Stores through junk financing, declared that he lacked enough capital to satisfy debt payments and was sweating units to raise badly needed cash. Fears surfaced regarding junk liquidity, prompting increased selling in October. The spread between junk and government bonds widened alarmingly, from slightly more than 200 basis points in January 1989, to 372 on November 15.

Reading such reports in the press and sensing that more were on the way, owners of shares in high-yield-bond mutual funds cashed them in, forcing the funds to cut back on positions and adding to the growing anxiety. Illiquidity compounded the problem of divestiture. As noted, high-grade corporate-bond markets were always thin, and the market for junk issued for public companies was thinner still; and junk placed for nonpublic companies was almost impossible to trade. Increased supply or demand usually resulted in high volatility. It was not surprising, then, that these developments dealt the junk market a hammer blow. Prices plummeted, taking the good with the bad.

During each of the eight months after passage of FIRREA, the high-yield funds experienced $300 million in redemptions. What Merrill Lynch banker Martin S. Fridson was to call "The Great Debacle" was on. Later, Senator D'Amato, who had warned against such drastic government actions throughout, said:

> Talk about exacerbating the problem. When we, the Congress of the United States, passed FIRREA legislation it forced—forced—the thrifts to sell these bonds, even if they're good, if they've been reporting good earnings, good interest, good income to those thrifts, if we didn't exacerbate this situation in the market by that action, I don't know what did.[33]

Secretary Brady now did what Congress had been unable to do: Act to eliminate junk as a tool in corporate takeovers. Together with the Fed, the FDIC, and the Comptroller of the Currency, the Treasury Department sent word to the commercial banks that loan criteria would be watched more carefully in the future. In January 1990, the Fed noted that more than 70 percent of the banks had tightened credit standards for loans granted for mergers and acquisitions.[34]

THE CRUSADE CONTINUES

The effective antijunk campaign in the states continued. New York ruled that state pension funds no longer could invest in junk bonds, and California declared that its pension funds would sell off its junk holdings, whose face value was $530 million, for $380 million. The Resolution Trust Company (RTC), which had seized many insolvent thrifts, also was selling junk, and dumped $5 billion in bonds on the market. The SEC ruled that as of May 1991, no more than 5 percent of the assets of money market funds could be dedicated to unrated or low-rated commercial paper. (Previously the figure had been 25 percent.) While this did not result in panic selling, it did dry up another market for junk paper. Most seriously, the insurance companies, a prime junk customer, were told by the National Association of Insurance Commissioners to limit junk holdings and were required to establish reserves against such investments.

The economy, which had been strong during the junk era, now entered a recession. Junk defaults, which hadn't been troublesome until 1988, rose as the economy declined. The failure rate on junk had averaged slightly under 2 percent during the 1978–1988 period. It would rise to more than 4 percent in 1989, and to 8.7 percent in 1990—the highest level since 1970's 11.4 percent.

What had caused the collapse of the junk market? Milken's defenders would point to FIRREA and related actions that prompted bondholders to dump their holdings, thus depressing prices. Critics would point to that massive wave of defaults that caused owners to lose confidence in the paper. Both were responsible. Either cause alone would have resulted in a sell-off. Taken together, they brought the junk era to a crashing close.

Critics and defenders also hold diametrically opposite views of the relationship between the disintegration of the junk market and the onset of the recession. Critics hold that the market's sell-off resulted from a realization by the public of the shaky and suspect nature of the instruments. Defenders believe that the collapse was caused both by those body blows from government and by fears engendered by the media. Once medium-sized businesses were cut off from sources of financing, they stopped expanding, and this was one of the reasons for the economy's problems. The latter position received unexpected support from Merton Miller of Modigliani-Miller fame, who received the Nobel Prize in Economic Science in 1990, largely due to his work in the bond field. "Capital markets have built-in controls against overleveraging," Miller said in his acceptance speech. He continued,

> Recent efforts by our regulators to override these built-in market mechanisms by destroying the junk bond market and by imposing additional direct controls over leveraged lending by banks will thus have all the unintended consequences

normally associated with such regulatory interventions. They will lower efficiency and raise costs.

It often is difficult to distinguish between cause and effect, and such is
the case with the junk market collapse. Noted historian-economist Charles
Kindleberger frequently pointed out that financial panics and crashes are
caused and deepened by the absence of both liquidity and a lender of last
resort. In the past, the Fed had come to the rescue of the broad market on
several occasions by acting as both. In the Penn Central collapse of 1972,
Chairman Arthur Burns saved the markets from panic by throwing open
the money window, and Chairman Alan Greenspan did the same during
"Black Monday," in 1987, when the market fell by 508 points and many
feared the financial end had arrived. During the panic of 1907, the worst
the country had known to that time, the aged J. P. Morgan gathered New
York's leading bankers in his office, locked the door, and refused to permit
them to leave until they agreed to contribute to a pool of funds he would
use to save important endangered banks and trust companies.

The faltering junk market of late 1989 had elements that made for panic.
Lacking was that old panacea, liquidity, of the type once provided by Morgan and, later, the Fed. But in the absence of a widespread collapse, the Fed
wasn't likely to intervene.

There was one person who might have performed for the junk market
in 1989 what Morgan did for the banks in 1907, and that was Michael
Milken. It was no mere coincidence that the instability of the junk sector
coincided with Milken's troubles with the Justice Department, which effectively removed him from the scene.

THE ACADEMIC EVIDENCE ON JUNK

In the midst of the deteriorating junk market came two academic studies in
the September 1989 issue of the *Journal of Finance,* which appeared to indicate that even those early junk bonds had performed poorly. These studies
shook many readers and caused further distress. In one article, by Paul
Asquith, David Mullins, and Eric Wolf, the authors studied the records of
junk bonds over their life span and reported that 29.3 percent of those issued in 1977–1979 had either defaulted or been exchanged during the ten
years after issuance. Asquith also noted that "issues underwritten by Drexel
exhibit lower default rates than do the aggregate issues of all other underwriters." The authors attributed this difference to "Drexel's expertise and
other underwriters attempts to penetrate the market with less creditworthy
issues."[42]

The second paper, by Edward Altman, entitled "Measuring Corporate
Bond Mortality and Performance," came to a similar conclusion, calculating

the rate at 30.9 percent. While this seemed a dreadful performance, another way to state the findings of both studies was that the default rate was little more than 3 percent per year—hardly disastrous. Saying that close to a third of all junk defaulted over a dozen years had one effect; saying that the rate was 3 percent a year sounded entirely different.

Other studies indicated that junk had been a fine investment until the late 1980s, but not afterwards. In taking the entire cycle into consideration, Lipper Analytical Services reported that for the ten years ending on September 30, 1990, the total return on junk bond funds came to 145 percent, or 9.4 percent annualized. In comparison, stocks rose 207 percent, or 11.9 percent annualized; A-rated corporates rose 202 percent, or 11.7 percent annualized; and Treasury bonds rose 177 percent, or 10.7 percent annualized. Indeed, Lipper showed that money market funds, the most mundane of investments, offered the same returns as junk bonds for that ten-year period. It would appear from this report that, taking the decline into consideration, junk investments hadn't lived up to the promise claimed by its advocates.[36]

This misses the point. For one thing, there is a cycle in most financings, and by the late 1980s, the junk cycle was ending. Then, too, most analysts during this time neglected to note that all junk was not the same. There was "good junk" and "bad junk," and a lot of the bad junk had come to market late in the decade.

More than 30 years ago, W. Braddock Hickman had warned of this, and said the cycle would end this way. In *Corporate Bond Quality and Investor Experience,* he had suggested that one of the worst times to purchase low-rated bonds was before the break in the market, because investor euphoria was such that inferior issues were presented:

> As a general rule, low grades fared better than high grades when purchased near troughs and sold near peaks of the investment cycle; but by the same token, losses were heavy on low grades purchased near peaks and sold near troughs. The same is true of investments in declining as against growing industries. Low-grade issues of a declining industry rarely worked out as well as high-grade issues.[37]

Hickman also noted, "The trends in default rates are roughly comparable with trends in net and gross new financing, default rates tending to be high on securities issued during years of high financial volume and vice versa. This would seem to suggest that some issues, perhaps those of marginal quality, can find a ready market only when the market is buoyant, and that in periods of market pessimism only the top grade issues can be placed."[38]

What it came down to was that the best time to buy, and for companies to issue, low-grade bonds was at the beginning or middle of the cycle.

When the mania took hold and buyers' demand could not easily be met, they should have been avoided. In other words, one had to be wary of purchasing any security when it became highly popular and celebrated. George Edwards, the co-author of the celebrated *The Principles of Bond Investment*, had commented on this principle in 1933:

> The history of business cycles shows that the stage of prosperity in general is marked by an ever-increasing inefficiency. In the field of security investment, the buying public, swayed by overoptimism, seeks more and more after securities of higher yield, and investment bankers, under the stress of competition, issue securities of higher yield, greater risk, and poorer quality.[39]

A study by Barrie Wigmore addressed the matter of quality. Wigmore demonstrated that the quality of bonds coming to market in the late 1980s was lower than those earlier in the decade. As the volume and size of junk offerings expanded, their earnings before interest on debt and taxes (EBIT), a standard measure, fell. In 1980, the figure for bonds rated B by Moody's was 1.64:1. By 1988, it was down to 0.731. Other scholars utilized a broader measure, which included depreciation of plant and equipment and amortization of such intangibles as good will (EBITA). By this measure, the average LBO in 1986 had been done at six times EBITA; by 1989, it had climbed to nine times, and some transactions had been done at 12 times EBITA. Equity accounted for 39 percent of capitalization in 1986; it was down to 4 percent by 1988. Moreover, there were fewer of those offerings for the medium-sized companies Milken so enjoyed financing.

Table 10–1

SPECULATIVE-GRADE NEW-ISSUE ACTIVITY, 1981–1988
(percent distribution)

Year	Total	Baa/BB Ba/BBB	Ba/BaNR NR/BB/ Ba/B B/BB	B/B NR/B B/NR	Caa and Under	Unrated
1981	100	6.56	19.03	61.67	—	12.74
1982	100	1.96	47.29	41.52	1.58	7.65
1983	100	13.92	35.95	33.81	6.50	9.82
1984	100	24.10	27.72	35.29	5.15	7.74
1985	100	3.18	34.56	39.66	13.94	8.66
1986	100	7.25	21.40	51.15	18.20	2.00
1987	100	3.90	13.07	64.75	17.10	1.18
1988	100	7.24	6.78	65.97	20.01	—

Source: Richard Wilson and Frank Fabozzi, *The New Corporate Bond Market* (Chicago: 1990), 260.

Table 10-2

HISTORIC DEFAULT RATES, 1970–1990

Year	Par Value Outstanding (millions of dollars)	Par Value Defaults (millions of dollars)	Default Rate
1970	6,996	797	11.3
1971	6,643	82	1.2
1972	7,106	193	2.7
1973	8,082	49	0.6
1974	11,101	123	1.1
1975	7,720	204	2.6
1976	8,015	30	0.4
1977	8,479	381	4.5
1978	9,401	119	1.3
1979	10,675	20	0.2
1980	15,126	224	1.5
1981	17,362	27	0.2
1982	18,536	577	3.1
1983	28,233	301	1.1
1984	41,700	344	0.8
1985	59,078	992	1.7
1986	92,985	3,156	3.4
1987	136,952	7,486	5.5
1988	159,223	3,944	2.5
1989	201,000	8,110	4.0
1990	210,000	18,354	8.7
1991	209,400	18,862	9.0

Source: Martin S. Fridson and Michael Cherry, "This Year in High Yield," in Merrill Lynch, *Extra Credit,* January/February 1992, 17.

During the 1986–1988 period, three-quarters of the issues were merger-related. It was then that flotations for the likes of Revco, Allied Stores, Federated Department Stores, SCI Television, Seaman Furniture, and Simplicity Pattern came to market. All had problems paying interest.[40]

In retrospect it could be seen that the quantity of junk offerings had increased after the middle of the decade, while the quality was declining. After it was all over, Edward Altman, who had been one of the most vocal and convincing academics favoring junk bonds, wrote, "There was a free lunch until 1988. But people got greedy."[41] Martin Fridson agreed and later would speak of the "bad cohort" of 1987–1988, which accounted for 39 percent of all junk issued, but 50 percent of the defaults and distressed issues.[42]

Lost in all of this postmortem analysis was the action in junk after the collapse. Several junk practitioners entered the market on the buy side. Leon Black and others made more money after the market breakdown than they had during its heyday, buying at the bottom and holding for the recovery that came in 1991, when junk was the best performing category of security in the markets.

MILKEN PREDICTS THE END
OF THE JUNK ERA

Among those cautioning against the use of junk was none other than Michael Milken. This should not have surprised anyone who had read his MBA thesis, "Managing the Corporate Financial Structure."[43] Recall that he had said there are times when markets and other circumstances call for debt, and times when they call for equity or some other instruments.

Milken hinted the idea in the April 1986 issue of Drexel's *High Yield Newsletter,* which, nonetheless, recommended convertible junk bonds like issues of Circus Circus, Wickes, Tesoro, and Manor Care. While saying "the high yield opportunity looks as good today as ever," the newsletter also concluded, "With equities at new highs, cash hoarders may decide that retiring their own debt—and possibly issuing equity for potential acquisitions—is now the way to go." The article intimated that the time was coming to retire, not issue, junk bonds.

There were few other statements on the matter, but the following April, the Drexel newsletter sent a clear signal: "The byword is 'equitize.'" In July 1987, Milken told journalist Allan Sloan that companies should use periods when their stock prices are high to call in their bonds and sell stock:

> When debt is cheap, debt should be a greater part of your capital structure. When equity is cheap, equity should be more of your capital. There's no fixed capital structure that's always right. Some days it should be debt, some days equity. You have to look at the markets every day.[43]

Now, a steady stream of pessimistic reports came out of Beverly Hills. In the autumn of 1988, when Robert Campeau took off after Federated, the *High Yield Newsletter* wrote, "cautious investors should avoid" that company's paper.

In February 1989, when the junk decline had begun and was attracting bargain hunters, Milken told an interviewer:

> Debt isn't good and it isn't bad. It depends on the type of business and the financial environment. Some companies can't afford it; they are not generating cash. Others are poorly managed. And there certainly is a time when it

makes sense to sell equity. There are some firms for which no debt is right. For others, it should be almost all of their capital.[44]

In a September speech, Milken said the market was demanding stock and sellers should provide it. "In today's environment, at least in the last 12 months, the market's been saying to you 'Please give us equity-based structures. Sell us converts . . . . Or sell me participation debt. Or sell me common stock. Or sell me preferred stock. I'm going to charge you too much if you keep trying to sell me straight debt.' So for 12 months the market's been saying that but very few people have been listening."[45]

Milken was particularly troubled by the large spread between junk and government bonds. The market was sending a message that it didn't make sense for companies to pay such rates. "Raising the yield on a deal from 16% to 17% doesn't make it a better credit," he said, charging that some bankers "keep 'xeroxing' the deals of 1985."[46]

Did Milken really mean it? Even while sounding these warnings, Drexel continued to underwrite junk issues. Buyers demanded more bonds, and sellers were willing to pay premium interest rates to obtain financing. Drexel underwrote some bad deals in the years when Milken was sounding these admonitions. There were underwritings for Bond Brewing, Eastern Airlines, Gillett Holdings, Integrated Resources, Koor Industries, and Southmark in 1986. The following year, the bank underwrote issues for Integrated Resources, Leaseway Transport, and SCI Television, plus a massive $500 million, 19$\frac{1}{2}$ percent undertaking for Western Union. With Drexel's assistance, Gillett purchased television station WTVT in Tampa for $385 million, raised through junk financing. At the time, the debt service on that amount exceeded WTVT's cash flow.[47]

All these firms fell into bankruptcy. The bankrupt firms of 1988 were Centrust Bank, Griffin Resorts, Hillsborough Holdings, Linter Textiles, Miramar Marine, Service Controls, and Univision. Even in 1989, under attack and with defaults mounting, Drexel underwrote a $200 million issue of 13 percent bonds for Ames Department Stores that would fall into Chapter 11 in less than a year.[48] In all, during the period after 1986, when Milken first sounded a warning about the deteriorating nature of the junk market, Drexel underwrote some $5.5 billion worth of bonds for companies that were in bankruptcy by 1990.

If Milken believed the market was worsening, as his words indicate, how can we account for Drexel's actions?

Some asserted that by mid-decade Milken had developed hubris and felt he had to be in on every deal, even questionable ones. In 1985, long before there was any trouble at Drexel, one of his associates said, "Mike Milken believes in 100% market share." Chairman Linton echoed the thought. "I don't think money has anything to do with what he does . . . . Michael wants to have it all. Michael wants to do every piece of business and every deal and make every dollar."[49]

Milken's associates suggest another motivation. Always a workaholic, he continued his intense pace while monitoring Giuliani's activities in New York. Perhaps in those last months at Drexel, Milken did not recognize that he was preoccupied and permitted worries regarding his own future to cloud his thinking at the office.

After Milken's departure, little could be done to prevent the meltdown of the web of buyers he had constructed. While an able banker, Kissick lacked Milken's imagination and dynamism when it came to structuring deals, making swaps, and massaging clients. Several of Drexel's star customers left the field. Would-be sellers found no market for their securities. Drexel was not alone; other banks felt the pinch. Companies had issued $27.6 billion in public non-investment-grade bonds in 1989. The figure for 1990 would be just $2.7 billion.

In Drexel's case, however, clients were reluctant to do business with a company clearly at odds with Washington. Said Managing Director David Hedley, "We've been told point blank by a number of utilities that they would like to do business with us, but because of the adverse press, they can't." New York City excluded Drexel from two of its bond offerings, and New Jersey placed a temporary prohibition on the firm's financing of gambling casinos there.[50]

Milken's empire had been cobbled together first by developing a strong network of customers for his services, and then by doing the same for clients. By 1989, both sides of the market had been crippled. Everything was falling apart. With the erosion of its customer base, Drexel was obliged to eat more of the bonds it had underwritten, undermining its own financial position. By the end of September 1989, Drexel had $1 billion in junk bonds and bridge loans on the books, and its liquidity was threatened.[51]

To increase liquidity, the bank had sold most of its retail operations to Smith Barney in June 1989, thus divesting itself of what had grown out of the old Burnham & Co. In December, S&P lowered the rating on Drexel's commercial paper from A-2 to A-3, which meant it was no longer eligible to be purchased by money market funds, and so a major customer was lost. Concerned investors refused to roll over their commercial paper, and the amount outstanding fell from $600 million to $180 million. The bank made this up by borrowing from its own commodities trading operation, which obtained most of the money from borrowing gold from overseas banks and then selling the metal on the open market.

Drexel was devastated by a combination of bad deals, government actions, and the absence of its chief player. Without Milken, the researchers and traders seemed to languish. "You used to be able to call up Drexel and find out what was going on at a small company that had issued bonds a few years before," complained Jim Caywood, a partner at Caywood-Christian Capital Management. "Mike kept track of that. Now you call up and nobody is up to date on the company."[52]

DREXEL'S DEMISE

The sell-off in junk continued, fueled by news of additional calamities. On January 15, 1990, Campeau Corp. filed for Chapter 11 bankruptcy. The following month, a proposed junk financing for UAL fell through. The market was in disarray. The continuous outpouring of criticism and hints of legislation to curb the market, together with attempts to link junk financings to the collapse of the thrifts, added to the nervousness.

In January, Drexel mailed out invitations to the annual Institutional Research Conference, which, as usual, was to be held in April in Beverly Hills. Joseph and his colleagues were sending a signal: "We're still here, and we intend to remain." Later that month, he told a reporter, "I see daylight. The worst is behind us."[53]

The firm's leadership knew this was not so. Drexel was in deep financial difficulties. It hadn't been able to cut back its portfolio of unsold bonds, which remained at $1 billion. Even as Joseph assured reporters of Drexel's health, he was taking $400 million out of its securities subsidiaries, which caused reserves to fall below capital requirements.[54]

In early February, Joseph learned that the creditors of Drexel's Belgian parent company had refused to extend their credit line for commercial paper. Drexel's capital, more than $1 billion, had been placed in its broker-dealer subsidiary. Ordinarily, this would have been available to the parent, but the SEC insisted that the parent raise the money on its own. Joseph and other top officials spent the weekend of February 10–11 attempting to get more than $300 million in the form of a loan, and no avail. Some of the troops were deserting. When Joseph asked Ackerman to assist, he tendered his resignation.

All the while, Joseph kept Federal Reserve Bank Chairman Alan Greenspan and E. Gerald Corrigan, head of the New York Fed, informed of Drexel's situation, perhaps hoping for a rescue, as was provided to Chrysler and other large companies. SEC Chairman Richard Breeden, no admirer of Drexel, offered no help. Secretary of the Treasury Brady agreed to take a call from Joseph, but he, too, refused aid, thereby settling the score for the Unocal fight. Drexel's opponents at the Business Roundtable sat back and watched the SEC finally put an end to their tormentor.

The investment banking industry also was delighted. Long resentful of the way Drexel had tried to monopolize the junk business, and hungry to scavenge the remains of the ailing firm, rivals eagerly spread baleful rumors. The major source was Salomon, where John Gutfreund was making an effort to become the new leader in junk, raiding Drexel for customers and bankers. Now, Gutfreund plunged his stiletto into Joseph's side, telling the Fed it was about to announce that Salomon would cease conducting business with Drexel, and other banks were likely to follow.[55]

As late as the evening of February 12, there was some talk of a bailout, for which there were precedents. In 1987, E.F. Hutton had been on the financial ropes, and with Washington's backing, other banks had pitched in and supported it until a buyer could be found. This wouldn't happen with Drexel. The financial establishment refused aid. NYSE Chairman John Phelan, Jr., denied that the Exchange had any responsibilities. "We didn't let a member firm fail," he said. "What went broke was a non-regulated company."[56] This was literally true, but the Drexel brokerage subsidiary was a member firm, so Phelan was begging the issue. "You have to ask, if it were Morgan Stanley, would it have gone under?" asked Roy Smith, of Goldman Sachs, rhetorically. "No," he replied, "It would have been saved by the Federal Reserve, the stock exchange, the banks, or someone. But Drexel had no friends."[65]

So, Joseph could expect no assistance from Wall Street, or from a government that had forced it to the wall. None of this surprised him. "There are constituencies out there that have reasons to dislike what Drexel has been able to achieve," he told a reporter. "We have found ways to finance medium-sized, growing companies. That has taken business away from the banks . . . . There are clearly companies that have been attacked in the takeover game that feel very bitter about us." "We were tough on the way up," recalled another Drexel officer. "We never made friends. We stole business from other firms. We made the banks look silly. This was payback time. The Establishment finally got us."[57]

On the evening of February 12, Joseph was told by the Fed and the Treasury that he must either file for Chapter 11 protection or accept a government-sponsored liquidation. Drexel's plight was the talk of the Street on Monday morning. At 6:00 A.M., Joseph told his board it was all over. "The four most powerful regulators [Brady, Corrigan, Breeden, and Phelan] have told us to go out of business." Without dissent, the board voted for bankruptcy.[58]

Later that day, Joseph informed Drexel's employees of the firm's collapse, and within hours, most were seeking employment elsewhere.

The *Wall Street Journal*'s lead editorial later in the week dealt with the Drexel bankruptcy. It noted that after three years of investigation, the government still hadn't brought Milken to court, and that Drexel was being blamed for deals in which it wasn't involved.

> When it comes to Drexel Burnham Lambert, there's only one thing everyone agrees on. The firm's troubles began with a federal prosecution, not some virus infiltrating all the companies that use junk bond financing. Rudolph

Giuliani's legacy now includes the collapse of a major securities firm and its 5,000 employees. Now someone from the Justice Department needs to explain what it was that Milken allegedly did to justify the punishment being inflicted on the capital markets.[59]

This was a paramount point. The onus was now on the Justice Department to demonstrate that Milken's crimes were so horrendous as to warrant the destruction of a major investment bank and the risk of a financial panic. There was no doubt the government would press hard to have Milken declared guilty of serious felonies. Moreover, there was pressure on the department to force Milken into a plea bargain. What if the case came to court and Milken was exonerated? How might the Justice Department defend itself against charges of judicial brutality and recklessness?

By Friday, only a skeleton force remained at Drexel's Manhattan headquarters and at the Beverly Hills enclave. Drexel clients were moving on to other houses. Its professionals, admired by rivals, would be snapped up, although many took pay cuts.

Salomon purchased the Drexel data base, which included client transactions and holdings. To no one's surprise, Joe Bencivenga and other Milken acolytes relocated there. The Resolution Trust Corp. took on Salomon as its adviser in disposing of its junk portfolio. Later, it would be revealed that Salomon had purchased for its own account a good deal of the junk in the RTC account for which it acted as adviser.[60] Ironically, Bencivenga was instrumental in assisting in the purchase of bonds he had been involved with while at Drexel.

Little more than a year after Milken's departure, the firm that was once the envy of Wall Street was no more. "The use of RICO destroyed two businesses [the other was Princeton/Newport] which would certainly be in existence but for the abuse of power," said white-collar criminal attorney Gerald B. Lefcourt.[61]

Integrated Resources filed for bankruptcy the same day Drexel failed. In an unrelated development, the nation's seventh-largest accounting firm, Laventhal & Horwath, also took shelter behind Chapter 11. In 1991, Columbia S&L would be taken over by the Resolution Trust Corp., after posting losses of $1.4 billion the previous two years, most of it due to the collapse of the junk market and enforcement of the FIRREA provisions.

More startling was the First Executive failure. At the end of 1989, after a half year of hemorrhaging funds and seeing new business dry up, the embattled insurance company still had $850 million in capital surplus and mandatory security valuation reserves, while stockholders' equity was $1 billion. Nine months later, after more torrents of bad publicity, the reserves had declined to $450 million, but, amazingly, First Executive was still viable. But the pounding continued, as troubled policyholders cashed in. On

April 1, 1991, the company revealed that it had lost $366 million in 1990, and stockholders' equity had fallen to $378 million.[62]

After surviving more than a year of bad publicity resulting in policy cancellations, transfers, and liquidations, in addition to the sharp decline in the value of its portfolio, Executive Life of California was seized by the regulatory commission on April 11, 1991. On May 13, the company filed for voluntary bankruptcy. It was the biggest insurance collapse in American history, caused in large part by the government's vendetta against junk.

By then, Mike Milken was behind bars, and the junk era had ended.

11
CRIME AND PUNISHMENT

Shortly after learning that Boesky had been arrested, Milken assembled an impressive legal team, whose considerable fees were paid by Drexel. Edward Bennett Williams, of Williams & Connally, one of the nation's premier trial lawyers, was his original lead attorney. Williams died in August 1988 and was replaced by Arthur Liman, of Paul, Weiss, Rifkin, Wharton & Harrison, who had represented such Drexel clients as Nelson Peltz and Ron Perelman. How Williams might have structured the defense will never be known, but, after it was all over, Milken's associates said they believed Liman had bungled the case.

Rudolph Giuliani had gathered much of the material he felt would justify an indictment, but he wouldn't be there to file the papers. Through the autumn and early winter of 1988, rumors circulated that he would seek the Republican nomination for mayor of New York. This appeared plausible after he announced his resignation on January 18, 1989, and was replaced temporarily by Benito Romano.

Romano offered Milken a deal. The government would drop most of the charges, including insider trading and racketeering. In return, Milken would be required to plead guilty to two felony counts. The charges against his brother would be dropped if he would plead guilty to a third count. Finally, Milken would have to agree to cooperate with the Justice Department by naming others involved in his crimes.

By offering this deal, the Justice Department all but conceded the weakness of its case, especially the idea of Milken as the ringleader of a gigantic conspiracy. By insisting upon Milken's cooperation in targeting others, Romano implied that, while Milken might be guilty of some misdeeds, they were not so severe as to have merited the scope of its crusade against junk, much less Drexel's destruction. Perhaps, the public would believe that the scope of the inquiry had been justified if others were implicated.

Milken was given a deadline of the afternoon of Wednesday, March 29, to accept. Believing this to be the best his client could hope for, Liman advised

Milken to take the offer. With close friends urging him to fight to the end, Milken hesitated. Finally, he agreed to the plea bargain, but only after the Justice Department's deadline had passed. The offer was withdrawn.

WHAT WAS MILKEN'S CRIME?

Why did Milken ultimately accept the plea bargain? And why had he hesitated? Later, associates would claim he had been under constant pressure and was severely stressed, and did so to end his agony. If it was expedient psychologically, it made no sense from a defense point of view. Attorney Alan Dershowitz, who later would be retained by Milken, faulted him and Liman for failing to act decisively. The decision whether to cooperate has to be made early, he said. "If you're going to cooperate, you have to be the world's greatest cooperator. And if you're going to fight, you have to be the world's greatest fighter. You can't give an inch. In the end, this case was too vacillating."[1]

Later that afternoon, March 29, Romano brought a 98-count indictment against Michael and Lowell Milken and Bruce Newberg. The charges included 54 for mail fraud, 33 for securities fraud, 5 for false filing of income taxes, 2 for RICO-related crimes, and 1 of assisting in the preparation of a bogus tax return. If Milken was found guilty, the government could strip him of every cent he had and put him away for up to 520 years. The government also announced it would attempt to obtain forfeitures from the three men of an astounding $1.8 billion, the total they received from Drexel from 1984 to 1987.

The public now learned of Milken's remuneration. Earlier, reporters had guessed that Milken's take had been on the order of $40 million. Five hundred and fifty million dollars was something else.[2]

Milken's compensation resulted from that deal with I. W. Burnham that permitted him to retain one dollar of every three he earned for the firm. He was given that amount to distribute among his unit. Milken had always retained the largest portion for himself. Accordingly, he made $46 million in 1983, the last year in which there were no hostile takeovers at Drexel. The amount rose to $124 million in 1984, $135 million in 1985, and $295 million in 1986. In 1987, Milken's bonus pool came to $700 million, and as noted his remuneration was $550 million. In addition, he earned large amounts from ancillary ventures, not counted in the $550 million.

Milken's personal earnings were more than the total profits of most firms on the Fortune 500 list. One reporter calculated that he received $1,046 a minute, based on a 14-hour workday. To mitigate the shock, Milken's public relations representative noted that he paid half of that in taxes and gave another 30 percent to charity. No matter. The image of the "$550 million man" was etched in the public consciousness and would haunt Milken in the years that followed.[3]

The numbers involved in Milken's wages set off a storm of criticism among Drexel's former eastern contingent. From the start there had been animosity between Beverly Hills and New York. The New Yorkers knew the salaries and bonuses paid to those in Beverly Hills were much higher than theirs, and resented this bitterly. On learning of the true amounts involved, one East Coast Drexel banker told *Institutional Investor,* "I had no idea [the West Coast was] earning so much more." Another banker added, "It was not just demoralizing. It raised the question, 'Who's in charge?'" "It was always we and they," griped an East Coast manager.[4] The loyalty they once had felt for Milken evaporated.

Milken had other matters to worry about. He seemed defiant regarding the charges, telling the press:

> In America, an indictment marks the beginning of the legal process, not the end. After almost two and a half years of leaks and distortions, I am now eager to present all the facts in an open and unbiased forum. I will plead not guilty to the charges and vigorously fight these allegations. I am confident that in the end I will be vindicated.[5]

Even so, negotiations with the U.S. Attorney's office continued.

News of the indictment delighted Fred Hartley, who told a reporter he thought the indictment was "marvelous." He denied that he felt this way because of the near takeover by Pickens of Unocal. Rather, Hartley said, "Junk bonds were destroying the central financial system of the country and he [Milken] initiated the whole concept."[6]

Milken had his defenders. On March 31, close to 100 former Drexel clients signed an advertisement sponsored by Integrated Resources's Selig Zises, which appeared in the *Wall Street Journal* and other newspapers, proclaiming, "Mike Milken, We Believe in You." John Kluge, Nelson Pelz, William McGowan, and many more signed the declaration. Absent were such celebrated client names as Icahn, Pickens, Steinberg, Perelman, and Spiegel.

The Milkens formally pleaded not guilty on April 7. Romano's office started playing hardball. It asked the judge to set a high bail, and this was done: $700 million.

Liman and his team fenced with the Justice Department for a year, as the public received an education in just what it was Milken had done, his significance in American financial history, and the nature of his alleged crimes. In the end, Milken accepted a plea bargain. On April 20, 1990, he agreed to plead guilty to six felony charges, none of which involved insider trading, bribery, racketeering, or manipulating the prices of stocks, the key elements of Boesky's plea bargain. He also agreed that, after sentencing, he would cooperate with the Justice Department. The government would not file additional criminal charges, but Milken remained subject to civil actions and criminal charges from other jurisdictions. It appeared he would be spending a good deal of time in the courts for the rest of his life. With this, the Justice Department might validate its actions, which had led to Drexel's failure.

The defense strategy was a blunder. The government had started out by suggesting that Milken was a master criminal. Now, it offered him a plea bargain on minor charges. Then and later, Milken believed he was guilty of nothing more than technical violations. Liman and other attorneys had persuaded him that an admission of guilt to minor infractions would result in a suspended sentence, or perhaps community service in lieu of imprisonment. How they could believe this, given the atmosphere of the time and the record of sentencing in the other cases, is a mystery.

Couldn't Milken's attorneys see the desperation in this government action? Later, it would be suggested that they permitted Milken to accept the plea bargain because he continued to unravel under the pressure. If so, the plea is understandable. If not, it is incomprehensible. What is clear about the plea bargain is that the government recognized the weakness of its case. Otherwise, how can one explain so drastic a reduction in charges? It was as if a prosecutor had brought charges of manslaughter against a reckless driver and then agreed to a guilty plea to running a red light.

The guilty plea was a mistake for other reasons. Had Milken stood his ground and gone the route Dershowitz suggested, he might have been found guilty of those infractions, but the debate regarding his position in financial history would be raging more passionately than it is today.

In reality, the Justice Department was in more trouble than Milken at that moment. Princeton/Newport was a memory. So was Drexel. Had Milken pleaded not guilty, heads might have rolled at Justice, and today Milken could have been a hounded victim, rather than a despised ex-con.

Milken's lawyers tried to put the best face possible on the deal. In a press release, Liman said:

> The charges speak for themselves. I urge you to read them and the allocution carefully. The charges are a far cry from the lurid, irresponsible and prejudicial accusations against Michael that have been made by anonymous sources to the press for the past three and a half years. The charges do not involve RICO or insider trading, nor do they reflect on the fundamentals of the junk bond market.

Some interested observers greeted the plea bargain with mixed feelings. The *New York Times* devoted an editorial to the subject on May 1:

> Michael Milken is a convicted felon. But he is also a financial genius who transformed high-risk bonds—junk bonds—into a lifeline of credit for hundreds of

emerging companies. Snubbed by the banks, these businesses would otherwise have shriveled.

In other words, the Milken case presents issues far more important than one person's slide from the financial pinnacle. There is no condoning Mr. Milken's criminality. But if overzealous Government regulators overreact by indiscriminately dismantling his junk bond legacy, they will wind up crushing the most dynamic part of the economy.

The charges themselves were minor, even trivial to those who understood the character of investment banking during the 1980s. Four concerned illegal securities transactions with Boesky and, clearly, had resulted from information provided to Giuliani by Boesky.

One of these four charges involved Victor Posner's takeover of Fischbach Corp. As part of the takeover strategy, Milken asked Boesky to make heavy, reported purchases of the firm's stock, with the promise that Drexel would make up any losses. This was done to create the impression that Boesky was making a play for that company, and free Posner from judicial constraints. Devious and reprehensible? Certainly. Illegal? No. Such practices were common during the takeover era. The problem here was that Boesky did not file a Schedule 13-D statement to reflect Milken's activity and his guarantee. Did Milken know this? Perhaps, and if so, that was a crime. But Milken pleaded guilty only to "aiding and abetting" Boesky, who conducted the purchases. Boesky was not charged with failure to file.

On another count, Milken acknowledged aiding Boesky in failing to file an X-17-A form, stating his net capital position. Again, Boesky wasn't indicted for this crime. Milken and Boesky worked together to support the price of MCA, which Steve Wynn's Golden Nugget, another Milken client, was selling after a failed attempt to capture MCA. Milken guaranteed that Drexel would make up any losses incurred by Boesky. Milken would purchase 1 million shares of Helmerich & Payne from Boesky, although Milken remained responsible for losses. This was done to enable Boesky to give the impression of being in compliance with SEC requirements.

That Boesky, cooperating fully with the government, still could not provide it with sufficient information to support more serious charges against Milken, was a measure of the weakness of the case. The Justice Department really had to stretch. This was the first time anyone had been obliged to plead criminally guilty to such securities violations. In the past, defendants had been permitted to plead on civil charges.

The information Boesky promised to reveal about others in the industry turned out to be equally disappointing. The plea bargain was another indication that Boesky was one of the winners in all of this maneuvering.

One of the two non-Boesky-related charges involved false reporting of the prices of Drexel trades with the Finsbury Fund. Instead of taking a commission, Drexel had charged Finsbury a fraction of a point more on purchases, although always within the market range for the security. If Milken had accepted the identical amount as a commission, no crime would have been committed. The charge for this offense was mail fraud. Therefore, if the necessary papers had been delivered by a private company or by hand, there would have been no crime.

Milken also had assisted David Solomon in reducing his income tax liability. In itself, this was not a crime; it was an issue of tax avoidance, not evasion. Solomon was never indicted for this action, nor was his tax statement challenged. Milken had promised to include him in deals in the future that would make up those losses. This was against the law.

These, in sum, were the charges to which Milken pleaded guilty, and for which the Justice Department was prepared to settle. "Did the crimes Milken confessed to, taken against the broad scope of the government's initial allegations, justify the war?" asked *Business Week,* implying they did not.[7] SEC chairman Richard Breeden, disagreed, telling the press that Milken's admissions "demonstrate that he stood at the center of a network of manipulation, fraud, and deceit."[8] Breeden did not say what there was in the six counts constituting manipulation, fraud, and deceit.

Louis Wolfson was 78 years old when the government went after Milken. The situation must have seemed more than slightly familiar to him, even down to the cast of characters. Michael Armstrong, who had prosecuted the Continental case against Wolfson, was defending Lowell Milken. Edward Bennett Williams had been Wolfson's attorney in several appeals in another case. Liman had represented Joseph Kosow, Wolfson's codefendant. So Wolfson, all but forgotten outside of the thoroughbred business, watched what, at times, must have seemed a rerun of his experiences. Another prominent businessman who had troubled entrenched interests had been hauled into court. But there was one important difference. Wolfson had pleaded innocent and had not backed down. Milken admitted that he had committed felonies. To this day, Wolfson protests he was guilty of no crime. Milken will never be able to do that.

The 58-year-old Jimmy Ling was still active in business when he learned of Milken's indictment. Ling refused to answer telephone callers interested in learning his opinions. In 1989, he was chairman of Hill Investors, a private, Dallas-based venture capital company. It engaged in relatively small deals—for example, in 1987, Hill joined with a finance company to purchase Aviation Technical Support, a defunct manufacturer of aircraft engine enclosures for $14 million.[9] Beyond a small circle of acquaintances and those with longer memories than usual (like Wolfson), the tycoon who, for many, symbolized the conglomerate movement is largely forgotten.

With Milken's guilty plea, he lost his last chance to claim that he had been railroaded, and reinforced the public's perception of him as its premiere white-collar criminal. On August 31, 1992, *Forbes* ran an interview with Milken in which it was suggested that the government had tormented him into confessions. "No intelligent American is going to buy the image" of Milken as having been harassed into the guilty plea, wrote David W. Hendry in a subsequent letter to the editor. "Soliciting and trading on inside information is not a skill; it is a crime." To this, the editor replied, "It is a matter of record that Milken did not plead guilty to violating insider trading laws nor was he found guilty of that crime."[10] No matter. By 1990, when Milken was going through his ordeal, Lou Wolfson was still threatening law suits against those who believed he had been guilty of securities manipulations, not the technical violations for which he had been sent to prison. For the rest of his life, Milken will be accused of crimes for which he was not charged and to which he did not plead guilty.

The public response to the plea bargain was mixed but, on balance, unfavorable to Milken. The court of public opinion found Milken guilty of crimes that it little understood. Instant experts on talk radio denounced him, and their listeners seemed to agree, although they often got the name wrong, calling him "Milliken."

THE FATICO HEARING

What of the original 98 counts, including insider trading? In dropping almost all of those charges, the government not only looked foolish but irresponsible. Something would have to be done about a situation that, coming after several reversals, appeared to give credence to those who said it was all a politically inspired witch hunt.

Justice Department attorneys asked Judge Kimba Wood, who was assigned to hear the case, for permission to present material regarding Milken's other activities. None of this had anything to do with the plea bargain. Rather, it was information the prosecution hoped would inform Judge Wood's sentence. The government asserted that, while the evidence in these areas was insufficient to indict, there would be enough information for her to justify giving Milken a stiff sentence. Perhaps, the prosecution was aware of just how minor the remaining six charges seemed and wanted to create the impression that Milken was indeed guilty of insider trading and other crimes. This way, the prosecution would come as close as possible to a ventilation of the original case.

To the layman, the presentation of evidence without an indictment might appear unfair, but there was a precedent for it in what was termed a "Fatico hearing." Such a special hearing was named after a case involving Carmine and Daniel Fatico, brothers with organized-crime connections. In 1979, a jury had found the Faticos guilty of hijacking a truck filled with furs at Kennedy Airport. After a trial in which the term "Mafia" was not mentioned, the Justice Department was permitted to introduce evidence at a special hearing so that the judge would conclude that the Faticos were members of the Gambino crime family.

Liman had expected something like this. He charged the Justice Department with reneging on the deal, but he was powerless to do any more. Later, during the sentencing, Judge Wood said she had agreed to the Fatico hearing because of the furor surrounding the case.

> It has also been suggested that the defendant was forced to plead guilty to minor technical violations because the government in bad faith hounded him with a massive amount of other misconduct which could theoretically take defendant years to defend and because the government allegedly had indicted his brother to put unfair pressure on defendant.

> The government in contrast claimed defendant was one of the most villainous criminals Wall Street had ever produced and he abused his position as head of the most powerful department in one of the most powerful firms on Wall Street to regularly distort the securities market and enrich himself and Drexel, and, finally, that he obstructed justice.[11]

The hearing began in October. After a lengthy opening statement, Assistant U.S. Attorney John Carroll claimed that Milken and Boesky had conspired to manipulate the stock of Wickes Corp., a Drexel client that had generated approximately $118 million in fees. "Milken provided Wickes with extraordinary investment banking services," said Carroll. "He committed crimes for his client. In doing so, he cheated the customers who had bought Wickes preferred stock from him out of millions of dollars in dividends." He had done this, Carroll charged, by driving up the Wickes price to the point where the company would not have to make a special payment.

After the presentation, Liman rose to concede that Wickes had been manipulated but denied that Milken had anything to do with it, demanding that Carroll produce evidence. This Carroll attempted to do by introducing the grand-jury testimony of Milken's former associate, Peter Gardiner, who had been threatened with an indictment unless he pointed the finger of blame at Milken. Earlier, Gardiner had admitted having committed perjury before the grand jury, and now he had been granted immunity for his testimony. Gardiner changed his testimony when presented with evidence regarding trades and admitted he hadn't even been in the office when they were made. Moreover, when Boesky was seeking to boost the price of Wickes, Milken's department had been a net *seller* of the stock, hardly the action of one colluding with the admitted manipulator.

The Justice Department hoped to prove that Milken was cognizant of all that transpired and, to this end, called James Dahl to the stand. Dahl seemed willing to say whatever it took to ingratiate himself with the Justice

Department and avoid prosecution. Recall that in the Staley Continental case in October 1987, he had testified that he had the authority to trade stock without authorization, on that occasion clearing Milken of responsibility. A year later, he changed his tune. Asked, "During the period of time you were working in the high-yield department at any time did Mr. Milken supervise your activities?" Dahl replied, "At all times."

"How did he go about supervising your activities, Mr. Dahl?"

"Each day all of us, including Mike, would receive a copy of the transaction report that gave an alphabetical listing of all the trades that had been done the previous day. And it was Mike's practice to go through all of the trades and make comments about them, suggest ways we could improve our business, increase our productivity, et cetera. On all trades salesmen did, including myself, we had to have approval from either Mike or one of the traders before we could exercise a trade."[12]

Cary Maultasch also was brought to the stand to corroborate the government's case. In cross-examining Maultasch, Liman asked, "Did he [Milken] ever ask you to close a stock at a particular price?" to which Maultasch replied, "Not to my recollection." Liman continued, "Or to manipulate a stock?" Maultasch: "No, sir." Judge Wood declared that the Justice Department's evidence on Wickes was "fairly ambiguous."

The government next contended that there had been irregularities in Drexel's support of KKR's 1985 uninvited bid for Storer Broadcasting at $75 a share, plus bonds with a face value of $25, which would require $2 billion. Soon after KKR had made its offer, rumors surfaced that another company was preparing a rival bid. In an attempt to mask his actions, Milken had arranged for Boesky to purchase some 124,000 shares of Storer, with the understanding that Drexel would receive any profits and pay for any losses. Comcast was the other bidder, coming in with an offer of $82 a share, plus bonds. Soon after, Boesky notified the SEC that he had more than 5 percent of the common.

The Justice Department alleged that Milken had hoped that Storer's management would accept the KKR offer, since KKR might permit it to remain in office. But a bidding war developed, which ended when KKR got the company for $91 and paper a share, which came to $2.4 billion.

As has been related, Milken then told KKR that, because of the higher price, some of his larger bond clients were troubled and would need sweeteners to take the bonds required to raise that amount. KKR agreed, and Milken had Drexel issue warrants to purchase the common stock, which were sold at discounts to those institutional investors who took an issue of preferred stock that was a tough sell, while many of the warrants went into in the accounts of fund managers.

When the Justice Department suggested that Milken had used the warrants as bribes, Liman retorted that there was no evidence. He had asked for a quid pro quo. Some of the warrants wound up in Milken's outside partnerships and those of other leading figures at Drexel. Banker Dean Kehler was irate at being left out. "Don't talk to me about warrants. I didn't get any," he said angrily. Peter Ackerman, who was cut in, told a critic, "Listen, you don't know all the facts. The facts are that we committed for a lot of the financing in this deal. We took risk. We had exposure, personal exposure, and, as a result, we were entitled to the warrants."

Ackerman did not explain how Drexel was at risk in the deal, probably because it was not true. He and others involved would have been embarrassed professionally if it fell through, but that was all the danger there was. Seen in this light, Milken's use of the warrants was ethically flawed. But it was not illegal.

Recall Benalder Bayse, who got his job as a portfolio manager at First Investors due to a Drexel recommendation. He continued that fund's warm relations with Drexel and was rewarded by being dealt in personally on some deals. Bayse would purchase warrants from Drexel and then sell them back for a profit. He took some of the Storer paper for his funds and soon called his Drexel contact, Roy Johnson, to ask about the warrants. "I knew I had been a good customer, that because I was trying to change the character of the portfolio in the last two quarters of 1985 that I had done a lot of business and I didn't feel it was out of line for me to ask to invest in an opportunity that I thought was a good one."

Bayse was permitted to purchase 100,000 warrants for $8,800. Other deals followed, all violations of Bayse's contract with First Investors. He avoided being criminally charged by agreeing to cooperate with the Justice Department. But Bayse also testified that Milken was not involved with these purchases. All were made through Johnson.

Richard Grassgreen, the former executive vice president for Kindercare, a Drexel client, testified after agreeing to plead guilty to two felony counts and to return illegally acquired moneys. Grassgreen said that in his capacity as portfolio manager at Kindercare, he regularly invested in Drexel offerings and provided financial assistance to Drexel clients seeking takeovers. In return, he and CEO Perry Mendel received payoffs in the form of warrants of such firms as Pantry Pride, Pacific Lumber, Midcon, and GAF. Grassgreen and Perry had made hundreds of thousands of dollars this way.

Grassgreen claimed that Milken had telephoned him during the Storer underwriting, telling him it was a great deal and to invest in it. "He then advised me, he said, there are warrants for you in the Storer deal. I asked him if he meant if it was for Kindercare. He said, no, it was for you and Perry. I said could Kindercare get some? He said, it's for you and Perry." Liman didn't even bother to question this claim, indicating that he knew there was no way to shake the testimony. Thus, at the very least, Milken had risked the appearance of making a payoff for past and future favors.

As with the Beatrice LBO, KKR was under the impression that the warrants were to be used to sweeten the deal for investors, not to further enrich Drexel bankers and other clients. On learning the facts, Henry Kravis and others were angered, but they soon cooled down. Said KKR banker R. Theodore Ammon, "I think it's fair to say we felt that there was no one better in the business, that they could provide the best service to us for the types of deals that we were doing."

A 1983 deal involving Caesar's Hotel and Casino was introduced. Dahl had told the grand jury that Milken had asked him to buy Caesar's World bonds for his customers. Before a meeting with Caesar's World CFO Stephen Ackerman, Milken hinted that he had inside information regarding the deal. But Liman had testimony that no inside information was revealed at that meeting. Moreover, when Drexel's pension fund wanted to purchase Caesar's World bonds, Milken cut the amount in half; this was not the action of someone acting on inside information. Once again, the Justice Department had chosen not to prosecute on these grounds. Nor did the prosecution call the one witness whose testimony it once had asserted would be the most damaging: Ivan Boesky. To do so would open Boesky to cross-examination by Liman.

After the government had made its case in the Fatico hearings, Judge Wood stated, "I am unable to find that Michael Milken traded on material, nonpublic information." In a way, this was a vindication. The government's attempts to implicate Milken in crimes other than those to which he had pleaded guilty had fallen flat.

Yet, the prosecution didn't suffer a complete defeat. If Milken wasn't guilty of additional offenses, the same could not be said for Drexel. That some at the firm had played fast and loose appeared abundantly clear. Milken was part of Drexel. On this part of the hearing, one might have concluded that a "Scotch verdict" would have made sense: "not proven."

In early 1913, J. P. Morgan had testified at a special investigation by a subcommittee of the House Banking and Currency Committee, which came to be known as the Pujo Committee, after its chairman, Representative Arsene Pujo (D. Louisiana). The 76-year-old banker seemed to realize that this was to be his swan song. When counsel Samuel Untermyer asked, "Is not commercial credit based primarily upon money or property?" Morgan replied, "No sir, the first thing is character."

"Before money and property?"

"Before money or anything else. Money cannot buy it."

What happens when a banker abuses his power and loses the trust of his fellows? Untermyer wanted to know. Does he lose his character? "Yes," Morgan replied, "and he never gets it back again, either."[13]

After his experiences in the courtroom, few would compare Milken with Morgan.

IN THE COURT OF PUBLIC OPINION

Michael Lewis, the author of *Liar's Poker,* wrote that for most people Milken's guilt rested in selling junk bonds, not in technical violations or what had been discussed in the Fatico hearing. "Of Mr. Milken's many disruptive deeds, none that truly angered people was illegal. Selling junk bonds to willing investors—even to savings and loans—was legal."[14]

This message was repeated over and over again by individuals who understood the market, to little avail. Milken was guilty of something, and those who had only a faint idea of what constituted junk seemed to believe that selling junk was his crime.

Nor was there much consideration of Milken's role in financing companies that otherwise might not have obtained needed funds. The list was impressive, including the likes of Comdisco, Barnes & Noble, MCI Communications, Viacom International, Duracell, and scores of others. Most people simply didn't know this. For example, in the January 1990 issue of *Playboy* magazine, Mark Hosnaball caricatured Milken as "Money Mad Mike," the symbol of what had gone wrong in the country during the 1980s. A second profile in the same magazine, by Joshua Hammer, concerned "Triumphant Ted" Turner, who "weakened the networks' hammerlock on news and entertainment broadcasting." Turner was praised for having founded the Better World Society, whose director described him as "two-thirds do-gooder, one-third entrepreneur." Milken, in contrast, was criticized for having involved his charities in junk bond deals. What neither writer seemed to know was that Milken was one of Turner's more important bankers and that without his efforts, the Turner empire could not have developed as it did.[15]

Hosnaball was not alone in viewing Milken's coming incarceration as a fitting end to a decade of avarice. As might have been expected, hyperbole was the rule of the day for the $550 million man. "The entire purpose of the plea arrangements made with Ivan Boesky, Drexel Burnham and others was to get at the man who is accused of masterminding what was by far the largest fraud ever perpetrated in modern history," a "man-in-the-street" told *Newsday.*[16]

KIMBA WOOD AND THE ART OF SENTENCING

In sentencing Milken on November 21, 1990, Judge Wood said, "I believe that a prison term is required for the purpose of general deterrence; that is, the need to deter others from violating the law and the possibility that the sentence given in one case will prevent others from violating the law." The Judge went out of her way to deny that she was pronouncing a "verdict on a decade of greed," but that is precisely what she wound up doing.

Milken was sentenced to ten years in the penitentiary, plus 1,800 hours of community service a year for three years, and he was fined $200 million. This was in addition to $400 million already extracted from him for a restitution fund. Later, there would be an additional $500 million fine to settle an anticipated 150 legal actions.[17] Six of those ten years were for assisting Boesky in committing felonies. Boesky had received a fine of $100 million, plus three years in jail.

The Judge was "sending a message," a term one heard often in the days that followed. Timothy Smith, Director of the Interfaith Center on Corporate Responsibility, supported Judge Wood. He thought the sentence "clearly sends a message to the business community that corporate crime is not to go unpunished." SEC chairman Richard Breeden echoed Smith. "This sentence should send the message that criminal misconduct in our financial markets will not be tolerated, regardless of one's wealth or power." Indeed, it was quite similar to the message Judge Palmieri had sent in the Wolfson case.

Securities attorney Thomas Russo had a different interpretation of the sentence. Russo told a reporter, "It does send a strong message when someone has that notoriety. So he's a victim of the publicity in that he probably got more than he deserves. In a sense, Milken and Drexel are becoming the fall guys for a large problem of leverage that goes well beyond anything created by Mike Milken." Dean John W. Rosenblum, of the Graduate School of Business at the University of Virginia, agreed. Speaking to a reporter before Milken's sentencing, he said, "The judge has to be careful not to send the message that one gets taken out and drawn and quartered for creating value and innovation. If the system is looking for scapegoats, then a lot of bright people will not take the risk of doing creative things."[18]

Judge Wood indicated that a primary consideration in the sentence was deterrence. Recall, however, the charges to which Milken pleaded guilty. Did the harsh sentence mean that, in the future, Wall Streeters would have to make certain their clients were not remiss in filing the proper papers or in labeling charges as fees? Hardly. What it came down to was that Milken was sentenced on the original, discarded indictment, and not on those six counts.

The Milken sentence was the most severe of the 70-odd handed down in Wall Street cases during the last ten years. (Paul Bilzerian, CEO of Singer, had the second-longest sentence, four years for having filed false statements with the SEC.) There simply was no clear rationale in the court's actions. Perhaps, Judge Wood had sent out another message. Milken had received a stiff sentence after a plea bargain. Might this not deter plea bargaining in the future?

Judge Wood had seemed indignant that Milken would not name names, as other defendants in such actions had. She even hinted that Milken's time could be shortened given proper cooperation. There were precedents for this. Judge "Maximum John" Sirica had used heavy jail time, which was then reduced, to convince Watergate criminals to cooperate with the Justice Department, and Wood had once clerked for Sirica. Judge Wood's justification for the sentence indicated as much. "I should note for the benefit of those who urge the court to sentence you to the full 28 years in an effort to force you to cooperate with the Justice Department in its investigation in the future, that a court is not permitted to do that." But she followed immediately by saying, "Where a defendant cooperates with the government fully and is of assistance to the government, the defendant deserves a significant reduction in sentence for assisting the government to uncover crimes that are otherwise very resistant to discovery." This, she said, was the grounds for the light Boesky sentence. "If you cooperate, and if the government moves for a reduction in your sentence based on your cooperation, the court can adjust your sentence accordingly."[19]

To his defenders, responding to his sentence, Milken was a hero brought low by enemies who did not understand and appreciate his vision. One defender, Martin Klein, wrote:

> Michael has been sentenced for the failings of the 1980s. He has been sentenced for the arrogance of some of his peers, and for the excessive and illegal acts of others. I ask you how this could happen in America? Perhaps because Michael wished to lead an anonymous life, he is being punished for not publicing his good works? Perhaps the American public and media are so cynical that they can only identify with arrogant, autocratic individuals?

It can be added to this statement that, in an industry where sidestepping rules during manias had been common, prosecutions for all such technical violations on Wall Street would have stripped several banking houses of their key personnel.

Milken's critics obviously had a different view. For journalist Robert Reno, who regularly pilloried Milken in his *Newsday* columns, the sentence wasn't stiff enough. Nor did the prosecution reach all of the guilty. Reno raged:

> Where are all the people in the Reagan administration whose policies and tax breaks helped Milken create [junk bonds]? Where are all the Drexel Burnham Lambert officials who shamelessly voted themselves huge bonuses before taking the firm into bankruptcy? Where are the corporate raiders who used Mike's invention to mercilessly destroy corporations and jobs as a maniac might rake a schoolyard with a legally purchased semi-automatic? Where are the savings-and-loan regulators, the savings-and-loan officers, who allowed a whole industry to mortgage the nation with its greed and incompetence? Where are all the brokers who packaged these junk bonds as mutual funds and sold them to old ladies and orphans?

Reno gloated. "Finally, we're going to see what Mike Milken looks like without his toupee."[20]

A *New York Times* editorial tried to be balanced. The editors noted that junk bonds did not contribute materially to the thrift calamity and that the tax code, not Milken, led companies to borrow. The editors also conceded that the leveraged companies introduced efficiencies. On the other hand, the leveraging may have caused investments in new technologies to be post-poned. "The long-term effects of such leveraged buyouts are uncertain," they said. "But if debt-ridden corporations ride out the recession, Mr. Milken's legacy will look brighter. He won't be able to erase his conviction but opin-ions of his financial contributions to upstart companies would soar."[21]

As it turned out, most heavily indebted corporations survived the reces-sion, and the market for junk has revived. In 1986, public junk financings had come in at a record $31.9 billion, and then the offerings declined. In 1989, the total came to $25.1 billion. In 1990, when the market received hammer blows by legislative and administrative actions, the total under-writings added up to a mere $1.4 billion, most for refinancing. Not until early 1991, did bargain hunters appear. Then, with the revival of RJR Nabisco and analyses of the First Executive failure and those of the thrifts, demand rose once again.

Leon Black has emerged as one of the more sophisticated individuals in this market, picking up hastily sold portfolios and making more money at it than he did during the 1980s. Forty billion dollars in junk was marketed in 1991; during the first nine months of 1992, the figure was close to $30 billion. Defaults in the latter period came to $5.6 billion, against $28.5 bil-lion for all of 1990.[22]

Junk is alive, even if Drexel is not. Now, Merrill Lynch and Goldman Sachs lead the way. Along with this revival have come some nagging ques-tions, in financial quarters at least: Was the antijunk crusade overdone? If so, to whose benefit?

PRISON

Milken entered prison at Pleasanton, California, on March 4, 1991. Already, Judge Wood was reconsidering her sentence. The financial harm resulting from Milken's crimes was far less than the $4.7 million the government at-torneys had claimed it was; the U.S. Parole Board estimated that losses re-lating to those six felonies came to $318,082. In light of this, Judge Wood recommended that Milken be incarcerated for from 36 to 40 months. Under parole guidelines, this meant that he would have been eligible for release after three years and four months in prison, October 30, 1994.

Milken was given menial tasks, which he performed without complaint. Then, perhaps to encourage cooperation, he was permitted to teach inmates mathematics and other subjects to assist them in earning high school equivalency diplomas.

Alan Dershowitz now was charged with attempting to further reduce Milken's sentence, while preparing for anticipated further criminal and civil actions. These were not long in coming. Drexel instituted a suit against the Milkens, charging that they were responsible for its downfall, and Milken countersued to obtain deferred compensation.

The search for scapegoats for the thrift and other financial debacles also intensified. The Justice Department announced plans to sue the defunct Drexel for $6.8 billion and involve Milken in a civil action, asserting that the bank had ravaged 40 thrifts. This attempt to switch blame for the S&L fiascoes from Washington to Wall Street, was labeled by the *Economist* as "blatant political opportunism."[23] The egregiousness of the charge was enhanced when the government announced that it had retained Cravath, Swaine & Moore to develop the civil case against Milken. Cravath was the law firm that had handled junk bond offerings for General Development Co. and Campeau, among others. Economist Paul Craig Roberts wondered if the Justice Department's contention was that Drexel bore responsibility for bad deals, "Why isn't the government suing Cravath for its corresponding junk bond role?"[24] For that matter, if collusion with clients and customers had taken place, why hadn't any of *them* been charged with wrongdoing? There never was a hint of civil prosecution against Lindner, Pickens, Icahn, Perelman, or any other client whom Milken had assisted through junk financing. Not until the summer of 1992, when Milken was behind bars, was Spiegel charged with any crime, and then the charge was misapplying Columbia S&L funds for his own uses, not investing in junk or in any way mismanaging the company through the use of junk. The failure of the government, after years of intense investigation, to demonstrate that Milken's web of influence had any criminal content or intent was one of the unspoken failures of its war against the empire of junk.

The assertion that Drexel was responsible for thrift failures was another of the transparently political ruses that appeared so often in the junk bond saga. Nothing further was heard regarding the thrift connection. Nine months later, Drexel settled all its tax claims with the Justice Department for $290 million.[25]

DEMONIZATION

After the sentencing, with Milken in prison, defense attorney Arthur Liman reflected on the experience. "I am convinced that society needs a certain number of demons," he told a reporter. "And if somebody becomes a demon, it is very hard for the process to operate the way it should on paper." As far as Liman was concerned, "the case took on the characteristics of a heresy trial." In other words, Milken lost because he had "become a symbol, the symbol of an era, and it was beyond any kind of control."[26]

Like Wolfson more than 20 years earlier, Milken had been stripped of his humanity and transformed into a mythic figure. As the *Economist* put it, "In many ways it was Wall Street's excesses of the 1980s that was on trial, not Mr. Milken." Rare is the person today, with more than a passing interest in finance, who can entertain a balanced view of Michael Milken.

It became apparent that Milken would not cooperate with the government when, in June 1992, he appeared in the government's case against Drexel banker Alan Rosenthal. On the face of it, Rosenthal was on trial for minor crimes, but the real offense was his prior refusal to testify against Milken. Journalist Reno had his wish about seeing a bald Milken. Stripped of his toupee, Milken seemed quite ordinary, thinner and frailer than he had been during his own sentencing. If he had looked that way two years earlier, he might have evoked sympathy. But Milken never wanted sympathy. Like Wolfson, he wanted justice and felt he had been denied it.

During the Rosenthal trial, additional allegations were made that Milken was involved with shady operations, in this case, a kickback scheme. David Solomon testified that Milken had threatened to remove him as manager of Solomon Assets Management if Solomon refused to pay Milken a cut of 1 percent. Solomon said he refused the first time he was asked, but then he gave in, saying the payment was made to offset fees Drexel was exacting against profits from junk underwriting and trading. Milken denied this claim, and, with his wife and sons in the courtroom, he refused to implicate Rosenthal. He denied having destroyed documents and rejected assertions that Lowell Milken had been involved with his transgressions.

In his brief appearance during the Rosenthal trial, Milken demonstrated the kind of approach that, had it been adopted earlier, might have spared his reputation some of the blows. Several of the jurors said they had been impressed with his intellect.

In the end, four of the more serious charges against Rosenthal were dismissed, and he was found guilty of one technical wrongdoing. Thus, he could claim victory. Milken had salvaged honor on this occasion, but by 1992, it mattered little to any except those closest to him.

Commentary on Milken's testimony at the Rosenthal trial was mixed. In March 1992, while preparing for the trial, Roger S. Hayes Acting United States Attorney for the Southern District, had expressed dissatisfaction with Milken's cooperation, but two weeks after the trial, in a memorandum to Judge Wood, he asserted that Milken's testimony had been useful, even though he had contradicted two other government witnesses. It seemed this might help Milken obtain an early release. But SEC Director William McLucas said, "At this time we cannot credit Mr. Milken with having exposed widespread corrupt industry practices, or with providing the commission with information that might lead to any significant corrective steps in regulatory policy."[27]

Rudolph Giuliani was asked his impression. In June of 1992, Giuliani was considering a second run for the New York mayoralty, and he chose his words carefully. After noting that Milken's only promise to the government had been to testify truthfully, Giuliani complained that he was not as forthcoming as he might have been, and that guilty people were walking free. One of these, he implied, was Rosenthal. John Carroll also was displeased, telling the press, Milken "would score not that high on the candor scale." Yet, Judge Wood thought Carroll's expectations might have been unreasonable.[28] All of this was puzzling. What was going on behind the scenes is unknown, but there was more to this affair than was made public that summer.[29]

There were other court appearances. On July 28, Patricia Ostrander was convicted of taking a bribe from Milken. Milken had testified that he had never given her a payoff or a bribe, and, in fact, he appeared as a witness for the defense. Again, he gave the government no satisfaction. Perhaps because of this, and his cooperation with Jesse Kornbluth in his generally pro-Milken book, *Highly Confident*, Milken was deprived of teaching duties and assigned to a weeding patrol.

Nonetheless, on August 5, 1992, after Milken had served 17 months, Judge Wood announced that she was reducing his sentence. On January 4, 1993, he entered a halfway house near his home. Once again, there was a split between the Justice Department and the SEC, with the former praising Milken for cooperating and the latter bluntly stating that he had not cooperated. On the public record, it would appear that the SEC was correct. The action on Judge Wood's part once again raised that question regarding Drexel. What had been done that was so appalling as to merit the death of that bank?

THE SHADOW OF ANTI-SEMITISM

With rare exceptions, Felix Rohatyn's worst fears were not realized: there was no real eruption of anti-Semitism, but there was a shadow of it. Some callers to radio talk shows pointed out that many Wall Street malefactors were Jews. Also, novelist and journalist Michael M. Thomas caused something of a sensation with his novel, *Hanover Place*. It tells the story, from 1924 to 1990, of a fictitious investment bank that begins as a Protestant, establishment operation, and winds up in the hands of Jews using junk bonds to finance hostile takeovers. Thomas presents cardboard characters. The "good Jews" among them think and behave like the Protestant heros; the bad ones are caricatures of East European Jews. There is anti-Semitic talk in the novel, and individual characters obviously modeled on Icahn, Milken, and others, but Thomas puts most of the bigoted statements into the mouths of miscreants. One of these, a rabid anti-Semite speaking to a Holocaust survivor, utters the kinds of words that troubled Rohatyn and others:

> Why is it, Mr. Lazlo, that if I point out in public that five out of six violent crimes are committed by blacks, even black people will concede I'm simply making an interesting sociological observation with an apparent basis in fact. But if I point out that nine out of ten of those indicted for insider trading and the like are Jewish, and that maybe there's a connection there, too, the world blows up in my face! Why is the one a mere statistic, but the other an act of bigotry! Why is it the police can beat a black youth half to death and no one says boo, but give a Jew a parking ticket, and he screams, "Holocaust!"[30]

Hanover Place disappeared from the bookstores without many outside of Wall Street even knowing it existed. Not so, *Den of Thieves,* by the *Wall Street Journal's* James B. Stewart, a work of nonfiction primarily concerned with the Levine-Boesky-Siegel-Milken connection. Much awaited, it received a laudatory review on the front page of the *New York Times* by Thomas himself, who called it a classic, comparing it to such major works as Henry and Charles Adams' *Chapters of Erie.* Others, however, noted that it seemed to be a restatement of the prosecution's case, rather than a fair attempt to freshly understand and evaluate the principal players.

More a crime story than a recitation of the whys and hows of the takeover phenomenon, *Den of Thieves* was insensitive regarding religious sensibilities tending to identify characters by their religion when it had no bearing on the story. In introducing Milken, his villain, Stewart writes:

> . . . Milken had grown up in a comfortable, upper-middle-class home. Encino, California, a town in the San Fernando Valley north of Los Angeles, had a sizeable Jewish population—the synagogue was near the Milken home—but was about as homogeneous as the rest of rapidly growing Southern California.[31]

When he describes Gary Lynch, one of the book's heros, Stewart says:

> The youngest of five children, Lynch had grown up in the countryside near Middletown, a small city in rural upstate New York near the Pennsylvania border. His father ran a small trucking operation and owned several other small businesses. Lynch was raised a Methodist.[32]

That Milken is a Jew is well known. But why did Stewart find it necessary to identify Lynch as a Methodist? It might appear that this was done to distinguish the good guys from the bad guys.

The title, *Den of Thieves,* was taken from the Gospel of Matthew and refers to Jesus' ejecting the moneylenders from the Temple in Jerusalem. It is possible to infer that the author was alluding to Giuliani and Lynch as doing the same for Wall Street. On one occasion in his book, Stewart refers to a "nest of vipers." Had he used this phrase as his title, there would have been no criticism on that score. In any case, the book drew attorney Alan Dershowitz's fire. He paid for a series of *New York Times* advertisements; on October 17, 1991, in a statement entitled "An Open Letter from Alan Dershowitz Concerning a Conflict of Interest Hidden from the Readers of the New York Times Book Review," he castigated both Thomas and Stewart as anti-Semites. In addition, he challenged them to debates. Stewart denied the charge and refused the dare unless Dershowitz withdrew the claim.

Den of Thieves became a national best-seller. Dershowitz's actions probably boosted rather than harmed sales. Nevertheless, throughout this period, little overt anti-Semitism appeared. As far as most Americans were concerned, Milken and the others were just criminals, not *Jewish* criminals.

THE VERDICT ON MILKEN

Years from now, assuming no major revelation is made, few will remember just what Milken pleaded guilty to. Rather, there will be a vague feeling that he did something terribly wrong; otherwise, why did he admit guilt, and why was he incarcerated? This was Wolfson's lot. Now and then, Wolfson is mentioned in the press. The writers usually say he was found guilty of stock manipulation or insider trading, which was not so. For example, Clark Clifford, an old acquaintance, wrote in his 1991 memoir that Wolfson went to jail for "perjury, stock manipulations, and conspiracy to violate the securities laws." None of this was true.[33]

Future generations likely will conclude that Milken's guilt was not a matter of law but of ethics or morality. The picture of life at Drexel that was described at the Fatico hearing will endure because it offers a far more vivid image than the technical one presented in the plea bargain.

Whether other aspects of the man will persist in the public mind is another matter. Milken deserves praise for his generosity and support for charitable and philanthropic causes, which began long before his troubles with the government. In late 1989, while the press buzzed about Malcolm Forbes' million-dollar birthday party, Milken hosted a dinner at which he dispensed four $250,000 checks to cancer researchers. The event did not make the press because, as a general rule, Milken considered his bequests to be a private matter. He avoided the spotlight, and he seemed embarrassed when praised and complemented.

Nor was avarice part of his personal way of life. Nothing about the man smacked of any of the seven cardinal sins. He was not like Levine and Boesky, who pursued wealth both for its own sake and to enhance their quality of life.

If Milken was principled in his goals, his means were suspect. The Beverly Hills operation was small enough for him to know everything that went on there. It strains credulity to believe that Milken was unaware of the bullying tactics used by Dahl and others. On one occasion, he told the SEC, "I have good hearing and over the years it has developed so that I can hear most of the conversations in the department."[34] From his X-shaped desk, Milken was at the center of things, and he must have seen and heard the rough attempts to use financial muscle on clients, customers, and others, and the destruction of values as well as their creation. It appears that he stood aside, saying nothing, when a word from him could have brought such activities to an end.

Some of Milken's defenders argue that he really had no taste for hostile takeovers and LBOs. In their scenario, Fred Joseph emerges as the key player in this area at Drexel. But according to all unbiased accounts, Milken was the prime mover at Drexel, capable of swaying the firm in any direction he wanted it to go.

What Milken's defenders and critics alike have ignored is the crucial element of motivation. What prompted him to take the chances he did? Why would a person of such talents, imagination, and wealth assume such risks? If Milken never financed a takeover, participated in an LBO, or engaged in any multibillion-dollar deal, he still would have had more than enough money to support himself in the way he wanted to live. Was it really necessary to make almost $2 million dollars a day, five days a week? Why this pursuit of wealth?

In his 1910 novel *Howards End,* E. M. Forster, the British son of a banker, has Ruth Wilcox, his symbol of virtue, ask her businessman husband, "Henry, why do people who have enough money try to get more money?" She doesn't receive a satisfactory answer. Had Forster provided one, perhaps we would have a better insight into Milken's motivations.

The Drexel affair was followed by revelations of Salomon's chicanery during Treasury auctions in 1990 and 1991. The bank was purchasing more two- and five-year Treasury notes than was permitted—in this way, dominating the aftermarket. This action resulted in a shortage of securities, which raised their prices. Those who expected the notes to fall, and so entered into short sales, would get hurt. Then they would have to cover by purchasing the notes at higher prices—from Salomon.

Salomon had been reprimanded several times before this scandal. For example, in 1989, the SEC censured the firm for having made illegal short sales during the October 1987 crash, which it had tried to cover up. When confronted with evidence of wrongdoing, John Gutfreund tried to conceal evidence; finally, he conceded what had happened and stepped down. No explanations were forthcoming. He and others at Salomon never maintained they were in business for anything but money and power. They took risks and lost, and that was that. This was, and probably still is, standard operating procedure on Wall Street.

Gutfreund and the others were not prosecuted, and, unlike Drexel, Salomon survived. Not until late 1992 was anyone in the Salomon affair brought to the bar. On this occasion Paul Mozer, former head of the government bond desk, pleaded guilty to criminal charges.[35] In common with a few other bankers, like Felix Rohatyn and Peter Peterson, Milken articulated a social vision. Such was alien to Gutfreund and most in the financial community. Milken entertained a concept of a future capitalism in which greed played no role. His insights were wider, if shallower, than those of Charles Merrill and Charles Wilson. But, while Milken was sufficiently powerful to hew to his own articulated standards, too often, he did not. This hypocrisy, not parking securities and other minor crimes, was Milken's real offense.

Milken's period of celebrity lasted slightly more than half a decade. What his career might have been without his guilty plea, sentencing, and incarceration will never be known. It is worth reflecting that after the Civil War, while in his 20s, J. P. Morgan was accused of having sold defective rifles to the Union Army. There was little to the charge. But if there had been an indictment, a trial, and a guilty verdict, American history might have been very different.

Imagine the scenario for Mike Milken without Dennis Levine and Ivan Boesky. Legislative action would have ended the hostile-takeover movement. Milken would have returned to financing midsized companies in emerging industries. He might have continued this and other positive activities well into the 21st century. Unquestionably, Milken would have been drawn to financing new enterprises in eastern Europe and Latin America, for he became involved in such matters after leaving Drexel and before going to jail. Given his abilities and intelligence, he might have become a figure of global importance. At the close of his career, quite plausibly he might have been viewed as the greatest banker of the age.

When he completes his sentence, Milken will be forbidden to re-enter the securities field. That won't prevent him from conducting other business. He has indicated a desire to "do something" in the area of education. This is not surprising, since even before his troubles, Milken devoted a good deal of time and thought to the subject, and schools and teachers received generous contributions from the Milken Family Foundation. "I think education in this country is going to be a multi-hundred-billion dollar industry. That's where I'm going to put my time and money."[36] Characteristically, Milken the visionary is inextricably coupled to Milken the businessman.

NOTES

CHAPTER 1

1. Stanford N. Sesser, "Wolfson Lawyers to Appeal His Conviction; Landmark Securities Law Ruling Possible," *Wall Street Journal*, Oct. 2, 1967.
2. "Indictments," *Time*, Sept. 30, 1966, 106–7.
3. "Exit for Wolfson," *Time*, May 2, 1969, 55.
4. Richard Phelon, "Wolfson Is Indicted in Sales of Stock," *New York Times*, Sept. 20, 1966.
5. Arnold Markowitz, "Wolfson's Ordeal," *Miami Herald*, April 12, 1970.
6. Richard Phelon, "Wolfson: Taste of Success Turns Sour," *New York Times*, Sept. 25, 1966.
7. Terry Robards, "Secrecy Hides Rittmaster Role," *New York Times*, June 19, 1969.
8. Terry Robards, "Wolfson and the Law," *New York Times*, Oct. 3, 1967.
9. Allan Sloan, "A Chat With Michael Milken," *Forbes*, July 13, 1987, 250–51.
10. Richard Hammer, "Why Things Went Sour for Louis Wolfson," *Fortune*, Sept. 1961, 133.
11. "The Bitterest Battle," *Forbes*, March 15, 1955, 19.
12. Hammer, "Why Things Went Sour for Louis Wolfson," 133.
13. "The Bitterest Battle," 23.
14. Ralph Ginzburg, "Capital Gainsmanship," *Playboy*, March 1960, 85.
15. Whetten, *Recent Proxy Contests: A Study in Management-Stockholder Relations* (Atlanta, 1959), 43–44.
16. *Moody's Industrial Manual*, 1961, 1892.
17. Whetten, *Recent Proxy Contests*, 39.
18. John Rothschild, *Going for Broke* (New York, 1991), 93, 107.
19. Montgomery Ward, Proxy Letter, March 14, 1955.
20. "Wolfson's Case," *Forbes*, March 15, 1955, 20.
21. "The Bitterest Battle," 21.
22. "The Bitterest Battle," 19.
23. Whetten, *Recent Proxy Contests*, 54.
24. "Avery Wins the Decision, But Challenger Wolfson Says He'll Wear the Crown after Next Year's Fight," *Wall Street Journal*, April 25, 1955.

CHAPTER 2

1. Moira Johnston, *Roller Coaster: The Bank of America and the Future of American Banking* (New York, 1990), 37.

2. B. C. Forbes, ed., *America's Fifty Foremost Business Leaders* (New York, 1948), 332.

3. "The Year on Wall Street," *New York Times,* Jan. 2, 1947.

4. Samuel L. Hayes III, "The Transformation of Investment Banking," *Harvard Business Review,* Jan.–Feb. 1979, 160.

5. Vincent Carosso, *Investment Banking in America* (Cambridge, 1970), 257.

6. Martin Mayer, *Wall Street: Men and Money* (New York, 1955), 1.

7. Paul Hoffman, *The Dealmaker: Inside the World of Investment Banking* (New York, 1984), 46–47.

8. Mayer, *Wall Street,* 46. For a good picture of what the NYSE was like in 1950, see Martin Mayer, *Stealing the Market* (New York, 1992), Chapter II.

9. Julius Grodinsky, *Investments* (New York, 1953), 375.

10. Benjamin Graham and David L. Dodd, *Security Analysis* (New York, 1934), 372.

11. United States, *Historical Statistics* (Washington, DC, U.S. Department of Commerce, 1970), II, 1003.

12. *Moody's Handbook of Widely Held Common Stocks, November 1957 edition.*

13. This attitude would linger at some newspapers into the early 1970s. In 1973, for example, business reporter Chris Welles wrote an article on what he called "The Bleak Wasteland of Financial Journalism" for the *Columbia Journalism Review* (Summer 1973). In conducting his research, he spoke with Richard Harwood, assistant managing editor for the prestigious *Washington Post,* which had just won praise for Bob Woodward and Carl Bernstein's reporting on the Watergate scandal. When Welles asked Harwood why his newspaper gave more space to sports than to finance, Harwood replied, "I guess it is because we think sports is more interesting to readers than business and economics. I know it is to me."

14. Robert Sobel, *NYSE: A History of the New York Stock Exchange, 1935–1975* (New York, 1975), 191, 194.

15. John Train, *The New Money Managers* (New York, 1989), 171–91.

16. Charles D. Ellis with James R. Vertin, eds., *Classics II* (Homewood, IL, 1991), 204, 208.

17. Sobel, *NYSE,* 179.

18. Ellyn E. Spragins, "At Merrill, A Frustrating Hunt for Profits," *New York Times Magazine,* June 10, 1990, 53.

19. New York Stock Exchange, *1975 Fact Book,* 48.

20. Lewis Kimmel, *Share Ownership in the United States* (Washington, 1952), 66; New York Stock Exchange, *1975 Fact Book,* 48.

21. Mayer, *Wall Street,* 120.

22. New York Stock Exchange, *1974 Fact Book,* 52.

23. Peter Drucker, *Adventures of a Bystander* (New York, 1981), 277–78.

24. NYSE, *1975 Fact Book,* 50; Raymond Goldsmith, ed., *Institutional Investors and Corporate Stock—A Background Study* (New York, 1973), 144.

25. Gabriel Kolko, *Wealth and Power in America: An Analysis of Social Class and Income Distribution* (New York, 1962), 69.

26. Peter Drucker, *The Unseen Revolution: How Pension Plan Socialism Came to America* (New York, 1979), 1; Peter F. Drucker, *Managing for the Future* (New York, 1992), 236.

27. United States, *Historical Statistics,* II, 10.

CHAPTER 3

1. The best source for Ling's early career is Stanley Brown, *Ling: The Rise, Fall, and Return of a Texas Tycoon* (New York, 1972).

2. Johnston, *Takeover: The New Wall Street Warriors, The Men, The Money, The Impact* (New York, 1985), 101.

3. Robert Sobel, *Money Manias* (New York, 1973), 149.

4. *Wall Street Journal,* Aug. 2, 1969.

5. Charles Bluhdorn, CEO of Gulf+Western, made runs at Armour & Co., Pan American Airways, Sinclair Oil, Allis Chalmers, and others, always saying he wanted to purchase them, or else looked upon his stakes as "investments." Whatever the reasons, these forays added to G+W's earnings in the late 1960s. In 1969, the firm reported earnings of $72.1 million, of which $21.1 million came from securities sales. Gulf+Western Annual Report, 1969, 30–31.

6. Senate, Committee on the Judiciary, *Hearings on the Nomination of Richard G. Kleindienst of Arizona to be Attorney General,* 92nd Cong., 2d Sess., 1972, 1651.

7. Brown, *Ling,* 169–70.

8. Ibid., 205; Robert Goolrick, *Public Policy Toward Corporate Growth: The ITT Cases* (Port Washington, NY, 1978), 98–100.

9. *Moody's Industrial Manual,* 1970.

10. Brown, *Ling,* 205.

11. Jeff Madrick, *Taking America: How We Got from the First Hostile Takeover to Megamergers, Corporate Raiding, and Scandal* (New York, 1987), 74.

12. "The Return of Ling, et al.," *Forbes,* Jan. 3, 1983.

13. John C. Coffee, Jr., Louis Lowenstein, and Susan Rose Ackerman, eds., *Knights, Raiders, and Targets: The Impact of the Hostile Takeover* (New York, 1988), 18.

CHAPTER 4

1. Jack Wilson, Richard Sylla, and Charles Jones, "Financial Market Panics and Volatility in the Long Run, 1930–1988," in Eugene White, ed., *Crashes and Panics: The Lessons from History* (Homewood, IL, 1990), 130.

2. "The Big Money in 'Junk' Bonds," *Forbes,* April 1, 1974, 26–27.

3. Samuel L. Hayes III, "The Transformation of Investment Banking," *Harvard Business Review*, January–February 1979, 153–54.

4. "Whose Firm, Whose Money?" *Economist*, May 5, 1990, 8.

5. All material on the Milkevitz family history is derived from Marie Brenner, "The Man Who Fell to Earth," *Vanity Fair*, August 1989, 103–9, 148–54.

6. Brian O'Reilly, "Mike's Midas Touch," *Fortune*, Oct. 10, 1988, 62.

7. Allan Sloan, "A Chat With Michael Milken," *Forbes*, July 13, 1987, 252.

8. Richard Greene, "Their Eyes Are on the Main Chance," *Forbes*, March 9, 1987, 69–70.

9. Isaiah Berlin, *The Hedgehog and the Fox* (New York, 1953), 2.

10. W. Braddock Hickman, *Corporate Bond Quality and Investor Experience* (Princeton, 1958), 14.

11. Ibid., 26–27.

12. Ibid., 19.

13. Thomas R. Atkinson, with the assistance of Elizabeth T. Simpson, *Trends in Corporate Bond Quality* (New York, 1967), 47.

14. O. K. Burrell, *A Study in Investment Mortality* (Eugene, OR, 1947), 7, 10.

15. Ibid., 37.

16. Ibid., 42–43.

17. Ibid., 43–44.

18. Barrie Wigmore, *The Crash and Its Aftermath* (Westport, CT, 1985), 604, 610–611.

19. Sidney Homer, *A History of Interest Rates* (New Brunswick, NJ, 1977), 348.

20. David Dreman, *The New Contrarian Investment Strategy* (New York, 1982), 170. Dreman offered the example of the Consolidated Edison $9^3/_8$ bond maturing in 2000, which was rated Baa in early 1974 and sold at 106. In April, the firm eliminated its dividend, and the bond was downrated to Ba, whereupon it fell by nearly half, even though interest payments continued. When the dividend was restored in 1977, the rating was raised to A, and the bonds moved back over 100.

21. Franco Modigliani and Merton Miller, "The Cost of Capital, Corporate Finance and the Theory of Investment," *The American Economic Review*, June 1958.

22. John C. Coffee, Jr., Louis Lowenstein, and Susan Rose Ackerman, eds., *Knights, Raiders, and Targets* (New York, 1988), 18.

23. "Survey of International Finance," *The Economist*, April 27, 1991, 14.

24. James E. Walter and Michael R. Milken, "Managing the Corporate Financial Structure" (Working Paper No. 26–73, Rodney L. White Center for Financial Research, University of Pennsylvania, 1974), 13.

25. "Boardinghouse Reach," *Grant's Interest Rate Observer*, Dec. 23, 1988, 3.

26. "History is Bunk. The Future is Junk," *New Perspectives Quarterly*, Fall 1989, 12.

27. Samuel L. Hayes III, "Investment Banking in Flux," *Harvard Business Review*, March–April 1971, 143, 146.

28. "Whose Firm, Whose Money?" 8.

29. O'Reilly, "Mike's Midas Touch," 62.

30. Arlene Hirshman, "High Risks—and Rewards—in High-Yield Bonds," *Dun's Review,* June 1977, 121.

31. Michael Lewis, "How Michael Milken Changed the World," *Business* [U.K.], May 1988, 86.

32. John Kobler, *Otto the Magnificent* (New York, 1988), 52.

33. "Drexel's Rise and Fall," *Wall Street Journal,* Feb. 14, 1990.

34. Glenn Yago, *Junk Bonds: How High Yield Securities Restructured Corporate America* (New York, 1990), 21.

35. Connie Bruck, *The Predators' Ball: The Inside Story of Drexel Burnham and the Rise of the Junk Bond Raiders* (New York, 1989), 44.

36. "Frederick Joseph, Chief Executive Officer, Drexel Burnham Lambert," *Institutional Investor,* June 1987, 364.

37. O'Reilly, "Mike's Midas Touch," 62.

38. Yago, *Junk Bonds,* 19.

39. "How Linton Made Drexel the Hottest Name on the Street," *Business Week,* April 1, 1985, 50.

40. "Power on Wall Street," *Business Week,* July 7, 1986, 58.

41. Bruck, *The Predators' Ball,* 44.

42. "Drexel Wins Big by Backing Dark Horses," *Business Week,* Feb. 20, 1984, 64.

43. "How Linton Made Drexel the Hottest Name on the Street," 51.

CHAPTER 5

1. In 1983, Milken would move the entire operation to larger quarters at the intersection of Wilshire Boulevard and Rodeo Drive. Along with others, he owned the building, which was leased to Drexel.

2. "Banker of the Year: Robert Linton of Drexel Burnham Lambert," *Institutional Investor,* August 1985, 62.

3. Drexel Burnham Lambert, "Financing America's Future," 1989 Report, pp. 13–15.

4. Glenn Yago, *Junk Bonds: How High Yield Securities Restructured Corporate America* (New York, 1990), 34.

5. William Meyers, "Down—But Not Out—in Beverly Hills," *Institutional Investor,* August 1989, 74.

6. Gary Schulte, *The Fall of First Executive: The House that Fred Carr Built* (New York, 1991), 28–29.

7. Jill Dutt, "What Happened to Me?" *Newsday,* June 17, 1991.

8. Schulte, *The Fall of First Executive,* 101–2.

9. Ibid., 190.

10. Jaclyn Fierman, "How Secure Is Your Nest Egg?" *Fortune,* Aug. 12, 1991, 53.

11. Richard W. Stevenson, "Insurer's Role Raises Pension Fear," *New York Times,* April 15, 1991.

12. Some of the material reported about Milken's quasi-legal activities is derived from a special hearing or "Fatico hearing," held as part of his trial, in which a number of Drexel employees and clients testified—many against Milken. United States v. Milken, D.N.Y., 589, Oct. 18 to Oct. 25, and Nov. 6, 1990.

13. "This Drexel Treasure Trove May Hold Fool's Gold," *Business Week,* April 1, 1991, 70; United States v. Michael Milken, Oct. 25, 1990, 1206.

14. United States v. Milken, Oct. 25, 1990, 1196.

15. Drexel Burnham Lambert, "Financing America's Future." 1989 Report, 13.

16. Stratford P. Sherman, "Drexel Sweats the SEC Probe," *Fortune,* March 16, 1987, 40.

17. "Comdisco Chief Thankful for Junk," *Chicago Sun-Times,* May 11, 1989.

18. Ben Weberman, "The King of the BBs," *Forbes,* Dec. 5, 1983, 113–14.

19. "This Drexel Treasure Trove May Hold Fool's Gold," 70.

20. United States v. Michael Milken, Oct. 25, 1990, 1188.

21. Sarah Bartlett, "A Straight Arrow's Inexplicable Fall," *New York Times,* March 24, 1991; James W. Michaels and Phyllis Berman, "My Story—Michael Milken," *Forbes,* March 16, 1992, 98; "The Drexel Debacle's 'Teflon Guy'," *Business Week,* June 8, 1992, 93.

22. Joel Dreyfus, "The Firm That Fed on Wall Street's Scraps," *Fortune,* Sept. 3, 1984, 90.

23. "Drexel Wins Big by Backing Dark Horses," *Business Week,* Feb. 20, 1983, 64.

24. Ellen Wojahn, "Paper Planes," *Inc.,* September 1985, 96–98.

25. Ibid., 100–6.

26. "The Flight Wall Street Missed," *Business Week,* July 5, 1982, 82–83; Cary Reich, "Milken the Magnificent," *Institutional Investor,* August 1986, 86.

27. Marlys Harris, "Crisis in the Courts (Part 1)," *Insurance Review,* April 1986, 52–57.

28. "Frederick Joseph, Chief Executive Officer, Drexel Burnham Lambert," 364, 366.

29. Sherman, "Drexel Sweats the SEC Probe," 41.

30. Dreyfus, "The Firm That Fed on Wall Street's Scraps," 91.

31. Paul H. Hunn, "The Evolution of Leveraged Buyout Financing," *Commercial Lending Review* (Spring 1987), 42.

32. Allan Sloan, "The Magician," *Forbes,* April 23, 1984, 32; "Metromedia Reaches Accord to Settle Suit Opposing Buyout Plan," *Wall Street Journal,* March 23, 1984.

33. "Metromedia Inc.'s Holders Approve $1.13 Billion Buyout," *Wall Street Journal,* June 21, 1984.

34. "Metromedia's Blockbuster Bid to Stretch Out Its Debt," *Business Week,* Nov. 26, 1984, 61.

35. Gary Hector, "Are Shareholders Cheated by LBOs?" *Fortune,* Jan. 19, 1987, 99.

36. "Survey of International Finance," *The Economist,* April 27, 1991, 17–18.

37. United States v. Michael Milken, Oct. 18, 1990, unpaginated.

38. Michael Lewis, "How Michael Milken Changed the World," *Business* [U.K.], May 1988, 86.

CHAPTER 6

1. Samuel L. Hayes III, "The Transformation of Investment Banking," 160.

2. Charles Anderson et al., *1989–90 Fact Book on Higher Education* (New York, 1991), 246.

3. Douglas Frantz, *Mr. Diamond: The Story of Dennis Levine, Wall Street's Most Infamous Inside Trader* (London, 1987), 137–38.

4. Justin G. Longnecker, Joseph A. McKinney, and Carlos W. Moore, "The Generation Gap in Business Ethics," *Business Horizons,* September–October 1989, 10.

5. Edward E. Scharff, *Worldly Power: The Making of the Wall Street Journal* (New York, 1986), 167–68.

6. Institutional Investor, *The Way It Was: An Oral History of Finance. 1967–1987* (New York, 1988), 176.

7. Edward N. Saveth, "Suicide of an Elite?" *Commentary,* August 1991, 44–47; William F. Buckley, "In Search of Anti-Semitism," *National Review,* Dec. 30, 1991, 22.

8. Bruck, *Predators' Ball,* 160, 205, 331.

9. "Founding Fathers First Insider Traders," *Chicago Tribune,* May 15, 1987.

10. H. Fenwick Huss and Burt A. Leete, "The Broadened Scope of Rule 10b-5: Analysis and Implications for Participants in the Securities Markets," *Business and Society,* Spring 1988, 2.

11. Morton Shulman, *The Billion Dollar Windfall* (New York, 1970), vii.

12. "Morality and Wall Street," *Chief Executive,* February 1989, 21.
M. P. Dooley, "Enforcement of Insider Trading Restrictions," *Virginia Law Review* (1980), 1–83.

13. Jennifer Moore, "What Is Really Unethical about Insider Trading?" *Journal of Business Ethics* (1990), 171.

14. Stevens, *The Insiders,* 58.

15. Lawrence J. Tell, "Inside Information: It Isn't Always Easy to Define," *Barron's,* Nov. 24, 1986, 56–57.

16. United States v. Michael Milken, Oct. 18, 1990, unpaginated.

17. Samuel L. Hayes III and Russell A. Taussig, "Tactics of Cash Takeover Bids," *Harvard Business Review* (March–April 1967), 135.

18. Adolph Berle and Gardner Means, *The Modern Corporation and Private Property* (New York, 1932).

19. Ibid., 75–76.

20. American Enterprise Institute, *Proposals Affecting Corporate Takeovers* (Washington, 1985), 11.

21. Robert W. McGee, "Ethical Issues in Acquisitions and Mergers," *Mid-Atlantic Journal of Business* (March 1989), 28, 31.

22. John Brooks, *The Takeover Game* (New York, 1987), 4–5.

23. "How Linton Made Drexel the Hottest Name on the Street," *Business Week,* April 1, 1985.

24. "Fast Growing Drexel Irritates Many Rivals With Its Tough Tactics," *Wall Street Journal,* June, 13, 1986.

25. Stratford P. Sherman, "Drexel Sweats the SEC Probe," *Fortune,* March 16, 1987, 41–42.
"Frederick Joseph, Chief Executive Officer, Drexel Burnham Lambert," 368.

26. "Did Drexel Bully Takeover Candidates?" *Business Week,* March 9, 1987, 43.

27. Michael Lewis, "How Michael Milken Changed the World," *Business* [U.K.], May 1988, 88–89.

28. "Houdini of the Drexel Scandal," *Business Week,* Dec. 9, 1991, 81.

29. Charles Bluhdorn often is credited with having invented greenmail, which became a feature of the LBO movement. As with so many matters, it had existed in the 19th century, when Jim Fisk, Jay Gould, and Daniel Drew paid a version of greenmail to Cornelius Vanderbilt during the Erie Wars of the post–Civil War period. Bluhdorn went after Allis-Chalmers in 1969. When rebuffed—A-C found a "white knight" (another term not used at the time) in White Consolidated—Bluhdorn sold his shares for a $5 million profit. He later would make profits of $6.5 million on a play for Pan Am and $24.2 million on a similar one for Sinclair Oil.

30. "Did Drexel Bully Takeover Candidates?" 43.

31. "Frederick Joseph, Chief Executive Officer, Drexel Burnham Lambert," 368.

32. Lewis, "How Michael Milken Changed the World," 87–88.

33. United States v. Michael Milken, Oct. 25, 1990, 599–612.

34. "Surviving the Drexel Whirlwind," *Economist,* March 24, 1990, 69.

CHAPTER 7

1. Edmund Faltmayer, "The Deal Decade: Verdict on the '80s," *Fortune,* Aug. 26, 1991, 58; Michael Jensen, "Corporate Control and the Politics of Finance," *Journal of Applied Corporate Finance* (Summer 1991), 88.

2. "Will Money Managers Wreck the Economy?" *Business Week,* Aug. 13, 1984, 87.

3. Jeff Madrick, *Taking America: How We Got from the First Hostile Takeover to Megamergers, Corporate Raiding, and Scandal* (New York, 1987), 14–15.

4. Allan Sloan, "Why Is No One Safe?" *Forbes,* March 11, 1985, 136.

5. "An Expert Tells Executives How to Invite—or Avoid—Raiders," *Business Week,* Oct. 26, 1957, 193.

6. Louis Wolfson, "Robot Executives," *Vital Speeches,* Dec. 1, 1959, 275–77.

7. Caroline Rawls, "From the Playing Fields of Andrew Jackson High . . ." *Suntime,* April 1955, 25.

8. T. Boone Pickens, "Boone Speaks," *Fortune,* Feb. 16, 1987, 43.

9. Ibid., 43.

10. Carl Icahn, "The Case for Takeovers," *New York Times Magazine,* Jan. 29, 1989, 34.

11. "Takeovers: What Next?" *CE Roundtable,* November/December 1988, 62, 69.

12. Neil Osborn, "The Furor over Shelf Registration," *Institutional Investor,* June 1982, 61–71.

13. Jack Wilson, Richard Sylla, and Charles Jones, "Financial Market Panics and Volatility in the Long Run, 1830–1988," in Eugene White, *Crashes and Panics: The Lessons from History* (Homewood, IL, 1990), 103–6.

14. As Nathaniel Rothschild once put it, efficiency results from the fact that "corporate managers can no longer sleep peacefully at night; this is because they are constrained to have nightmares regarding a potential takeover." Abraham J. Briloff, "Cannibalizing the Transcendent Margin: Reflections on Conglomeration, LBOs, Recapitalizations and Other Manifestations of Corporate Mania," *Financial Analysts Journal* (May–June 1988), 78.

15. Glenn Yago, *Junk Bonds: How High Yield Securities Restructured Corporate America* (New York, 1990), 112, 119.

16. General Accounting Office, *Financial Markets, Issuers, Purchases, and Purposes of High Yield, Non-Investment Grade Bonds* (Washington, 1988).

17. "Frederick Joseph, Chief Executive Officer, Drexel Burnham Lambert," 368.

18. Sherman, "Drexel Sweats the SEC Probe," 41.

19. Sloan, "Why Is No One Safe?" 137. Institutional Investor, *The Way it Was: An Oral History of Finance: 1967–1987* (New York, 1988), 714.

20. Neil R. Gazel, *Beatrice from Buildup to Breakup* (Urbana, 1990), 202 ff.

21. Leonard Sloan, "Cashing Out Beatrice, Ringing Out an Era," *Newsday,* 17 June 1990.

22. Abraham Briloff, "Drexel's Greediest Deal," *Barron's,* Dec. 5, 1988, 26.

23. Keystone Fixed Income Group, "The High Yield Bond Market in Perspective," 1990, 29.

24. "The Great Takeover Debate," *Time,* April 22, 1985, 52.

25. "Drilling for Oil on Wall Street," *Economist,* Feb. 20, 1988.

26. Kenneth M. Davidson, *Mega-Mergers: Corporate America's Billion-Dollar Takeovers* (Cambridge, MA, 1985), 253–54.

27. Ibid., 258.

28. Peter Nulty, "Boone Pickens, Company Hunter," *Fortune,* Dec. 26, 1983, 57.

CHAPTER 8

1. Wallace N. Davidson III and James L. McDonald, "Evidence of the Effect on Shareholder Wealth of Corporate Spinoffs: The Creation of Royalty Trusts," *Journal of Financial Research* (Winter 1987), 321–22.

2. T. Boone Pickens, *Boone* (New York, 1987), 2.

3. Institutional Investor, *The Way it Was,* 106.

4. Sloan, "Why Is No One Safe?" 137.

5. T. Boone Pickens, "The Continuing Struggle to Restore Management Accountability and Competitiveness in Corporate America," *Executive Speeches*, November 1988, 15–16.

6. Johnston, *Takeover*, 127; Tim Metz and Doron P. Levin, "Cities Service Imposed Accord Ending Mesa Bid," *Wall Street Journal*, May 3, 1982.

7. Charles F. McCoy and G. Christian Hill, "Pickens Likely to Go Hunting with Gulf Profit," *Wall Street Journal*, 7 March 1984; L. J. Davis, "The Biggest Knockover," *Harper's*, January 1985, 58.

8. Pickens, "The Continuing Struggle," 15–16. By 1991, Pickens had softened this view somewhat. On a panel, he sparred with Johnson & Johnson CEO James E. Burke, who said: "We lay out the responsibilities to our people. You put the customer first, the employees next, then the community, and finally the shareholders. People say to us all the time, Why do you put the shareholders last? And we say: If you serve all the stakeholders better than the competition, you'll beat them at the bottom line." Apparently in agreement, Pickens replied, "I see all of these things as just good management." "Are Shareholders the Primary Constituency? Pickens, Burke Debate," *Ethikos* (July/August 1991), 13.

9. T. Boone Pickens, "I Called My Guys Together and said, 'Fellas, We Need a Home Run.' And that was Gulf Oil," *Institutional Investor*, June 1987, 79.

10. Ralph Nader and William Taylor, *The Big Boys: Power and Position in American Business* (New York, 1986), 434.

11. Doron P. Levin and Richard B. Schmitt, "Gulf Oil is Accused by Mesa's Pickens of Getting Four Banks to Cancel Credit," *Wall Street Journal*, Oct. 19, 1983.

12. Nader and Taylor, *The Big Boys*, 517–18.

13. T. Boone Pickens, "Boone Speaks," *Fortune*, Feb. 16, 1987, 45; Sloan, "Why Is No One Safe?" 137.

14. "The Deal Maker," *Wall Street Journal*, March 1, 1984.

15. Pickens, "Boone Speaks," 45.

16. Sloan, "A Chat With Michael Milken," *Forbes*, July 13, 1987, 250.

17. Johnston, *Takeover*, 148–49.

18. Pickens, *Boone*, 212.

19. "Gulf Oil Stock Rises Partially on Rumor," *Wall Street Journal*, Jan. 30, 1984.

20. Monci Jo Williams, "The Pickens Plot that Has Gulf Gulping," *Fortune*, March 5, 1984, 34.

21. Two-tier offers were made earlier in the century, but the modern form appeared in 1977–1978, when McDermott International acquired Babcock & Wilcox in this fashion. The structure was perfected in 1981, in the U.S. Steel-Marathon deal. Mary Greenbaum, "Tips for Takeover Targets' Stockholders," *Fortune*, Dec. 28, 1981, 109.

22. Doron P. Levin and Tim Metz, "Gulf Oil Unveils Moves to Block Pickens Group," *Wall Street Journal*, Feb. 13, 1984.

23. Pickens, "I Called My Guys Together," 78.

24. "Pickens Group Bids to Lift Stake in Gulf to 21.3%," *Wall Street Journal*, Feb. 23, 1984.

25. Pickens, *Boone*, 214.

26. Kenneth Labich, "How Jimmy Lee Let Gulf's Shareholders Win Big," *Fortune*, April 2, 1984, 23.

27. Daniel Yergen, "The Oil Wars," *Investment Vision*, June/July 1991, 53.

28. Pickens, *Boone*, 216; "The Biggest Paychecks," *Wall Street Journal*, March 7, 1984.

29. Pickens, "Boone Speaks," 48; Subrata W. Chakravaty, "Fred Raises the Flag Again, but Nobody's Saluting," *Forbes*, June 13, 1988, 42.

30. Pickens, "Boone Speaks," 45.

31. Davis, "The Biggest Knockover," 53.

32. Johnston, *Takeover*, 80.

33. "How Drexel's *Wunderkind* Bankrolls the Raiders," *Business Week*, March 4, 1985.

34. John D. Williams, "Takeover Tactics: How 'Junk Financings' Aid Corporate Raiders in Hostile Acquisitions," *Wall Street Journal*, Dec. 6, 1984.

35. Ibid.

36. Ida Picker, "Picking Up the Pieces at Drexel," *Institutional Investor*, May 1989, 102.

37. J. Ernest Beazley and Doron P. Levin, "Gulf's Failure to Take Bold Defensive Steps Set It Up for Takeover," *Wall Street Journal*, March 7, 1984.

38. Yergen, "The Oil Wars," 53.

39. "Knights of the Roundtable," *Business Week*, Oct. 21, 1988, 39.

40. "T. Boone Pickens," *Institutional Investor*, June 1987, 79.

41. Ibid., 42.

42. Yago, *Junk Bonds*, 176.

43. Sloan, "Why Is No One Safe?" 137.

44. Pickens, "Free Enterprise Without the Entrepreneur," *Vital Speeches*, July 1, 1985, 565–66.

45. Pickens, "Boone Speaks," 44.

46. Ken Wells, "Big Oil Firms Will Find Unlikely Foes as They Make Pitch for Large Mergers," *Wall Street Journal*, March 15, 1984.

47. "Pickens on Prowl," *Wall Street Journal*, Oct. 11, 1984.

48. Nader, *The Big Boys*, 518.

49. Randall Smith, "Several Institutional Holders of Phillips Haven't Made a Decision on Pickens' Bid," *Wall Street Journal*, Dec. 6, 1984.

50. Fred R. Bleakley, "A Trustee Takes on the Greenmailers," *New York Times*, Feb. 10, 1985.

51. Pickens, *Boone*, 227–32.

52. Tim Metz, "Phillips Petroleum, Mesa Partners, Reach Agreement that Ends Hostile Takeover Threat by Pickens Group," *Wall Street Journal*, 24 Dec. 1984; Charles F. McCoy, "Phillips Is Seen Possibly Exposed to a New Offer," *Wall Street Journal*, Dec. 26, 1984.

53. Pickens, *Boone,* 235.

54. "Frederick Joseph, Chief Executive Officer, Drexel Burnham Lambert," 368.

55. "How Drexel's *Wunderkind* Bankrolls the Raiders," 90.

56. House Committee on Energy and Commerce, Subcommittee on Telecommunications, Consumer Protection, and Finance, "Corporate Takeovers (Part One)," 99th Cong., 1st sess., 1985, 56.

57. Johnston, *Takeover,* 83–87.

58. "Fast-Growing Drexel Irritates Many Rivals with Its Tough Tactics," *Wall Street Journal,* June 13, 1986.

CHAPTER 9

1. William Hall, "Independence Comes at a Punitive Cost," *Financial Times,* Jan. 16, 1987.

2. Nader and Taylor, *The Big Boys,* 188.

3. Ibid., 518.

4. Fenton Bailey, *The Junk Bond Revolution,* (London, 1991), 117.

5. Yago, *Junk Bonds,* 177.

6. "Unocal Tells Its Holders Pickens Invested Wisely," *Wall Street Journal,* Feb. 20, 1985.

7. Debra Whitefield and Nancy Rivera, "Takeover War: Unocal Saw Pickens Bid, Trumped It," *Los Angeles Times,* 2, June 1985.

8. "It's Official: Pickens Going After Unocal," *Chicago Tribune,* March 29, 1985.

9. Charles F. McCoy, "Pickens Group Boosts Stake in Unocal to 13.6% with $322 Million Purchase," *Wall Street Journal,* March 28, 1985.

10. Pickens, *Boone,* 239; Johnston, *Takeover,* 90. Frederick Rose, "Fred L. Hartley's Dominance at Unocal Could Cause Problem When He Retires," *Wall Street Journal,* Jan. 3, 1985.

11. Fred Williams, "Pickens Takes Up New Battle," *Pensions and Investment Age,* Oct. 31, 1988.

12. Pickens, "Free Enterprise Without the Entrepreneur?" 25.

13. T. Boone Pickens, J., "Takeovers: A Purge of Doc Managements," *Management Review,* January, 1988, p. 54.

14. Jennifer Bingham Hull, "Unocal Sues Bank That Made Loans to Pickens Group," *Wall Street Journal,* March 13, 1985.

15. "The Raiders," *Business Week,* March 4, 1985, 80.

16. Whitefield and Rivera, "Takeover War."

17. *Financial Times,* Dec. 10, 1985.

18. *Washington Post,* April 3, 1985.

19. "Unocal Changes Its Bylaws to Thwart Pickens," *Los Angeles Times,* April 3, 1985.

20. House Committee on Banking, Housing, and Urban Affairs, Subcommittee on Securities, "Impact of Corporate Takeovers," 99th Cong., 1st Sess., April

3, 4 and June 6, 12, 1985, 4; "The Great Takeover Debate," *Time,* April 22, 1985, 52.

21. William Proxmire, "Hostile Corporate Takeovers and Raids," *Vital Speeches,* April 15, 1985, 388.

22. Ehrbar, "Have Takeovers Gone Too Far?" 20.

23. Ann Reilly, "Lobbyists Cash in on Takeovers," *Fortune,* June 10, 1985, 129.

24. Yago, *Junk Bonds,* 182. The bill failed passage, but in 1987, Domenici came back with a new one, called "The Junk Bond Limitation Act," which would have limited the amount of capital that federally insured banks could invest in those instruments. It received little attention at the time, aimed as it was to limit the market for junk, and not to save the S&Ls. It would reappear later on with the latter objective in mind.

25. "Why Congress Could Let the Raiders Run Free," *Business Week,* June 10, 1985, 54.

26. Al Ehrbar, "Have Takeovers Gone Too Far?" 24.

27. *Washington Post,* May 9, 1985.

28. McCoy, "Pickens Group Boosts Stake in Unocal."

29. Charles F. McCoy, "Pickens Weighs Bid to Acquire Unocal," *Wall Street Journal,* March 29, 1985; Bruck, *Predator's Ball,* 130.

30. "Some Big Unocal Holders, Unsure of Plans of Pickens and Takeover Prospects, Sell Stakes," *Wall Street Journal,* March 1, 1955.

31. Whitefield and Rivera, "Takeover War."

32. Charles F. McCoy, "Unocal and a Group Headed by Pickens Move Closer to Fight for Control of Firm," *Wall Street Journal,* April 1, 1985.

33. "Unocal Targets Mesa and Pickens in Antitrust Suit," *Wall Street Journal,* April 12, 1985.

34. Whitefield and Rivera, "Takeover War."

35. "Unocal Discloses Details of Stock Offer Aimed at Halting Takeover by Pickens," *Wall Street Journal,* April 18, 1985.

36. Frederick Rose and Charles F. McCoy, "Unocal Sets Plan to Buy 49% of Its Stock to Thwart Takeover by Pickens," *Wall Street Journal,* April 17, 1985; "Unocal Proposal Doesn't Deter Pickens Offer," *Wall Street Journal,* April 22, 1985.

37. Laurie P. Cohen and Michael Cicily, "Unocal Is Ordered to Include Pickens in Buyback Offer," *Wall Street Journal,* April 30, 1985.

38. Pickens, *Boone,* 260.

39. Allan Sloan and Jack Willoughby, "T. Boone Pyrrhus," *Forbes,* Aug. 12, 1985, 34–35.

40. Laurie P. Cohen, "Mesa to Post $83 Million Gain on Unocal Bid," *Wall Street Journal,* July 2, 1985.

41. William Hall, "Independence Comes at a Punitive Cost," *Financial Times,* Jan. 16, 1987.

42. "T. Boone Pickens," 79.

43. "The World According to Pickens," *Barron's,* Sept. 23, 1985, 8–9.

44. "Fed Acts to Curb 'Junk Bonds,'" *Facts on File News Digest*, Dec. 13, 1985.

45. Senate Committee on Banking, Housing, and Urban Affairs, "Hostile Takeovers," 100th Cong., 1st sess., 1987, 625.

46. Ibid., p. 620.

47. Bruck, *Predator's Ball*, 259–60. Bailey, *Junk Bond Revolution*, 126.

48. David A. Vise, "Merger Bill Chances Held Dim in '86," *Washington Post*, Jan. 29, 1986.

49. James W. Michaels and Phyllis Berman, "My Story—Michael Milken," *Forbes*, March 16, 1992, 95.

50. House Committee on Energy and Commerce, Subcommittee on Telecommunications, Consumer Protection, and Finance, "Conglomerate Mergers and High Yield [Junk] Bonds: Recent Market Trends and Regulatory Developments," 99th Cong., 2d sess., 1986, 54.

51. William A. Niskanen, *Reaganomics: An Insider's Account of the Policies and the People* (New York, 1988). 96–113; Michael J. Boskin, *Reagan and the Economy* (New York, 1987), 157–63.

52. Edward Markey, "A View from Washington on the High-Yield Debt Market," in Altman, *The High Yield Debt Market*, 132.

53. "States vs. Raiders: Will Washington Step In? *Business Week*, Aug. 31, 1987, 56.

54. John Robinson, "Nicholas Brady: Child of the Privileged," *Boston Globe*, Nov. 16, 1988.

CHAPTER 10

1. Michael Barone and Grant Ujifusa, *The Almanac of American Politics, 1986* (Washington, 1986), 697–98.

2. Glenn Yago, "The Credit Crunch: A Regulatory Squeeze on Growth Capital," *Journal of Applied Corporate Finance* (Spring 1991), 99–100.

3. Dennis B. Levine, "The Inside Story of an Inside Trader," *Fortune*, May 21, 1990, 82.

4. Kathryn M. Welling, "Ivan the Terrible," *Barron's*, Nov. 24, 1986, 16.

5. Kurt Eichenwald, "Key Figure in Insider Case Gets 2-Month Prison Term," *New York Times*, June 16, 1990.

6. Anthony Bianco, *Rainmaker: The Saga of Jeff Beck, Wall Street's Mad Dog* (New York, 1991), 370–71.

7. L. Gordon Crovitz, "Milken's Tragedy: Oh, How the Mighty Fall Before RICO," *Wall Street Journal*, May 2, 1990.

8. Yago, *Junk Bonds*, 181.

9. Unless otherwise indicated, information contained in this section is derived from Paul A. Batista, *CIVIL RICO Practice Manual* (New York, 1987), especially Chapter 2, "The Statutory Background: Basic Concepts and the Enigmatic Legislative History." In addition, see "Report of the Ad Hoc Civil RICO Task Force of the ABA Section of Corporation, Banking and Business Law," March 28, 1985.

10. William Glaberson, "Racketeering Cases Are Popping Up in Several Varieties," *New York Times,* Feb. 18, 1990.

11. Donald R. Lorelli, "Sword, Shield or Albatross?" *Best's Review,* April 1985, 26.

12. Peter H. Gunst and Robert B. Levin, "RICO: A Runaway Anticrime Law," *Nation's Business,* January 1990, 61.

13. Bruck, *Predator's Ball,* 160.

14. Crovitz, "Milken's Tragedy"; "Did Drexel Bully Takeover Candidates?" *Business Week,* March 9, 1987, 43.

15. "More Reversals of Fortune," *Economist,* Aug. 3, 1991, 74; Ronald Sullivan, "U.S. Will Not Seek Retrial in Securities-Scandal Case," *New York Times,* Jan. 9, 1992.

16. "'Guilty, Your Honor,'" *Business Week,* May 7, 1990, 34.

17. Jill Dutt, David Henry, and John Riley, "Milken's World," *Newsday,* Oct. 28, 1990; United States v. Michael Milken, Oct. 25, 1990, 1222.

18. Bailey, *The Junk Bond Revolution,* p. 250.

19. There were some Drexel defenders at the hearings. Representative Thomas J. Bliley (R. Virginia), fresh from speaking at Drexel's 1988 Institutional Research Conference, said, "High yield bonds have become an essential type of financing mechanism for many companies. This financing has produced employment and growth in our economy. I've learned that in my own State of Virginia, 162 corporations headquartered or with significant operations in the State, have issued high yield securities since 1977, raising over $31.9 billion. This number, by the way, does not include financing for hostile takeovers." House Committee on Energy and Commerce, Subcommittee on Oversight and Investigations, "Securities Markets Oversight and Drexel Burnham Lambert," 100th Cong., 2d sess., 2, 5, 21.

20. Gretchen Morgenson, "We're All Right, Jack," *Forbes,* May 13, 1991, 76.

21. Kurt Eichenwald, "Business and the Law: U.S. Treatment of Milken Brother," *New York Times,* Oct. 15, 1990.

22. Jude Wanniski, "Trial by Press: James B. Stewart vs. Michael Milken," *Polyconomics,* Oct. 9, 1991.

23. Brett Duval Fromson, "Did Drexel Get What It Deserved?" *Fortune,* March 12, 1990, 88; Monci Jo Williams, "Can Fred Joseph Save Drexel?" *Fortune,* May 8, 1989, 90; "I Woke Up with my Stomach Churning," *Fortune,* July 3, 1989, 120.

24. Proxmire "Hostile Corporate Takeovers and Raids," 388.

25. Thomas G. Donlan, "Dividing Up the Spoils," *Barron's,* Dec. 26, 1988, 10.

26. Roy C. Smith, *The Money War* (New York, 1990), 242.

27. Bailey, *Junk Bond Revolution,* 232–33.

28. "Could Fred Joseph Have Saved Drexel?" *Business Week,* March 5, 1990, 73.

29. Kevin Winch, "Junk Bonds: 1988 Status Report," Congressional Research Service, Library of Congress, Dec. 30, 1988.

30. "Survey of International Finance," *Economist,* April 27, 1991, 23; Keystone Fixed Income Group, "The High Yield Bond Market in Perspective," 1990, 19.

31. General Accounting Office, "Issues Concerning the Thrift Industry's Investments in High Yield Bonds" (Washington, 1989), 3–4.

32. Gary Hector, "S&Ls: Where Did All Those Billions Go?" *Fortune,* Sept. 10, 1990, 84–88.

33. Senate Committee on Banking, Housing, and Urban Affairs, "The Issues Surrounding the Collapse of Drexel Burnham Lambert," 101st Cong., 2d sess., 1990, 70.

34. Stephen R. Waite, "The Eclipse of Growth Capital," *Journal of Applied Corporate Finance* (Spring 1991), 80.

35. Paul Asquith, David Mullins, and Eric Wolf, "Original Issue High-Yield Bonds: Aging Analysis of Defaults, Exchanges, and Calls," *Journal of Finance* (September 1989), 118.

36. George Anders and Constance Mitchell, "Milken's Sales Pitch on High-Yield Bonds Is Contradicted by Data," *Wall Street Journal,* Nov. 20, 1990.

37. Hickman, *Corporate Bond Quality and Investor Experience,* 15.

38. Ibid., 109.

39. *Grant's Interest Rate Observer,* Oct. 27, 1989, 3.

40. *Grant's Interest Rate Observer,* Feb. 2, 1990, 9–10; Faltermayer, "The Deal Decade: Verdict on the '80s," 62.

41. Ibid., 68.

42. Martin S. Fridson, "Agency Costs: Past and Future," in *Extra Credit,* June 1991, 5.

43. Allan Sloan, "A Chat With Michael Milken," 34.

44. "No Bad Debt—Only Bad Managers," *U.S. News & World Report,* Feb. 13, 1989.

45. "History is Bunk. The Future is Junk," 17.

46. Phyllis Berman and Katherine Weisman, "Be Wise, Equitize," *Forbes,* Nov. 17, 1989, 39.

47. The most spectacular failures, however, were taken to market by investment banks that came late to the game and had far less experience in evaluating risk. Goldman Sachs, one of the Street's most prestigious banks, underwrote junk issues for Southland and for Macy's. First Boston, Paine Webber, and Dillon Read were involved with Allied and Federated, and Ohio Mattress. Salomon turned in one of the worst records, having underwritten issues for Revco, Grand Union, and TVX.

48. David Six, "Due Diligence," *Forbes,* Oct. 15, 1990, 123; Phyllis Berman, with Jean Sherman Chatzky, "Warming Up for the Big Ones," *Forbes,* March 2, 1992, 42.

49. "How Linton Made Drexel the Hottest Name on the Street," *Business Week,* April 1, 1985, 91.

50. Picker, "Picking Up the Pieces at Drexel," 105.

51. Phyllis Berman and Roula Khalaf, "We're Doing Just Fine," *Forbes,* March 18, 1991, 52; Bailey, *Junk Bond Revolution,* 229, 232; Waite, "The Eclipse of Growth Capital," 78.

52. Gary Hector, "Junk After Milken," *Fortune,* Nov. 6, 1989, 76.

53. Fromson, "Did Drexel Get What It Deserved?" 88.

54. Bianco, *Rainmaker,* 446–47.

55. "The Issues Surrounding the Collapse of Drexel Burnham Lambert," 11–19ff; Michael Lewis, *The Money Culture* (New York, 1991), 58.

56. Fran Hawthorne, "Could Drexel Have Been Saved?" *Institutional Investor,* March 1990, 44.

57. "Could Fred Joseph Have Saved Drexel?" *Business Week,* 73; Fromson, "Did Drexel Get What It Deserved?" 88.

58. James B. Stewart, *Den of Thieves* (New York, 1991), 433.

59. "Drexel: Prosecution and Fall," *Wall Street Journal,* Feb. 15, 1990.

60. Paul Craig Roberts, "Mike Milken, Scapegoat for the Feds," *Business Week,* Sept. 30, 1991, 12.

61. David E. Kalish, "Did U.S. Get Its Money's Worth From Boesky in Plea Bargain?" *Newsday,* July 15, 1990.

62. Schulte, *The Fall of First Executive,* 272.

CHAPTER 11

1. Jennet Conant, "The Trials of Arthur Liman," *Vanity Fair,* June 1991, 46; Leslie Wayne, "Several Morals for Milken's Story," *New York Times,* Nov. 23, 1990.

2. Smith, *The Money Wars,* 247.

3. Bailey, *Junk Bond Revolution,* 206.

4. Picker, "Picking Up the Pieces at Drexel," May 1989.

5. Laurie P. Cohen, "The Other Shoe," *Wall Street Journal,* March 30, 1989.

6. *Los Angeles Times,* March 30, 1989.

7. "'Guilty, Your Honor,'" *Business Week,* May 7, 1990, 33.

8. Crovitz, "Milken's Tragedy: Oh, How the Mighty Fall Before RICO," May 2, 1990.

9. Irwin Frank, "Oklahoma City Supporters to Join Ling in Business Deal," *Dallas Times Herald,* March 10, 1987.

10. "Incredulous," *Forbes,* Sept. 28, 1992, 22.

11. United States of America v. Michael Milken, Nov. 21, 1990, 40–41. Unless otherwise noted, the facts and quotations in this chapter are derived from the record of the hearing that took place in October and November of 1990.

12. "Houdini of the Drexel Scandal," *Business Week,* Dec. 9, 1992, 81.

13. Carosso, *Investment Banking in America,* 150.

14. Michael Lewis, "Milken's Morals, and Ours," *New York Times,* Nov. 23, 1990.

15. Joshua Hammer, "Triumphant Ted"; Mark Hosnaball, "Money-Mad Mike," both in *Playboy*, January 1990, 76, 78ff.

16. David Henry and John Riley, "Lots of Advice for Milken, Judge, in 'Junk Mail,'" *Newsday*, Sept. 26, 1990.

17. Alison Leigh Cowan, "Milken to Pay $500 Million More in $1.3 Billion Drexel Settlement," *New York Times*, Feb. 18, 1992.

18. Leslie Wayne, "Several Morals for Milken's Story," *New York Times*, Nov. 23, 1990.

19. United States of America vs. Michael Milken, November 21, 1990, pp. 51–52.

20. Robert Reno, "Up the Creek But Pals Stay Safe on Shore," *Newsday*, Nov. 22, 1990.

21. "Too Much Milken Moralizing," *New York Times*, Nov. 27, 1990.

22. Allen R. Myerson, "As Defaults Drop, Junk Bonds Make a Comeback," *New York Times*, Sept. 23, 1992.

23. "Junked," *Economist*, Nov. 24, 1990, 90.

24. Paul Craig Roberts, "Mike Milken, Scapegoat for the Feds," *Business Week*, Sept. 30, 1991, 12.

25. Floyd Norris, "Drexel Set to Pay I.R.S. $290 million," *New York Times*, July 30, 1991.

26. Conant, "The Trials of Arthur Liman," 42.

27. Ronald Sullivan, "Kickback Plan is Described at Trial," *New York Times*, May 22, 1992; Murray Kempton, "What Milken Would Do for a Buddy," *Newsday*, June 3, 1992.

28. "Ledger," *Newsday*, June 26, 1992.

29. Ronald Sullivan, "Testimony by Milken Wins U.S. Approval," *New York Times*, June 20, 1992; Ronald Sullivan, "Testimony by Milken Unhelpful, S.E.C. Says," *New York Times*, June 23, 1992.

30. Michael M. Thomas, *Hanover Place* (New York, 1991), 387.

31. James B. Stewart, *Den of Thieves* (New York, 1991), 43–44.

32. Ibid., 234.

33. Clark Clifford, *Counsel to the President* (New York, 1991), 558.

34. Bailey, *The Junk Bond Revolution*, 33.

35. "Plea Bargain Cited in Salomon Corp.," *New York Times*, Dec. 19, 1992.

36. James W. Michaels and Phyllis Berman, "My Story—Michael Milken," *Forbes*, March 16, 1992, 100.

SELECTED BIBLIOGRAPHY

Adams, James R. *The Big Fix: Inside the S & L Scandal.* New York, 1990.

Adams, Walter, and James W. Brock. *Dangerous Pursuits: Mergers and Acquisitions in the Age of Wall Street.* New York, 1989.

Altman, Edward, and Scott A. Nammachere. "The Default Rate Experience on High-Yield Corporate Debt." *Financial Analysts Journal* (July–August 1985).

———, eds. *The High Yield Debt Market: Investment Performance and Economic Impact.* New York, 1990.

———. "Measuring Corporate Bond Mortality and Performance." *Journal of Finance* (September 1989).

American Enterprise Institute. *Proposals Affecting Corporate Takeovers.* Washington, 1985.

Aranow, Edward Ross, and Herbert A. Einhorn. *Proxy Contests for Corporate Control.* New York, 1957.

Araskog, Rand. *The ITT Wars: A CEO Speaks Out on Takeovers.* New York, 1989.

Asquith, Paul, David Mullins, Jr., and Eric D. Wolff. "Original Issue High Yield Bonds: Aging Analysis of Defaults, Exchanges and Calls." *Journal of Finance* (September 1989).

Atkinson, Thomas R., with the assistance of Elizabeth T. Simpson. *Trends in Corporate Bond Quality.* New York, 1967.

Auerbach, Alan J., ed. *Corporate Takeovers: Causes and Consequences.* Chicago, 1988.

Bailey, Fenton. *The Junk Bond Revolution: Michael Milken, Wall Street, and the 'Roaring Eighties'.* London, 1991.

"Banker of the Year: Robert Linton of Drexel Burnham Lambert. *Institutional Investor,* August 1985.

Barone, Michael, and Grant Ujifusa. *The Almanac of American Politics, 1986.* Washington, DC, 1986.

Bartlett, Sarah. *The Money Machine: How KKR Manufactured Power & Profits.* New York, 1991.

Batista, Paul A. *Civil Rico Practice Manual.* New York, 1987.

Berle, Adolph, and Gardiner Means. *The Modern Corporation and Private Property.* New York, 1932.

Berlin, Isaiah. *The Hedgehog and the Fox.* New York, 1953.

Berman, Phyllis, and Jean Sherman Chatzky. "Warming Up for the Big Ones." *Forbes,* 2 March 1992.

———, and Roula Khalaf. "We're Doing Just Fine." *Forbes,* 18 March 1991.

———, and Katherine Weisman. "Be Wise, Equitize." *Forbes,* 27 Nov. 1989.

Bianco, Anthony. *Rainmaker: The Saga of Jeff Beck, Wall Street's Mad Dog.* New York, 1991.

Block, Dennis J., and Harvey Pitt. *Hostile Battles for Corporate Control: 1986.* New York, 1986.

Boesky, Ivan. *Merger Mania.* New York, 1985.

Bose, Minir, and Cathy Gunn. *Fraud: The Growth Industry of the Eighties.* London, 1989.

Boskin, Michael J. *Reagan and the Economy.* New York, 1987.

Brenner, Marie. "The Man Who Fell to Earth." *Vanity Fair,* August 1989.

Briloff, Abraham J. "Cannibalizing the Transcendent Margin: Reflections on Conglomeration, LBOs, Recapitalizations and Other Manifestations of Corporate Mania." *Financial Analysts Journal* (May–June 1988).

———. "Drexel's Greediest Deal." *Barron's,* 5 Dec. 1988.

Brooks, John. *Once in Golconda: A True Drama of Wall Street.* New York, 1969.

———. *The Takeover Game.* New York, 1987.

Brown, Stanley. *Ling: The Rise, Fall, and Return of a Texas Tycoon.* New York, 1972.

Bruck, Connie. *The Predator's Ball: The Inside Story of Drexel Burnham and the Rise of the Junk Bond Raiders.* New York, 1989 ed.

Buckley, William F. "In Search of Anti-Semitism." *National Review,* 30 Dec. 1991.

Burrell, O.K. *A Study in Investment Mortality.* Eugene, Oregon, 1947.

Burroughs, Bryan, and John Helyar. *Barbarians at the Gate: The Fall of RJR Nabisco.* New York, 1990.

Carosso, Vincent. *Investment Banking in America.* Cambridge, Mass., 1970.

Chakravaty, Subrata W. "Fred Raises the Flag Again, but Nobody's Saluting." *Forbes,* 13 June 1988.

Coffee, John C., Jr., Louis Lowenstein, and Susan Rose-Ackerman, eds. *Knights, Raiders, and Targets: The Impact of Hostile Takeovers.* New York, 1988.

Conant, Jennet. "The Trials of Arthur Liman." *Vanity Fair,* June 1991.

Davidson, Kenneth. *Mega-Mergers: Corporate America's Billion-Dollar Takeovers.* New York, 1985.

Davidson, Wallace N. III, and James L. McDonald. "Evidence of the Effect on Shareholder Wealth of Corporate Spinoffs: The Creation of Royalty Trusts." *Journal of Financial Research* (_____).

Davis, L.J. "The Biggest Knockover," *Harper's,* January 1985.

Donlan, Thomas G. "Dividing Up the Spoils." *Barron's,* 26 Dec. 1988.

Dooley, M.P. "Enforcement of Insider Trading Restrictions." *Virginia Law Review* (1980).

Dreman, David. *The New Contrarian Investment Strategy.* New York, 1982.

Drexel Burnham Lambert. "Financing America's Future." 1989 Report.

Dreyfus, Joel. "The Firm That Fed on Wall Street's Scraps." *Fortune,* 3 Sept. 1984.

Drucker, Peter. *Adventures of a Bystander.* New York, 1981.

———. *Managing for the Future.* New York, 1992.

———. *The Unseen Revolution: How Pension Plan Socialism Came to America.* New York, 1979.

Ehrbar, Al. "Have Takeovers Gone Too Far?" *Fortune,* 27 May 1985.

Ellis, Charles D., with James R. Vertin. *Classic II: Another Investor's Anthology.* Homewood, Ill., 1991.

Fabozzi, Frank, and Rayner Cheung, eds. *The New High-Yield Debt Market: A Handbook for Portfolio Managers and Analysts.* New York, 1990.

Faltmayer, Edmund. "The Deal Decade: Verdict on the '80s." *Fortune,* 26 Aug. 1991.

Ferris, Paul. *The Master Bankers: Controlling the World's Finances.* New York, 1984.

Fierman, Jaclyn. "How Secure Is Your Nest Egg?" *Fortune,* 12 Aug. 1991.

Forbes, B.C., ed. *America's Fifty Foremost Business Leaders.* New York, 1948.

Frantz, Douglas. *Mr. Diamond: The Story of Dennis Levine, Wall Street's Most Infamous Inside Trader.* London, 1987.

"Frederick Joseph, Chief Executive Officer, Drexel Burnham Lambert." *Institutional Investor,* June 1987.

Fridson, Martin S. "Agency Costs: Past and Future." In Merrill Lynch *Extra Credit,* June 1991.

———, and Michael Cherry. "This Year in High Yield." In Merrill Lynch *Extra Credit,* January–February 1992.

Friend, Irwin, et al. *Investment Banking and the New Issues Market.* New York, 1967.

Fromson, Brett Duval. "Did Drexel Get What It Deserved?" *Fortune,* 12 March 1990.

Gazel, Neil R. *Beatrice from Buildup to Breakup.* Urbana, IL, 1990.

Goldsmith, Raymond, ed. *Institutional Investors and Corporate Stock—A Background Study.* New York, 1973.

Goodman, Lauri S. "High Yield Default Rates: Is There Cause for Concern?" *Journal of Portfolio Management* (Winter 1990).

Goolrick, Robert. *Public Policy Toward Corporate Growth: The ITT Cases.* Port Washington, NY, 1978.

Graham, Benjamin, and David L. Dodd. *Security Analysis,* 2nd ed. New York, 1940.

Graves, Samuel B., and Sandra A. Waddock. "Institutional Ownership and Control: Implications for Long-Term Corporate Strategy," *Academy of Management Executive* (1990), No. 1.

Greenbaum, Mary. "Tips for Takeover Targets' Stockholders." *Fortune,* 28 Dec. 1981.

Greene, Richard. "Their Eyes Are On The Main Chance." *Forbes,* 9 March 1987.

Greider, William. *Secrets of the Temple: How the Federal Reserve Runs the Country.* New York, 1987.

Grodinsky, Julius. *Investments*. New York, 1953.

Gunst Peter H., and Robert B. Levin. "RICO: A Runaway Anticrime Law." *Nation's Business*, January 1990.

Hammer, Joshua. "Triumphant Ted." *Playboy*, January 1990.

Hawthorne, Fran. "Could Drexel Have Been Saved?" *Institutional Investor*, March 1990.

Hayes, Samuel L. III, A. Michael Spence, and David Van Praag, eds. *Competition in the Investment Banking Industry*. Cambridge, Mass., 1983.

Hayes, Samuel L. III, and Russell A. Taussig. "Tactics of Cash Takeover Bids." *Harvard Business Review* (March–April 1967).

———. "Investment Banking in Flux." *Harvard Business Review* (March–April 1971).

———. "The Transformation of Investment Banking." *Harvard Business Review* (January–February 1979).

Hecht, Henry, ed. *A Legacy of Leadership*. New York, 1985.

Hector, Gary. "Are Shareholders Cheated by LBOs?" *Fortune*, 19 Jan. 1987.

———. "Junk After Milken." *Fortune*, 6 Nov. 1989.

———. "S&Ls: Where Did All Those Billions Go?" *Fortune*, 10 Sept. 1990.

Hickman, W. Braddock. *Corporate Bond Quality and Investor Experience*. Princeton, NJ, 1958.

Hirshman, Arlene. "High Risks—and Rewards—in High-Yield Bonds." *Dun's Review* (June 1977).

"History is Bunk. The Future is Junk." *New Perspectives Quarterly* (Fall 1989).

Hoffman, Paul. *The Dealmaker: Inside the World of Investment Banking*. New York, 1984.

Homer, Sidney. *A History of Interest Rates*. New Brunswick, NJ: Rutgers University Press, 1977.

Hosnaball, Mark. "Money-Mad Mike." *Playboy*, January 1990.

Hunn, Paul H. "The Evolution of Leveraged Buyout Financing." *Commercial Lending Review* (Spring 1987).

Huss, H. Fenwick, and Burt A. Leete. "The Broadened Scope of Rule 10b-5: Analysis and Implications for Participants in the Securities Markets." *Business and Society*, Spring 1988.

Institutional Investor. *The Way it Was: An Oral History of Finance. 1967–1987*. New York, 1988.

Jensen, Michael. "Corporate Control and the Politics of Finance." *Journal of Applied Corporate Finance* (Summer 1991).

———. "The Distribution of Power Among Corporate Managers, Shareholders and Directors." *Journal of Financial Economics* (January–March 1988).

———. "Eclipse of the Public Corporation." *Harvard Business Review* (September–October 1989).

————. "Takeovers: Their Causes and Consequences." *Journal of Economic Perspectives* (Winter 1988).

Johnston, Moira. *Roller Coaster: The Bank of America and the Future of American Banking.* New York, 1990.

————. *Takeover: The New Wall Street Warriors, The Men, The Money, The Impact.* New York, 1985.

Kaplan, Gilbert E., and Chris Welles. *The Money Managers.* New York, 1969.

Kimmel, Lewis. *Share Ownership in the United States.* Washington, DC, 1952.

Kobler, John. *Otto the Magnificent.* New York, 1988.

Kolko, Gabriel. *Wealth and Power in America: An Analysis of Social Class and Income Distribution.* New York, 1962.

Kornbluth, Jesse. *Highly Confident: The Crime and Punishment of Michael Milken.* New York, 1992.

Kuhn, Robert L. *Investment Banking.* New York, 1990.

Labich, Kenneth, "How Jimmy Lee Let Gulf's Shareholders Win Big." *Fortune,* 2 April 1984.

Levine, Dennis B. *Inside Out: An Insider's Account of Wall Street.* New York, 1991.

————. "The Inside Story of an Inside Trader." *Fortune,* 21 May 1990.

Lewis, Michael. *Liar's Poker.* New York, 1989.

————. "How Michael Milken Changed the World." *Business* [U.K.]., May 1988.

————. *The Money Culture.* New York, 1991.

Longnecker, Justin G., Joseph A. McKinney, and Carlos W. Moore. "The Generation Gap in Business Ethics." *Business Horizons,* September–October 1989.

Lorelli, Donald R. "Sword, Shield or Albatross?" *Best's Review* (April 1985).

Lowenstein, Louis. *Sense and Nonsense in Corporate Finance.* Reading, MA, 1991.

Madrick, Jeff. *Taking America: How We Got from the First Hostile Takeover to Megamergers, Corporate Raiding, and Scandal.* New York, 1987.

Margotta, Donald G. "The Separation of Ownership and Responsibility in the Modern Corporation." *Business Horizons,* January–February 1989.

Masulis, Ronald W. *The Debt/Equity Choice.* Cambridge, MA, 1988.

Mayer, Martin, *Stealing the Market.* New York, 1992.

McGee, Robert W. "Ethical Issues in Acquisitions and Mergers." *Mid-Atlantic Journal of Business* (March 1989).

McWade, Kim. "The Roundtable: Getting Results in Washington," *Harvard Business Review* (May–June 1981).

————. *Wall Street: Men and Money.* New York, 1955.

Meyers, William. "Down—But Not Out—in Beverly Hills." *Institutional Investor,* August 1989.

Michaels, James W., and Phyllis Berman. "My Story—Michael Milken." *Forbes,* 16 March 1992.

Michel, Allen, and Israel Shaked. *Takeover Madness: Corporate America Fights Back.* New York, 1986.

Modigliani, Franco, and Merton Miller. "The Cost of Capital, Corporate Finance and the Theory of Investment." *The American Economic Review* (June 1958).

Moore, Jennifer. "What is Really Unethical About Insider Trading?" *Journal of Business Ethics* (1990).

Morgenson, Gretchen. "We're All Right, Jack." *Forbes,* 13 May 1991.

Nader, Ralph, and William Taylor. *The Big Boys: Power and Position in American Business.* New York, 1986.

Needleman, Jacob. *Money and the Meaning of Life.* New York, 1991.

Niskanen, William A. *Reaganomics: An Insider's Account of the Policies and the People.* New York, 1988.

Nulty, Peter. "Boone Pickens, Company Hunter." *Fortune,* 26 Dec. 1983.

O'Reilly, Brian. "Mike's Midas Touch." *Fortune,* 10 Oct. 1988.

Osborn, Neil. "The Furor over Shelf Registration." *Institutional Investor,* June 1982.

Pickens, T. Boone. *Boone.* New York, 1987.

———. "Boone Speaks." *Fortune,* 16 Feb. 1987.

———. "Free Enterprise Without the Entrepreneur?" *Vital Speeches.* 1 July 1985.

———. "I Called My Guys Together and said, 'Fellas, We Need a Home Run,' And that was Gulf Oil." *Institutional Investor,* June 1987.

———. "Takeovers: A Purge of Poor Managements," *Management Review.* January, 1988.

———. "The Continuing Struggle to Restore Management Accountability and Competitiveness in Corporate America." *Executive Speeches.* November 1988.

Picker, Ida. "Picking Up the Pieces at Drexel." *Institutional Investor,* May 1989.

———. "The Temptations of Jim Stewart." *Institutional Investor,* April 1992.

Practicing Law Institute. *Hostile Battles for Corporate Control. 1986.* 2 vols. New York, 1986.

Proxmire, William. "Hostile Corporate Takeovers and Raids." *Vital Speeches.* 15 April 1985.

Reich, Cary. "Milken the Magnificent." *Institutional Investor,* August 1986.

Reilly, Ann. "Lobbyists Cash in on Takeovers." *Fortune,* 10 June 1985.

Roberts, Paul Craig. "Mike Milken, Scapegoat for the Feds." *Business Week,* 30 Sept. 1991.

Rothschild, John. *Going for Broke.* New York, 1991.

Saveth, Edward N. "Suicide of an Elite?" *Commentary,* August 1991.

Scharff, Edward E. *Worldly Power: The Making of the Wall Street Journal.* New York, 1986.

Schisgall, Oscar. *The Magic of Mergers: The Saga of Meshulam Riklis.* Boston, 1968.

Schulte, Gary. *The Fall of First Executive: The House that Fred Carr Built.* New York, 1991.

Schwartz, Robert, and David K. Whitcomb. *Transaction Costs and Institutional Investor Trading Strategies.* New York, 1988.

Seligman, Joel. *The Transformation of Wall Street: A History of the Securities and Exchange Commission and Modern Corporate Finance.* New York, 1982.

Sherman, Stratford P. "Drexel Sweats the SEC Probe." *Fortune,* 16 March 1987.

Shulman, Morton. *The Billion Dollar Windfall.* New York, 1970.

Six, David. "Due Diligence." *Forbes,* 15 Oct. 1990.

Sloan, Allan. "A Chat With Michael Milken." *Forbes,* 13 July 1987.

————."The Magician." *Forbes,* 23 April 1984.

————. "Why Is No One Safe?" *Forbes,* 11 March 1985.

————, and Jack Willoughby. "T. Boone Pyrrhus." *Forbes,* 12 Aug. 1985.

Smith, Adam. *The Roaring Eighties.* New York, 1988.

Smith, Roy C. *The Money Wars.* New York, 1990.

Sobel, Robert. *NYSE: A History of the New York Stock Exchange, 1935–1975.* New York, 1975.

————. *The Big Board: A History of the New York Stock Market.* New York, 1965.

————. *The Money Manias.* New York, 1973.

————. *Salomon Brothers, 1910–1985: Advancing to Leadership.* New York, 1986.

Spragins, Ellyn E. "At Merrill, A Frustrating Hunt for Profits." *New York Times Magazine,* 10 June 1990.

Stevens, Mark. *The Insiders: The Truth Behind the Scandal Rocking Wall Street.* New York, 1987.

Stewart, James B. *Den of Thieves.* New York, 1991.

Stone, Dan G. *April Fools.* New York, 1991.

"T. Boone Pickens." *Institutional Investor,* June 1987.

"Takeovers: What Next?" *CE Roundtable,* November–December 1988.

Taylor, William. "Crime? Greed? Big Ideas? What Were the '80s About?" *Harvard Business Review* (January–February 1992).

Thomas, Michael M. *Hanover Place.* New York, 1990.

Tidwell, Gary L., and Abdul Aziz. "Insider Trading: How Well Do You Understand the Current Status of the Law?" *California Management Review* (Summer 1988).

Train, John. *The New Money Managers.* New York, 1989.

Unger, Irwin, and Debi Unger. *Turning Point, 1968.* New York, 1988.

U.S. Department of Commerce. *Historical Statistics of the United States, Colonial Times to 1970.* 2 vols. Washington, DC, 1975.

U.S. General Accounting Office. *Financial Markets, Issuers, Purchases, and Purposes of High Yield, Non-Investment Grade Bonds.* Washington, DC, 1988.

U.S. General Accounting Office. "Issues Concerning the Thrift Industry's Investments in High Yield Bonds." Washington, DC, 1989.

U.S. Congress. Senate. Committee on Banking, Housing, and Urban Affairs. Subcommittee on Securities. "Impact of Corporate Takeovers." 99th Cong., 1st sess., 1985.

U.S. Congress. House. Subcommittee on Telecommunications, Consumer Protection, and Finance. Committee on Energy and Commerce. "Corporate Takeovers (Part 1)." 99th Cong., 1st sess., 1985.

U.S. Congress. House. Committee on Energy and Commerce. Subcommittee on Telecommunications, Consumer Protection, and Finance. "Conglomerate Mergers and High Yield [Junk] Bonds: Recent Market Trends and Regulatory Developments." 99th Cong., 1st sess., 1986.

U.S. Congress. Senate. Subcommittee on Securities. Committee on Banking, Housing, and Urban Affairs. "Definition of Insider Trading." 100th Cong., 1st sess., 1987.

U.S. Congress. Senate. Committee on Banking, Housing, and Urban Affairs. "Hostile Takeovers." 100th Cong., 1st sess., 1987.

U.S. Congress. Senate. Committee on Banking, Housing, and Urban Affairs. "Regulating Hostile Corporate Takeovers." 100th Cong., 1st sess., 1987.

U.S. Congress. House. Subcommittee on Oversight and Investigations. Committee on Energy and Commerce. "Securities Market Oversight and Drexel Burnham Lambert." 100th Cong., 2d sess., 1989.

U.S. Congress. Senate. Committee on Banking, Housing, and Urban Affairs. "The Issues Surrounding the Collapse of Drexel Burnham Lambert." 101st Cong., 2d sess., 1990.

U.S. Congress. Senate. Committee on Banking, Housing, and Urban Affairs. "Report on the Corporate Debt: A Perspective on Leverage." 102d Cong., 1st sess., 1991.

United States v. Michael Milken, D.N.Y. S89. October 18–25, 1990.

Waite, Stephen R. "The Eclipse of Growth Capital." *Journal of Applied Corporate Finance* (Spring 1991).

Wanniski, Jude. "Trial by Press: James B. Stewart vs. Michael Milken." Polyconomics, 9 Oct. 1991.

Walter, James E., and Michael R. Milken. "Managing the Corporate Financial Structure." Working Paper No. 26-73, Rodney L. White Center for Financial Research, University of Pennsylvania. 1974.

Weberman, Ben. "The King of the BBs." *Forbes,* 5 Dec. 1983.

Welles, Chris. "The Bleak Wasteland of Financial Journalism." *Columbia Journalism Review* (Summer 1973).

———. *The Last Days of the Club.* New York, 1975.

Welling, Kathryn M. "Ivan the Terrible." *Barron's,* 24 Nov. 1986.

White, Eugene, ed. *Crashes and Panics: The Lessons from History.* Homewood, IL, 1990.

Wigmore, Barrie. *The Crash and Its Aftermath.* Westport, CT, 1985.

Williams, Fred. "Pickens Takes Up New Battle." *Pensions and Investment Age,* 31 Oct. 1988.

Williams, Monci Jo. "Can Fred Joseph Save Drexel?" *Fortune,* 8 May 1989.

———. "The Pickens Plot That Has Gulf Gulping." *Fortune,* 5 March 1984.

Wilson, Richard, and Frank Fabozzi. *The New Corporate Bond Market.* Chicago, 1990.

Wojahn, Ellen. "Paper Planes." *Inc.,* September 1985.

Yago, Glenn. "The Credit Crunch: A Regulatory Squeeze on Growth Capital." *Journal of Applied Corporate Finance* (Spring 1991).

————. *Junk Bonds: How High Yield Securities Restructured Corporate America.* New York, 1990.

Yergen, Daniel. "The Oil Wars." *Investment Vision,* June–July 1991.

INDEX

Printed in the United States
125852LV00008B/115/A

9 781587 980299